THE NAME GAME

Football, Baseball, Hockey & Basketball — How your favorite sports teams were named

MICHAEL LEO DONOVAN

W

Warwick Publishing
Toronto Los Angeles

THE NAME GAME: Football, Baseball, Hockey & Basketball —
How Your Favorite Sports Teams Were Named

ISBN 1-895629-74-8

Published by Warwick Publishing Inc.
24 Mercer Street, Toronto, Ontario M5V 1H3
1424 N. Highland Avenue, Los Angeles CA 90027

Distributed by Firefly Books Ltd.
3680 Victoria Park Avenue, Willowdale, Ontario M2H 3K1

Originating Publisher: McGraw-Hill Ryerson Limited
300 Water Street
Whitby, Ontario L1N 9B6

Editor: *Erin Moore*
Production Coordinator: *Sharon Hudson*
Cover Design: *Marc Mireault*
Interior Design/Composition: *Lynda Powell*
Editorial Services: *Rachel Mansfield*

This book was composed in Plantin and ITC Machine using
Adobe PageMaker 6.0.1 and Illustrator 6.0.

Printed and bound in Canada by Webcom Ltd. using acid-free
paper.

To Kayleigh and Matthew

The brightest stars in my sky,
When you shine, the others fade.

And to Jane

The wind beneath our wings.

ABOUT THE AUTHOR

Michael Leo Donovan is a scriptwriter with more than thirty hours of produced television, including episodes of *Lassie, Top Cops, White Fang,* the American Cable Ace Award-winning *Chris Cross* and the PBS WonderWorks mini-series *African Journey.* He has a CD ROM interactive children's story in development, and in 1996 had published the historical novel *A Shamrock in the Snow.* A graduate of the University of Southern California, he has been a Communications Professor at Concordia University in Montreal for ten years. *The Name Game* is Donovan's first published work of non-fiction.

ACKNOWLEDGEMENTS

As with most people of my ilk, full of bright ideas and with no clue where to begin, I am forever in the debt of another. Without the wisdom, commitment and dedication of Patricia Lynn Dozois, this book would still be no more than a sparkle in my eye.

I would like to acknowledge also the hundreds of individuals for their contributions to my inquiries about their team names; from college sports info departments to media relations officers, sportswriters to retired athletes — many of whom didn't know the answers themselves and had to search out hundred-year-old files for long-forgotten origins. This book is for your team effort, and for all of us who love to cheer out loud.

CONTENTS

PREFACE

Perhaps never before has the concept of name-calling been more lucrative. The merchandising of sports team-name paraphernalia is a multi-billion dollar business. Where the names of some sports franchises are rich with tradition, others simply hope to *get* rich in a world where merchandising is king, cashing in on eye-catching marketing concepts to sell T-shirts and baseball caps.

In any case, no name is an accident, and many even teach us a lesson. Study the American history in the story behind the Charlotte Hornets' moniker. Appreciate the geography in the New York Islanders or Colorado Rockies. The Santa Cruz Banana Slugs, named after a mollusk, are a lesson in marine biology. Industry? We've got the Milwaukee Brewers, Detroit Pistons, and Edmonton Oilers. Music appreciation? Hum along with the melodic St. Louis Blues or New Orleans Saints. How about patriotism? Look no further than the jewels of pro sports, the New York Yankees and Montreal Canadiens. I offer the Maritime Keelhaulers, Irvine Anteaters, and Trinity Christian Trolls for just plain daffiness. Or perhaps you think the Mighty Ducks of Anaheim fill that bill. Regardless, from Aztecs to Zips, I guarantee that some of these nickname histories will stump even the most trivia-obsessed among you.

TEAM ROSTER

Why are they called the ...?

BASEBALL

BLUE JAYS

BREWERS

ANGELS

ORIOLES

METS

RED SOX

TIGERS

CARDINALS

BRAVES

REDS

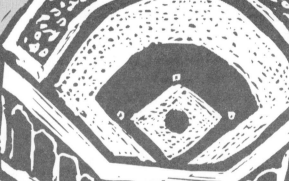

YANKEES

EXPOS

A'S

DODGERS

ROYALS

WHITE SOX

MAJOR LEAGUE BASEBALL

Arizona Diamondbacks

Atlanta Braves

Baltimore Orioles

Boston Red Sox

California Angels

Chicago Cubs

Chicago White Sox

Cincinnati Reds

Cleveland Indians

Colorado Rockies

Detroit Tigers

Florida Marlins

Houston Astros

Kansas City Royals

Los Angeles Dodgers

Milwaukee Brewers

Minnesota Twins

Montreal Expos

New York Mets

New York Yankees

Oakland A's

Philadelphia Phillies

Pittsburgh Pirates

St. Louis Cardinals

San Diego Padres

San Francisco Giants

Seattle Mariners

Tampa Bay Devil Rays

Texas Rangers

Toronto Blue Jays

ARIZONA DIAMONDBACKS

A popular name-the-team contest for this new Major League Baseball expansion team in Phoenix was finally reduced to these names in late 1995 — Arizona COYOTES, SAGUAROS, SCORPIONS, DIAMONDBACKS, RATTLERS, and even the Arizona PHOENIX! Team ownership was looking for a name that evoked local color, a moniker that would draw attention to the Arizona desert made famous in legend and lore. Also, marketing strategy informs contemporary sports franchises that animals make good copy. Therein came the Diamondbacks, a local poisonous snake with a diamond pattern on its back. Team owner Jerry Colangelo said, "We wanted to put a little bite into our name, and I think we've done that." Coincidently, sports fans in the state of Arizona were busy looking for a new name for the Winnipeg JETS National Hockey League franchise moving to Phoenix in 1996. A virtually simultaneous name-the-team contest attracted 10,000 entries, with the front-runners including SCORPIONS, MUSTANGS, POSSE, OUTLAWS, and DRY ICE. But COYOTES beat the other finalist, the Phoenix PHREEZE. Now the NHL and Major League Baseball have to watch out for two new predators — the COYOTES and DIAMONDBACKS. The DIAMONDBACKS are planning to field a team in 1998.

ATLANTA BRAVES

This team originated in Boston as the BEANEATERS. The franchise was not a success on the field and many fans claimed the moniker was offensive. After that the franchise was known as the Boston RED STOCKINGS until 1907. When they dropped that name, the American League Boston PILGRIMS snatched it up, becoming the Boston RED SOX. The National League team from Boston took on their new name, the BRAVES, in 1911. James E. Gaffney, nicknamed the "Political brave from Tammany Hall," had bought the RED STOCKINGS and named them after himself. Just from 1936 until 1940, the team was known as the Boston BEES. The Boston BRAVES became the Milwaukee BRAVES in 1953, the first major-league franchise shift in half a century. And in 1966, the

Milwaukee BRAVES moved to Atlanta, where they are today. Atlanta fielded the BLACK CRACKERS in the Negro American League in 1938.

Nickname: America's Team (II) — NFL Cowboys were first

BALTIMORE ORIOLES

The first franchise in Baltimore was in 1872 till 1874, called the LORD BALTIMORES, nicknamed at various times the MARYLANDS, YELLOW STOCKINGS, and CANARIES. Lord Baltimore founded the city in the 1600s. From 1875 until 1881 there was no pro ball in Baltimore. In 1882 the six-club American Association was formed, and Baltimore was a last-minute substitute for Brooklyn. The Baltimore Base-Ball Club was its name at that time. In 1883 there was a call for new owners, manager, and ballpark. The Von der Horst family, famous as beer brewers, took over ownership of the team with Bill Barney as Manager. A new field called Oriole Park was built. The park was named after the Order of the Oriole Parade, which was a Northern Autumnal Mardi Gras. There used to be a specific bird that nested in Baltimore, and it was called the Baltimore Oriole. This particular breed of oriole unfortunately no longer exists. Everything connected with the franchise, the park, and the parade, was named for that bird. In January of 1903, this club left town to establish a franchise in the northeast — the New York HIGHLANDERS, who became the YANKEES. Today's Baltimore ORIOLES began their major league lives as the St. Louis BROWNS. As the BROWNS they won the American League Pennant in 1944, then played the St. Louis CARDINALS in the World Series, losing 4 games to 2. All games were played in the same stadium, Sportsman's Park, the only time this has ever occurred in World Series history. In 1954 the St. Louis BROWNS became the Baltimore ORIOLES, in honor of a bird that had long ago left town.

Nicknames: Birds, O's

BOSTON RED SOX

The club started in the Western Association as the Buffalo BISONS. As one of four new ball clubs to enter into the newly formed American League in 1901, the RED SOX were then known as the Boston AMERICANS. Previous to that the club had been called the SOMERSETS, after original owner Charles W. Somers, the PLYMOUTH ROCKS, the SPEED BOYS, and the PURITANS. For a while they settled on the PILGRIMS. When the Boston PILGRIMS won the American League Pennant in 1903, they challenged the National League champion Pittsburgh PIRATES — the first true World Series. The PILGRIMS won the best-of-nine series five games to three! No World Series was played in 1904 because of a dispute between the leagues, but by 1905 the annual fall classic was here to stay. Various names were applied to the club until 1907 when the current name RED SOX was adopted. The origin of this name is traced to the Boston RED STOCKINGS, a powerful club of the National League in the 1870s and 80s. In 1907 the RED STOCKINGS abandoned the red hosiery they customarily wore because Manager Fred Tenney believed that the red dye in the socks could possibly cause infection in spike wounds. So, they changed their name to the BRAVES. That's when the owner of the Boston PILGRIMS in the American League, John I. Taylor, said, "From now on we'll wear red stockings, and I'm grabbing that name RED SOX!"

Nickname: *Bosox*

CALIFORNIA ANGELS

Radio, recording, movie and television star Gene Autry rekindled an old flame of his when he acquired the ANGELS franchise at an American League expansion meeting late in 1960. The club was named the Los Angeles ANGELS — remember, "Los Angeles" is Spanish for "The Angels" — to preserve and continue the legacy of a popular Pacific Coast League team which had departed Los Angeles when the DODGERS arrived from Brooklyn in 1957. To escape the DODGERS, whose park they shared during the 1962 through 1965 seasons, the team moved to suburbia. Anaheim Stadium was erected within the shadow of Disneyland, and the team became known as the California ANGELS. Still very much alive and still principal owner in 1996, Gene Autry has only recently hinted at putting his shares up for sale.

Nicknames: Halos, Seraphs, Cherubs

CHICAGO CUBS

They were originally named the Chicago WHITE STOCKINGS by owner William Hulbert, and they kept that moniker for almost twenty years. But the flurry of names that followed make the CUBS the most nicknamed in baseball. Most of these names were created by the Chicago newspapers, each with their own idea as to what name best suited "their" team. So, at various times, the *Chicago Tribune*, the *Daily News*, the *Journal*, and the *Interocean* referred to the club as the COLTS (1887-1906), SWALLOWTAILS (1888), BLACK STOCKINGS (1888-1889), EX-COLTS (1898), RAINMAKERS (1898), ORPHANS (1898-1902), COWBOYS (1899), ROUGH RIDERS (1899-1900), DESERT RANGERS (1899), REMNANTS (1901-1902), RECRUITS (1902), PANAMAS (1903), SELEE'S COLTS (1902-1905), ZEPHYRS (1905), NATIONALS (1905-1907), SPUDS (1906), the TROJANS (1913), and, again, the Chicago WHITE STOCKINGS, a moniker later lifted and still in use by their cross-town rivals in the American League — the Chicago WHITE SOX. They were nicknamed ANSON'S COLTS from 1887-97 because Manager Cap Anson had starred in a silent film called *A Runaway Colt*. In 1902, a sports columnist for the *Chicago Daily News* referred to the team's newest players as cubs. Sports editor Fred Rayner liked the name and so continued to use it. The name stuck. While every other club had succumbed to night games by 1946, Chicago's Wrigley Field didn't turn on the lights until 1988. 1908 was the club's last championship year.

Nickname: Cubbies

CHICAGO WHITE SOX ⎯⎯⎯⎯⎯⎯⎯

In the 1890s, the one-time player and manager after whom Comiskey Park was named, Charles Comiskey, invested in an eight-team circuit called the Western League. For reasons that remain unclear, Comiskey decided to purchase the ailing Sioux City club and transfer it to St. Paul. There, the newly baptized SAINTS prospered enough to attract the attention of Chicago CUBS' owner James Hart. Mr. Hart was looking for a "farm" club, but Comiskey would have nothing of it — he had his eyes on a move to Chicago and the big leagues where his club could challenge the CUBS themselves. In 1900, an enterprising young journalist named Ban Johnson, with Charles Comiskey, created the American League. The winners of the American League pennants in 1900 and 1901 were Comiskey's former St. Paul SAINTS, now the Chicago WHITE STOCKINGS, having lifted the very same moniker the Chicago CUBS had dropped a few years earlier. In 1906 the Chicago WHITE STOCKINGS won the American League Pennant three games ahead of the New York HIGHLANDERS, later to be known as the YANKEES. The STOCKINGS then met and defeated their cross-town rivals, the National League Champion Chicago CUBS, four games to two in the World Series. Comiskey's dream had been fully realized.

Nicknames: *Sox, Chisox, The Hitless Wonders (affectionately in 1906), Pale Hose, Go-Go Sox (1959 A.L. Champions), Uniques*

CINCINNATI REDS ⎯⎯⎯⎯⎯⎯⎯⎯

The world's first pro baseball club, in 1869 the team was called the Cincinnati RED STOCKINGS because they wore red stockings. For a while in the 1870s they flirted with two other monikers, the PORKOPOLITANS and the PIONEERS. They merged with the National League Washington SENATORS in 1890, and in the early 1900s the name was shortened to the Cincinnati REDS. Major League Baseball's first night game was played in Cincinnati's Crosley Field on May 24, 1935, with the hometown REDS besting the Philadelphia

PHILLIES, 2-1. In the 1950s, they became the RED STOCKINGS again because of the McCarthy era, when Reds and communism became synonymous, and there was a fear about the association. After two seasons with this old moniker, they were rechristened as the RED LEGS. In 1959 the club felt secure enough to return to its REDS nickname.

Nicknames: Redlegs, Reds, Big Red Machine

CLEVELAND INDIANS

While sliding past the SPIDERS and into the BLUES (named after the color of the letters on their uniforms), the team was originally called the NAPS, after a player on the team, Napoleon Lajoie. When Napoleon was cut in 1915, the Cleveland club had to unload its moniker. Briefly, they bounced between nicknames like the LAKESHORES, BLUEBIRDS, BRONCOS, and MOLLY MAGUIRES after the coal miners. Then a local newspaper, the *Plain Dealer,* had a naming contest. It was decided to honor a Penobscot Indian, Louis Francis Sockarlexis, nicknamed Chief because he was the first American Indian to play in the majors, who starred on the SPIDERS in 1898-99. Sock, as he was also known, along with the nickname Deerfoot, had been a phenom for the SPIDERS during the first half of his first season in 1897, hitting .413 by late July. After falling to alcoholism, newspaper accounts found at Cooperstown state that he spent time living in hobo jungles, as an umpire, as a basket weaver, as a canoeist, as a woodsman, and as a ferryman on the Penobscot River. He died at 42 working at a logging camp in Bangor, newspaper clippings from his glory days found in his pocket. Since then the INDIANS have changed leagues — from the National to the American in the late 1800s — but not their name. This team has the added distinction of bringing the first black player into the American League, Larry Doby in 1947. The team mascot is named Slider.

Nicknames: Blues, Tribe

COLORADO ROCKIES

There were few teams in professional sports today that could make the claim that Colorado did when they were awarded their Major League Baseball franchise: they were the only ball team within a thousand-mile radius! Marketing and management obviously took this fact into consideration when they called their club the ROCKIES, after North America's largest mountain range, therefore appealing to the entire region and generating more interest across the state borders. The region sure loves its mountain nicknames, as the 1995 Denver entry into the National Hockey League Colorado AVALANCHE can attest. The first NHL franchise, which moved to Kansas and then New Jersey, was called — that's right —the Colorado ROCKIES.

Nickname: Rox

DETROIT TIGERS

In its early years, the team was simply called DETROIT; The DETROITS; sometimes the WOLVERINES, perhaps after the team that played in the N.L. from 1881-88; and at other times, the CREAMS. The CREAMS broke into print in 1894, when a new owner out from Los Angeles arrived with an aggregation "... purported to be the cream of California baseball players." Baseball historians long credited Philip J. Reid, city editor of the *Detroit Evening News*, with first using the TIGERS moniker in print in 1896. He thought that the yellow and black socks were like those worn by the Princeton University TIGERS football team. But George Stallings, Manager of the Detroit team which was then a member of the Western League, took credit for the nickname. He had put his players in black-and-brown striped stockings which, he said, reminded fans of TIGER stripes. But still later evidence makes it appear that an unidentified headline writer at the *Detroit Free Press* actually originated the TIGERS nickname in 1895, a year before Stallings became Manager and before the team was wearing striped stockings. From then on, the *Detroit Free Press* regularly called them the TIGERS, and in May of 1895, *Sporting Life* began using TIGERS in its dispatches from Detroit. Thus it seems that the *Detroit Free Press* must get credit originating the TIGER nickname in 1895.

Nickname: Bengals

FLORIDA MARLINS

Though a number of minor league clubs in 1956 and 1970, 1982 and 1988 had MARLIN in their name it wasn't until owner Walter Huizenga, founder of the Blockbuster Video rental chain, chose the name for his Florida team that it appeared in the major leagues. For years Mr. Huizenga had enjoyed the sport of deep-sea fishing, appreciating especially the spirit of one particular dweller of the deep. Here's the metaphor that became his reason for the name, "I chose MARLIN because the fish is a fierce fighter and an adversary that tests your mettle." The Marlin is any of several large, slender, deep-sea fishes of the genus *Makaira,* related to the sailfish and spearfish. Other pro teams to have played in Florida include the Jacksonville RED CAPS, Fort Myers SUN SOX, Bradenton EXPLORERS, Orlando JUICE, West Palm Beach TROPICS, Gold Coast SUNS, St. Lucie LEGENDS, St. Petersburg PELICANS, mostly in the now defunct Senior Professional Baseball Association.

HOUSTON ASTROS

The Houston franchise was originally called the COLT 45'S after their first home field, Colt Stadium. When a new stadium was built in New Mexico, the team name changed to the Houston ASTROS because of the area's association with astronauts and the aerospace industry. The Astrodome was the Major League's first domed stadium. Originally, grass grew under the Texas dome, bathed in brilliant sunlight. But ballplayers complained about the glare, and the entire dome was painted opaque — causing the grass to stop growing! Thus emerged "Astroturf," another Texas first, the "grass" that revolutionized baseball. Houston fielded the Houston EAGLES in the American Negro League in 1949-50.

Nicknames: Colts, Stro's

KANSAS CITY ROYALS ————————

A city-wide contest was held in 1968 to select the name of the new Kansas City baseball club. The team's board of directors took the fan's choices into a meeting and emerged with a winner — the ROYALS. The moniker was a nod in the direction of the state's billion-dollar livestock industry, and its livestock parade. Kansas City is very proud of the annual event with its western theme, the famous American Royal Parade. Long before the ROYALS, the Negro National League and the American Negro League had teams all over the country, including the Kansas City MONARCHS. Kansas City also sported other pro baseball teams over the years, including the COWBOYS, BLUES, and PACKERS. Other clubs playing in the black leagues across the country included the Philadelphia STARS, New Orleans SECRET NINE, Pittsburgh CRAWFORDS, Chicago AMERICAN GIANTS, Cuban STARS, Homestead GRAYS, New York BUSHWICKS, and Newark EAGLES.

Nickname: K.C.

LOS ANGELES DODGERS ————————

In 19th century America there were plenty of amateur clubs playing the east coast circuit, and many with inspired nicknames. Consider the Hartford WIDE AWAKES — so eager to play, they got up at dawn to get in a game before work! But it was in 1890 that a professional team from Brooklyn first stepped out onto legendary Ebbets Field. The Brooklyn BRIDEGROOMS, named after the four players who married in the off-season, GLADIATORS, ATLANTICS, ROBINS, for Manager Wilbert Robinson, and HANLON'S SUPERBAS, for a popular vaudeville acrobatic troupe when Ned Hanlon was Manager, settled on a moniker the local citizenry had acquired. Because of the overwhelming number of streetcars at that time, including a wild maze of trolley-lines near the Brooklyn Bridge, and the need to stay alive by avoiding — or dodging — them, the good citizens of Brooklyn became known as "trolley dodgers." It seemed only natural then to call the team representing the area the Brooklyn TROLLEY DODGERS, a label that was shortened just before the turn of the century to Brooklyn DODGERS. Then in 1936, Jimmy Powers of the *Daily News* decided the basement-dwelling DODGERS needed a new name and appealed to his readers. Out of the seven thousand responses he chose ten, all of which he submitted to the team players. From these, they selected the ACES. But more than two million Brooklynites disagreed, and the team has remained the DODGERS — even after the move to Los Angeles in 1957. The Brooklyn DODGERS also had the distinction of using the Major League's first black player, a first baseman brought up from the Montreal ROYALS named Jackie Robinson.

Nicknames: Church City Nines, Brooklyn Kings, Brooklyn Foutz's Fillies (Manager Dave Foutz), Brooks, Daffiness Boys, Dem Bums (with affection), Big Blue Wrecking Crew

MILWAUKEE BREWERS

In 1968 the city of Seattle fielded an American League team called the PILOTS, named by Dewey Sariano, a former ship pilot with the coast guard (not, as generally believed, a nod in the direction of the huge Boeing air industry located in Seattle) and a minority owner of the new franchise. After a disastrous season on the field and at the box office, the American League demanded that the PILOTS meet three conditions — including the groundbreaking of a new proposed stadium. When none of the conditions were met after that first season, a battle erupted over a new home for the Seattle PILOTS. Though bitterly fought until the end, Texas lost, and the BREWERS were born in Milwaukee. The BREWERS took to the field just two years after the Milwaukee BRAVES had left town for Atlanta, where that franchise now flourishes. New Milwaukee owner Allan

H.(Bud) Selig called his team the BREWERS because of the city's long association with the brewing industry. Milwaukee had been the home of other pro teams, including KELLY'S KILLERS, relocated from Cincinnati in 1891, and the CREAM CITYS, or Milwaukee CREAMS, named for the color of Milwaukee-made bricks.

Nickname: The Brew Crew

MINNESOTA TWINS

This team originated in the nation's capital as the Washington SENATORS — a nickname with the obvious "political" appeal. When the franchise was moved to the State of Minnesota in 1961, new owner Calvin Griffiths baptized them the Minnesota-St. Paul TWINS. Still thinking about appealing to local flavor, by embracing the twin cities of Minneapolis and St. Paul in this manner, he hoped to attract fan support from both. Bloomington, a suburb of both cities was the home of Metropolitan Stadium, where the TWINS played from 1961 until 1981. They now play in Minneapolis, 15 miles from the old park, in the Hubert H. Humphrey Metrodome and are called simply the MINNESOTA TWINS. The old Metropolitan Stadium is now a shoping mall.

Nickname: Twin Cities

MONTREAL EXPOS

In 1967 the country of Canada celebrated its one hundredth birthday with two outstanding events in Montreal. They started by hosting one of the most outstanding World Fairs ever. Fifty million people made their way through the Expo '67 turnstiles, enjoying the award-winning architecture of the international pavilions. Much of this enormously successful fairground still exists today as the "Man and His World" complex. The second major event occurred with the introduction of Major League Baseball to Canada, the first franchise ever granted outside of the United States. Taking to the field in 1968, the Montreal EXPOS name was and continues to be a celebration of this dual "centennial" occurrence. Selected from the thousands of contest submissions sponsored by the new club by then owner Charles Bronfman, the moniker is also consistent with all the pro sport names that come out of bilingual Montreal — it is both a French and English word. Previously, the Montreal ROYALS of the semi-pro International League had fed the majors with such high-profile players/managers as Jackie Robinson and Tommy Lasorda and actor Chuck Connors.

Nickname: Spo's

NEW YORK METS

In 1961 the owner of the National League's newest entry, Mrs. Joan Payson, had five stipulations for a name for the team. There must be: 1. public press acceptance; 2. a close relationship to the team corporation name "Metropolitan Baseball Club Inc."; 3. a descriptive connection with the metropolitan area; 4. a brevity that would delight copyreaders; 5. a historical relationship to the Metropolitans team of the 19th century American Association. The METS came closest to filling the bill. Other names considered at the time: the REBELS, the SKYLINERS, the NYB'S, the BURROS, the CONTINENTALS, the AVENGERS, the JETS, and the ISLANDERS. Another team called the New York METROPOLITANS played in the American Association from 1883-87. New York has supported many other pro teams including the Cuban STARS, the Lincoln GIANTS, and the Troy HAYMAKERS.

Nickname: Amazins (1969 World Champions)

NEW YORK YANKEES

There have been four National League franchises in the Big Apple: the MUTUALS, named after the firemen of the Mutual Hook & Ladder Co., and nicknamed the CHOCOLATE SOX (1876); GIANTS, or New York GOTHAMS (1883-1957); Brooklyn DODGERS (1890-1957); and METS (1962 to present).

The Syracuse STARS, nicknamed the TWINKS, played only the 1879 season, and the Troy TROJANS, from 1879-82. In 1903 a team moved to New York from Baltimore, and has stayed through 33 American League pennants and 22 world championships. The most successful franchise in baseball history, and second in all professional sports, began its storied existence at Hilltop Park as the New York HIGHLANDERS. When a fire forced the team to accept an invitation from the GIANTS to play at the Polo Grounds, a name-change seemed necessary. Sports editors, weary of attempts to fit HIGHLANDERS into headlines, had already started to call the team the YANKEES. YANKEES they remain. The YANKS played in the big Harlem Horseshoe for ten years till, in 1920, they out-drew their hosts by 350,000 fans. Yankee Stadium was then built, and at the home-opener on April 18, 1923, Babe Ruth took the dimensions of the new stadium by hitting one out of the park.

Nicknames: Burglars, Porchclimbers, Hilltoppers (from the Hilltop Park days), Invaders (used by the Giants and other Highlander detractors), Bronx Bombers, Bombers, Yanks, Pinstripes

OAKLAND A'S

In the late 1800s, sports enthusiasts from various men's Athletic Clubs in Philadelphia got together and decided to form a professional baseball team. They called themselves the ATHLETICS — as did many different sports clubs around that time. They became part of the National Association, baseball's first professional league, which was formed on St. Patrick's Day, 1871, in New York. Along with the Philadelphia ATHLETICS, other charter member teams were the Boston RED STOCKINGS, Chicago WHITE STOCKINGS, Cleveland FOREST CITYS, Fort Wayne KEKIONGAS, Brooklyn ECKFORDS, New York MUTUALS, Rockford FOREST CITYS, Washington NATIONALS, Washington OLYMPICS, and the Troy HAYMAKERS. The Philadelphia ATHLETICS won the first National Association Championship. The League folded in 1875. In 1901 Connie Mack and his Philadelphia ATHLETICS helped form the American League, and it was the New York GIANTS' Manager

John McGraw who dismissed the A's as "white elephants," implying Mack shouldn't be allowed to spend money without supervision. The "white elephant" has since, on and off, been the team's mascot and jersey insignia. In 1957 the Philadelphia ATHLETICS moved to Kansas City. Charles Finley purchased the Kansas City ATHLETICS in December 1960, and moved the franchise to Oakland in 1968. Once there, he shortened the team name to the A's.

PHILADELPHIA PHILLIES

The PHILLIES weren't the first or only pro baseball team to play in Philadelphia. The ATHLETICS started here before making their way west to Oakland. How about the Philadelphia PEARLS? FILLIES? WHITES? DARBY DAISIES? Also, the Negro National League and the American Negro League had teams all over the east, including the Philadelphia STARS and BACHARACH GIANTS. Other clubs playing in the black leagues included the Baltimore ELITE GIANTS, New York BLACK YANKEES, Chattanooga WHITE SOX, Memphis RED SOX, Cincinnati TIGERS, and the St. Louis GIANTS. The Philadelphia PHILLIES franchise came into the league in 1883, having moved from Worcester, Massachusetts, where the baseball club was known as the BROWN STOCKINGS and RUBY LEGS. The National League club was immediately dubbed the PHILLIES — a takeoff on the state capital name of Philadelphia — by owner Alfred Reach. In 1944 and 1945 the club was known as the BLUE JAYS, but the nickname was never "officially" changed from the PHILLIES. So, it remains the longest running nickname in pro sports.

Nicknames: Whiz Kids, Fighting Phils

PITTSBURGH PIRATES

In the 1800s the pro ball club out of Pittsburgh was called the ALLEGHENIES, a geographical reference to the Allegheny Mountain range of the Appalachian system that runs through Pennsylvania. When another pro league, the Players League, folded in 1890 after just one year, players were expected to return to the team they played for before the new league folded. Second baseman Lewis Bierbauer was to return to Philadelphia, but was stolen — or "pirated" away — by the Pittsburgh team. Trying to cast suspicion elsewhere, the club called themselves the INNOCENTS, but in 1891 Bierbauer took to the field with the newly christened Pittsburgh PIRATES. Other pro franchises, from the Oakland RAIDERS to the Tampa Bay BUCCANEERS, have more traditional interpretations of this old "sea bandit" moniker. Other monikers included the POTATO BUGS (1887-89); ZULUS (1887-89); SMOKED ITALIANS (1887-89); CORSAIRS (1940s).

Nicknames: Bucs, Buccos, Lumber Company (1970s)

ST. LOUIS CARDINALS

Relocated from the Cleveland BLUES of 1887-98, this club was first named the BROWNS, and then briefly, the PERFECTOS. The St. Louis franchise became permanently known as the CARDINALS in 1899. Legend has it that the *St. Louis Republic* newspaper reporter Willie McHale overheard a female fan react to the color on the uniforms "Oh, what a lovely shade of cardinal!" From then on, McHale called the team the CARDINALS, and the nickname stuck. Never underestimate the power of the press! It was only after the need arose to find an insignia for the club uniform that the bird was born. So named because it is colored like a cardinal's robe, the Cardinal is a bright-red crested American songbird related to the finch. Other St. Louis pro teams over the years have included the MAROONS, ONIONS, BLACK DIAMONDS, TERRIERS, STARS, and BROWNIES.

Nicknames: Cards, Redbirds, The Gashouse Gang (1930s)

SAN DIEGO PADRES

This franchise in the southwest settled on its name as the result of a local newspaper contest. PADRES is a geographical reference to the Missions that were built in early California. Mexican settlers had established their first Mission in San Diego, bringing with them their own religious leader, or father — padre, in Spanish. The moniker was also a nod in the direction of the hugely popular Pacific League PADRES that had entertained San Diego baseball enthusiasts in the early fifties before the Major League came to town in 1968. The Swinging Friar cartoon character, who represented the PADRES from 1958 to 1984, will be reintroduced to mark the nickname's 60th birthday. The stout, be-robed man swinging a bat was first introduced in 1958 when the PADRES were part of the Pacific Coast League.

Nickname: Pads

SAN FRANCISCO GIANTS

During the 1883-1885 seasons the team out of the Big Apple was called the New York GOTHAMS. In turn, the club was called the New York MAROONS (1880s), GOTHAM GIANTS (1880s), and MUTRIE'S MULES (1890), named after the Manager, Jim Mutrie. But in 1886 the name was changed to GIANTS when Mutrie, the manager at the time, shouted at his players in victory, "My big fellows! My giants! We are the people!" In 1957 the New York GIANTS left the Polo Grounds in the Big Apple to be reborn out west as the San Francisco GIANTS. They brought with them a grand old winning tradition, and over a half-century's worth of healthy competition with their cross-town, and now cross-state rivals, the Los Angeles DODGERS, another team that made the trip from back east the same year. A 1996 rumor turning the team into the San Jose GIANTS never materialized.

Nickname: Jints

SEATTLE MARINERS

The American League Seattle PILOTS were moved after only one season to Milwaukee where they became known as the BREWERS. That was in 1969. Seattle, upset with the demands put on their

PILOTS by the American League, sued. The A.L. promised to deliver another franchise. But it wasn't until eight years later, in 1977, that Seattle had its next taste of professional baseball. The Seattle MARINERS were introduced in the Kingdome, a stadium originally meant for the PILOTS. A name-the-team contest was held by a local newspaper, and the new ownership picked the club's moniker from the 15,000 entries and 1600 different names. MARINERS is a response to the team's Pacific Northwest location, and the marine history of Seattle. The team mascot is called Moose!

Nickname: M's

TAMPA BAY DEVIL RAYS ————

It was actually the neighboring city of St. Petersburg that first flirted with the game way back in 1914 at a field near Coffee Pot Bayou when the St. Louis BROWNS lost 3-2 to the Chicago CUBS in the city's first spring training game. But it was Tampa Bay that was granted a major league franchise on March 9, 1995. During the weeks surrounding that date, more than 7,000 names were submitted by fans. Suggestions included such creative choices as FRUIT BLOSSOMS, PTERODACTYLS, BIGFEET, BACKCRACKERS, SNOWBIRDS, and TOADS. The largest percentage included the word "rays," an order of large, graceful fish that live primarily in the tropical waters off Florida's coast. In a telephone contest more than 50,000 calls supported DEVIL RAYS over MANTA RAYS. Both names are actually used to describe the same fish. Devil Rays are the largest member of the Ray family measuring 19 feet long. They are found in Florida waters, the Gulf of Mexico, and along the Atlantic coasts of the southern United States. They are massive but gentle creatures, harmless to humans. The Devil Ray got its name from the cephalic fins on the head that looked like devil's horns to the early explorers who first saw the bat-shaped creatures. Although they are quite large, Devil Rays are known to leap from the water and can sail up to 20 feet in the air! Tampa Bay managing general partner Vince Naimoli wanted a name and colors which reflected the geographical area. The DEVIL RAYS are planning to field a team in 1998.

TEXAS RANGERS

Shortly after the original Washington SENATORS left the nation's capital for Minnesota and the TWINS in 1960, baseball opted for expansion and a new SENATORS team took to the Washington field at the start of the 1961 season. Remember, one N.L. SENATORS team had folded in 1899, and another had become the Cincinnati REDS in 1890. Then, despite the efforts of such luminaries as Richard Nixon and Bowie Kuhn, the second SENATOR team in ten years left town in 1971! — this time for Arlington, Texas, much to the pleasure of Mayor Tom Vandergriff who had been pursuing a Major League franchise for the Dallas/Fort Worth area for 13 years. He'd already failed in his earlier bid for the Seattle PILOT franchise, which had gone to Milwaukee to become the BREWERS. The new Major League franchise had the distinction of being the second team to honor the legendary Texas Ranger law agency. The first was the New York RANGERS hockey team! The Texas RANGERS baseball club was named by Robert Short, the SENATORS/ RANGERS owner. RANGERS ownership built a new stadium in Arlington. It is called "The Ballpark."

TORONTO BLUE JAYS

In 1976 the city of Toronto held a "name the team" contest. Thirty thousand were submitted, and of those, 4,000 were different. One hundred and fifty-four fans submitted the name BLUE JAYS. After the selection was narrowed down by management to ten possibilities, BLUE JAYS came out on top. Labatt's Breweries, which owned a percentage of the club at the time, has a popular beer known as "Blue." The rumor was that some brewery officials were very pleased to make that word prominent. In 1944-45 the Philadelphia PHILLIES were known as the BLUE JAYS, but the name didn't stick. The Toronto BLUE JAYS were the second franchise granted outside of the United States (after the Montreal EXPOS), and the first non-American club to win a World Series.

Nickname: Jays

BASKETBALL

MAVERICKS   CELTICS   HORNETS   MAGIC

KNICKERBOCKERS   CLIPPERS

NUGGETS   76ERS   HEAT   BUCKS   SPURS

SUNS

RAPTORS   PISTONS   LAKERS   WIZARDS

GRIZZLIES   TIMBERWOLVES   PACERS   JAZZ

NATIONAL BASKETBALL ASSOCIATION

Atlanta Hawks

Boston Celtics

Charlotte Hornets

Chicago Bulls

Cleveland Cavaliers

Dallas Mavericks

Denver Nuggets

Detroit Pistons

Golden State Warriors

Houston Rockets

Indiana Pacers

Los Angeles Clippers

Los Angeles Lakers

Miami Heat

Milwaukee Bucks

Minnesota Timberwolves

New Jersey Nets

New York Knickerbockers

Orlando Magic

Philadelphia 76ers

Phoenix Suns

Portland Trail Blazers

Sacramento Kings

San Antonio Spurs

Seattle Supersonics

Toronto Raptors

Utah Jazz

Vancouver Grizzlies

Washington Wizards

ATLANTA HAWKS

A banjo box gymnasium called Wharton Field House seating 6,000 on hardwood benches in a city, or rather, three cities, straddling the Mississippi River, is where the Atlanta HAWKS have their roots. They were known as the Tri-City BLACK-HAWKS, one of the original members of the NBA after a mid-summer merger in 1949 of the 12-year-old National Basketball League and the four-year-old Basketball Association of America formed the new league. The Illinois cities of Moline and Rock Island, plus Davenport, Iowa across the river formed the neo-phyte BLACKHAWKS, coached by Roger Potter. Potter was replaced by Red Auerbach who led into the playoffs only to drop out in the first round to the ANDERSON DUFFY PACKERS. Auerbach left for the CELTICS, and after two years and a gram-matical change to Tri-Cities, the BLACKHAWKS packed their bags and moved to Milwaukee. There, they shortened the nick-name to the Milwaukee HAWKS. In 1955 they moved again, this time to St. Louis. There, led by Bob Petit, the HAWKS won their lone World Championship by beating the formidable Boston team. The St. Louis HAWKS turned sour during the 1961-2 sea-son, and if not for the expansion Chicago PACKERS, would've dropped from first to last in just one year. 1968 was the best year in franchise history, and then came the shocker. During the broadcast of an Atlanta BRAVES baseball game, announcer Milo Hamilton told Atlanta fans the city was going to have a profes-sional basketball team. It was, of course, the HAWKS, a peren-nial NBA powerhouse, moving from St. Louis to Atlanta. After finishing last in 1976, changes came fast, starting with the hiring of Hubie Brown, who coached the Kentucky COLONELS to the 1975 American Basketball Association Championship. Still, rumors abounded that another move was imminent, and that a new owner was soon to purchase the team. But when R.E. "Ted" Turner bought the club, he promised the HAWKS would stay in Atlanta.

BOSTON CELTICS

The Boston CELTICS and the National Basketball Association came into being on the same day, June 6, 1946. According to the arena owners of the time, the idea behind basketball was to create tenants that would fill empty dates in their respective buildings — between the popular hockey and boxing matches. The original owner of the Boston CELTICS franchise was Walter Brown — a man who uniquely would be elected to both the hockey and basketball halls of fame. He owned the team from 1947-1964. He and publicity staff member Howie McHugh, a captain and star goaltender of Dartmouth College's 1934 Ivy League hockey champions, took it on themselves to come up with a nickname. Among the suggestions were the WHIRLWINDS, OLYMPICS, and UNICORNS. Then Brown thought of CELTICS, and McHugh balked. Brown reminded him that the name already had a wonderful tradition. The New York CELTICS were a successful basketball franchise in the 1920s. And, Brown continued, Boston is full of Irish. "We'll put them in green uniforms and call them the Boston CELTICS!" McHugh was sceptical, telling his boss, "No team with an Irish name has ever won a damned thing in Boston — including a pro football team named the SHAMROCKS that fell flat." The CELTICS lost their first home game to the Chicago STAGS, a game delayed when the glass backboard was shattered by a CELTIC who would make an even greater impression elsewhere — Chuck Connors of *The Rifleman* fame. They also lost to the Providence STEAMROLLERS, and then the St. Louis BOMBERS. Other teams in the new 11-franchise league included New York, Philadelphia, Pittsburgh, Washington, Cleveland, Detroit, and Toronto. Only Boston, New York, and Philadelphia would survive five years. The Boston CELTICS went on to become the winningest team in all of basketball.

Nickname: Celts

CHARLOTTE HORNETS

When George Shinn selected the HORNETS nickname for his NBA franchise, he knew that Charlotte's affiliation with the aggressive, pain-inflicting insect had implications of historical significance dating back to the American Revolution. After one especially bitter skirmish, British General Charles Cornwallis discovered that his expected push through the Carolinas was to end in Charlotte. Though there were few soldiers to oppose him, his troops were harried on all sides and soon, the British were running out of provisions. Patrols sent out to obtain supplies were fired upon. "There's a rebel behind every bush," Cornwallis declared in a letter. "It's a veritable nest of hornets." At a two-story log home seven miles from Charlotte, the Britishers were fired upon by a group of 14 youthful Americans. So much confusion followed that the pillaging soldiers overturned several bee hives in the yard, which added considerably to the confusion. This skirmish, locally famous, came to be known as the "Battle of the Bees." The name HORNETS also has significance in Charlotte's sports history. For many years, local baseball fans turned out to see the Charlotte HORNETS, a Minnesota Twins farm club, play minor league ball at Griffith Park, later to become known as Crockett Park. Charlotte was also home to the HORNETS of the World Football League. Then owner Shinn first tried to launch a local entry of the United States Football League, but as the fledgling league fell upon hard times, he turned his attention to a sport for which expansion was imminent, the NBA. The effort to "Bring the NBA to Basketball Country" caused the community to explode with civic pride. The original name for the team was the SPIRIT, selected by a committee from a pool of suggested names. But due to popular demand, Shinn held another "Name-the-Team" campaign, soliciting suggestions from the community via *The Charlotte Observer*. An overwhelming number of votes for HORNETS poured in and Charlotte's NBA team had a new name.

CHICAGO BULLS

According to the media relations department of the Chicago BULLS there is no official written documentation available that gives the history of the team nickname — one of the three best selling logos in all of sports. There are two theories offered, however.

One is that the team used to play in the Ampitheater, and live bulls were regularly led through the stockyard next door — Chicago is known for its stockyards, the Packingtown heritage. Dick Klein, the team owner in 1966, wanted a "ferocious" name for his club, and thought BULLS to be apropos. The other theory is that Klein's son came up with the nickname in response to his father's suggestions of MATADORS and TROUBADOURS. Young master Klein called these choices a load of bull.

CLEVELAND CAVALIERS

Cleveland was granted a National Basketball Association franchise, along with the Portland TRAILBLAZERS and the Buffalo BRAVES (now the Los Angeles CLIPPERS), to begin the 1970-71 season. The *Cleveland Plain Dealer* had a contest to name the team. The winning name CAVALIERS was chosen by more than one-third of the 6,000 voters. The other four finalists were the JAYS, FORESTERS, TOWERS, and PRESIDENTS. Jerry Tomko, who was the contest winner, wrote that "the CAVALIERS represent a group of daring, fearless men, whose life's pact was never surrender, no matter what the odds." In the mid-1980s, CAVALIERS was shortened to CAVS for marketing purposes and the two nicknames are now interchangeable. The team's colors were wine and gold through the 1982-83 season, and were changed to burnt orange, white, and royal blue for the 1983-84 season. Then in 1994 a new logo and yet another color change occurred. The CAVS new colors are orange, blue, and black.

Nickname: Cavs

DALLAS MAVERICKS

In March 1980, radio station WBAP conducted a name-the-team contest for their new National Basketball Association franchise. Over 4,600 entries were received and turned over to a five-person committee. The committee narrowed the choices to MAVERICKS,

WRANGLERS, and EXPRESS, ultimately recommending MAV-ERICKS to owner Donald Carter. This moniker actually began its life as a person's name. Samuel Maverick, a Texas rancher who died in 1870, refused to brand his cattle. This non-conformist "attitude" made the rancher's name a word firmly embedded in the English language. A maverick is defined as a person who takes an independent stand, refusing to conform to that of his party or group. That is to say, unbranded. All 41 persons who suggested the name MAVERICKS were given two tickets to the charter season opener. In a drawing of those 41, Carla Springer was awarded a pair of season tickets.

Nickname: The Mavs

DENVER NUGGETS

The American Basketball Association was established in 1967, with eleven teams. When owner Mr. Ringsby brought an ABA team to Denver, he named it after his truck company, ROCKET. He changed the ROCKETS' nickname to the NUGGETS in 1974-75 — feeling it was more in keeping with the mining tradition of Colorado. Also, at the time, there was a National Basketball Association team called the San Diego ROCKETS — later, the Houston ROCKETS. In 1976-77, four of the ABA's eleven teams merged with the NBA. The Denver NUGGETS were one of the clubs invited to change leagues at that time. The NUGGETS won the Midwest Division Title their first year in the NBA. The NUGGETS mascot is called Rocky the Mountain Lion.

DETROIT PISTONS

Fred Zollner lived in Fort Wayne, Indiana, and it was there that the factory he owned manufactured pistons for the engines of automobiles and tractors. And it was there, in the war-stricken and prosperous 1940s, that Zollner founded his basketball team. He named them in reference to his company (Zollner Machine Works), the

Fort Wayne Zollner PISTONS, and played in an industrial conference called the National Basketball League. Then another group of adventurers with larger venues available to them formed the Basketball Association of America, introducing teams with names like the KNICKS of New York, the CELTICS in Boston, the WARRIORS in Philadelphia — and such other clubs as the Pittsburgh IRONMEN, the Toronto HUSKIES, the Cleveland REBELS, the Detroit FALCONS, and the Providence STEAMROLLERS. Zollner saw his club's future in the BAA, joining with another NBL team, the Chicago American GEARS, who became the Minneapolis LAKERS. By 1956 Zollner started considering transferring his club out of Fort Wayne. That year was the last NBA Championship the Fort Wayne PISTONS would challenge. They lost to the Philadelphia WARRIORS, 4-1. The Detroit auto companies were Zollner's major customers for the pistons manufactured in his plant. Detroit was a town with a large, sports-oriented population and a rich sporting heritage. The LIONS and RED WINGS were winning championships, and the struggling TIGERS were one of the most valuable franchises in baseball. On February 15, 1957, Fred Zollner signed the deal to switch his beloved basketball team's base to red-brick Olympia Stadium, the new home of the Detroit PISTONS.

GOLDEN STATE WARRIORS

The Golden State WARRIORS are descendants of an original National Basketball Association team. It was back in 1946-47, and they were known as the Philadelphia WARRIORS — a team that won the first NBA Championship ever 4-1 over the Chicago STAGS. *That* Philly team got its name from a pro-basketball franchise, also called the Philadelphia WARRIORS, that played in the City of Brotherly Love in the 1920s, and there was some fan recognition involved. The last NBA Championship played by the Philly WARRIORS was in 1955-56, 4-3 over the Fort Wayne PISTONS (later the Detroit PISTONS). In 1962-63, the team moved to San Francisco, bringing the nickname along with it. The San Francisco WARRIORS took a much shorter trip in 1971-72, across the bridge to Oakland, becoming the Golden State WARRIORS. Before the WARRIORS came to town, Oakland had played host to another pro club, the Oakland OAKS of the American Basketball Association. That franchise left town in 1970, becoming the Washington CAPITALS (a name soon adopted by a National Hockey League franchise). The team that originated in Oakland moved once more before folding in 1977, as the Virginia SQUIRES. Meanwhile, the city of Oakland didn't have to wait long, after their ABA OAKS left, to capture an even bigger prize.

HOUSTON ROCKETS

The American Basketball Association had a team in Houston in 1967 called the MAVERICKS. That team moved to North Carolina, becoming the Carolina COUGARS. In 1974 the COUGARS left for Missouri, and became the SPIRITS of St. Louis. But Houston didn't have to wait long after the MAVERICKS left before pro ball returned to that Texas city. Sometimes a sports franchise nickname is moved from one part of the country to another and makes just as much sense at its new location as its last! Take the Houston ROCKETS, which began its National Basketball Association life as an expansion team from San Diego. On January 4, 1967, the nickname was chosen in a contest that attracted 10,000 entries. The San Diego ROCKETS moniker was in keeping with the city's theme of a "City in Motion," and reflected the tremendous growth of the space industry in San Diego — Atlas rockets were being built here. When they moved to Houston in 1975, the ROCKETS' nickname took on even greater relevance, and Houston Control took on a second meaning.

INDIANA PACERS

When professional basketball came to Indianapolis in 1967, one of the key decisions would be what to call the new American Basketball Association franchise. According to Indianapolis attorney Richard D. Tinkham, the nickname PACERS was decided on through a collective decision of the original investors. Tinkham, one of those investors, recalled that the nickname was a combination of the state's rich history with the harness racing pacers and the pace car used for the running of the Indianapolis 500. Tinkham said the PACERS decision was an easy one, but the real debate was whether the team should be called the Indiana PACERS or the Indianapolis PACERS. Since one of the original ideas for the team was to have it playing throughout the state with its base in Indianapolis, the official team name became the Indiana PACERS. In 1976 the PACERS changed leagues, joining the National Basketball Association.

LOS ANGELES CLIPPERS

In 1970 the National Basketball Association expanded, introducing the Buffalo BRAVES, a nickname chosen through a contest. In 1978 the team moved to San Diego and renamed themselves the CLIPPERS. The new nickname was in reference to the ships that frequented the sea port in the 19th century. Plus, to this day, there is always a working clipper ship in the harbor. The CLIPPERS were not the first pro team in town. The San Diego CONQUISTADORS played for the American Basketball Association in 1972. In 1975 they changed their name to the San Diego SAILS. That team folded twelve games into their fourth season. The NBA franchise hung around until it sailed up the coast to Los Angeles. In 1984-85 they became known as the Los Angeles CLIPPERS.

Nickname: Clips

LOS ANGELES LAKERS

They started playing in the National Basketball League as the Chicago American GEARS. When they jumped to the Basketball Association of America they also changed cities. Minneapolis was their new home town, where they became the LAKERS. Choosing their state rather than their city to baptize the franchise, the team was called the Minnesota LAKERS in 1948-49. The franchise was named after the team's close vicinity to the Great Lakes. A laker is also the word used to describe one of those big, ocean-going sized cargo carriers that used to travel the Great Lakes and St. Lawrence Seaway in large numbers. They carried coal, iron ore, bauxite, wheat, corn, and numerous other mining and agricultural products. There was a time when a major portion of the U.S. economic output was shipped on these waters, and the lakers were a symbol of the upper midwest's strength and vitality. The last NBA Championship in Minneapolis was in 1953-54, 4-3 over the Syracuse NATIONALS (later the Philadelphia 76ERS). In 1960, the franchise moved to Los Angeles, becoming the Los Angeles LAKERS. It is assumed that the new L.A. team wanted to cash in on an established name, because there are no lakes to speak of in the area. By the way, former LAKERS star Jerry West is the model for the NBA logo.

MIAMI HEAT

Billy Cunningham and Lewis Schaffel, who had both been associated with the National Basketball Association in various capacities for many years, had thought for some time about pursuing an NBA franchise. In 1986, Cunningham and theatrical producer Zev Buffman announced plans to bring an NBA expansion team to South Florida. Schaffel, then vice president of the New Jersey NETS, resigned to officially join the ownership. In October of 1986 the Miami franchise selected the name HEAT from over 20,000 entries, submitted by Stephanie Freed — a moniker in reference to the notorious climate of southern Florida. And it wasn't until March of 1988 that Mark Henderson's flaming basketball was selected from 1,000 entries as the HEAT's official logo. The HEAT's mascot is called Burnie.

MILWAUKEE BUCKS

Milwaukee's first professional major league basketball team was the Milwaukee HAWKS, who played in the Milwaukee Arena from 1951 through 1956 before moving to St. Louis, where a fellow by the name of Bob Petit led them to great prominence and an NBA

Championship in 1958. On that original Milwaukee team, one of the HAWKS backcourt aces was 5'10" guard William "Red" Holzman, who went on to coach the New York KNICKERBOCK-ERS to NBA Championships in 1970 and 1973. On January 22, 1968, the National Basketball Association awarded a second franchise to a Milwaukee group headed by Wesley D. Pavalon and Marvin L. Fishman. The group, called Milwaukee Professional Sports and Services, Inc., named Pavalon its president and Fishman executive vice president. More than 14,000 fans participated in a team-naming contest. According to the 1969-70 Milwaukee BUCKS yearbook, R.D. Trebilcox of Whitefish Bay, Wisconsin, was one of 45 persons who suggested the name BUCKS. His reasoning — "Bucks are spirited, good jumpers, fast and agile." Mr. Trebilcox won a new car for his efforts in helping to position Milwaukee's entry into the professional sports world with an enduring nickname. In 1992 a new logo and team colors were introduced. According to Creative Director Tom O'Grady, the "contemporary but not trendy" logo design represents the theme of solidarity, strength, and focused determination. The colors of hunter green, purple, and silver, display a regal spirit of character.

MINNESOTA TIMBERWOLVES

Four months before the NBA awarded Minnesota a franchise, a contest drew 6,076 entries with a total of 1,284 different nicknames. Among the intriguing suggestions were FAT CATS, KILLER KARPS, PURPLE COWS, and ZIPS. The Minnesota climate seemed to be on the minds of many voters as well, with DEEP FREEZE, DRIZZLERS, FRIGID FIVES, FROSTBITE, SNOWBOUND-ERS, SNOWPLOWERS, THERMOSTATS, and WEATHER-MEN. Fish or fowl? How about the BURBOTS, FISHER PRACTICES, DUCKSTERS, GOERS, and FIGHTING WALL-EYES? And what exactly are LUCUSTRIANS, MAELSTROMS, and YUAAS? Though the most popular submission was BLIZ-ZARDS, the contest was reduced to two finalists, the POLARS and the TIMBERWOLVES, because "we didn't want to be associated with blizzards, and both reflect the state's strong orientation toward outdoor recreation, and both have excellent mascot potential." The final decision was left to the 842 city councils throughout the state. They went with TIMBERWOLVES, reflecting the animal's presence in the state. Minnesota is the only one of the 48 contiguous states that has roving packs of timberwolves. About 1,200 live here, while only 75 inhabit the rest of the continental states. Seventeen people submitted the winner, and a drawing awarded Tim Pope of Brooklyn Center (MN) first prize: a trip to the 1987 NBA All-Star weekend in Seattle.

Nicknames: The Pack, T-Wolves, Wolves

NEW JERSEY NETS

In 1967-68 the New Jersey AMERICANS were born into the American Basketball Association. One year later the franchise moved to New York. There they became known as the New York NETS, in reference to the silken ropes commonly referred to as a basketball net. Rhyming with both the METS and the JETS just seemed like a New York thing to do. In 1976 the team changed leagues, joining the National Basketball Association. Another move the following year prompted another name change. In 1977-78 they became the New Jersey NETS. Other clubs invited to leave the American Basketball Association for the NBA were the Indiana PACERS, San Antonio SPURS, and the Denver NUGGETS.

NEW YORK KNICKERBOCKERS

The term KNICKERBOCKERS traces its origins back to the Dutch settlers who came to the New World — and especially to what is now New York — in the 1600s. Until a British change of name in 1664, New York used to be called New Amsterdam. Specifically, the word refers to the style of pants the settlers wore — pants that rolled up just below the knee, which became known as knickerbockers, or knickers. Through history, the Dutch settler Knickerbocker character became synonymous with New York City. The city's most popular symbol of the late 19th and early 20th centuries was "Father Knickerbocker," complete with cotton wig, three-cornered hat, buckled shoes, and, of course, knickered pants. The Knickerbocker name had its first use in the world of sports in 1845, the Alexander Cartwright's Manhattan-based baseball team — the first organized team in baseball history — was named the New York KNICKERBOCKERS or the KNICKERBOCKER NINE. The KNICKERBOCKER name stayed with the team even after it moved its base of operations to Elysian Fields at Hoboken, N.J., in 1846. Thus the KNICKERBOCKER name was an integral part of the New York scene when the Basketball Association of America granted a charter franchise to the city in the summer of 1946. As can be best determined, the final decision to call the team the KNICKERBOCKERS was made by the club's founder, the legendary Ned Irish. Irish's longtime right-hand man, Fred Podesta, was present at the KNICK'S birth and recalls that the name selection was easy, quick, and uncomplicated. "The name came out of a hat," he says. "We were all sitting in the office one day — Irish, P.R. Director Lester Scott, and a few others on staff. We each put a name in the hat, and when we pulled them out, most of them said KNICKERBOCKERS, after Father KNICKERBOCKER. It soon was shortened to KNICKS."

Nickname: Knicks

ORLANDO MAGIC

The Orlando MAGIC was a National Basketball Association expansion team, arriving in 1989. They were not the first pro club in Florida, however. The American Basketball Association formed in 1967 with eleven teams. Among them were the Minnesota MUSKIES (a fish). The MUSKIES moved to Miami in 1968, becoming the Miami FLORIDIANS. In 1970, the franchise changed its location name, becoming the Florida FLORIDIANS. They folded after five years in 1973. In 1986 Orlando Mayor Bill Frederick presented a check for $100,000 and a set of Mickey Mouse ears to NBA Commissioner David Stern, officially entering the race to bring a franchise to Orlando. One month later former 76ERS General Manager Pat Williams announced that the Orlando franchise would be named the MAGIC. The name was chosen from 4,296 entries submitted in a contest held by the *Orlando Sentinel.* The NBA MAGIC nickname is a nod in the direction of the entertainment giant in Orlando, Walt Disney World and its famous MAGIC Kingdom. Team mascot is STUFF, the MAGIC dragon.

PHILADELPHIA 76ERS

Professional basketball in its modern phase has had two stages in this city. The first section comprised the career of the WARRIORS between 1946 and 1962 with two titles, 1947 and 1956. The WARRIORS were transferred to San Francisco after the 1961-62 campaign. The Philadelphia 76ERS franchise actually began in 1949, when six teams from the midwest-based National Basketball League joined the Basketball Association of America to form the 17-team National Basketball Association. One of those teams was the Syracuse NATIONALS. The NATS were very successful in Syracuse, reaching the finals in 1951 and 1953, losing both times to the Minneapolis LAKERS — the team that left for Los Angeles in 1960. The NATS won their first and only NBA title in 1954, defeating the Fort Wayne PISTONS 92-91 to take the series 4 games to 3. Philadelphians Irv Kosioff and Ike Richman teamed up to purchase the Syracuse NATS in the spring of 1963 and bring the franchise to Philadelphia with league approval May 22, 1963. These NATIONALS had their nickname changed to the 76ERS, in appreciation of the national association of Philadelphia with American Independence. Ironically, it was the ex-Philly San Francisco WARRIORS the Wilt Chamberlain-led 76ERS beat in 1967 for their first NBA Championship.

Nickname: Sixers

PHOENIX SUNS

Although the name-the-team contest generated an impressive 28,000 entries, the name SUNS —the Star of the Solar System — wasn't just picked out of a hat. Considerable thought went into the selection of not only the name but also the colors of Arizona's National Basketball Association franchise. In fact, the SUNS' young General Manager, Jerry Colangelo, was on the cutting edge of a marketing science that integrated a team's logo, nickname, colors, and merchandise with the character of the team's city. "The purpose is to develop a strong bond, a two-way sense of identity, between the fans and their team." The idea for the SUNS' purple and orange came from those spectacular Arizona sunsets. The name SUNS not only identified with the city and state, it was also short. "When thinking in terms of newspapers and headline space, editors like team names with three, four, or five letters," Colangelo said. "Since the exposure of our team through the media is vital to a new club, a short name was a must." Of course, with 28,000 entries, SUNS was not the only name suggested. Some were too long, some were inappropriate, and some were downright strange. Some of the more creative Phoenix rejects included the GRANDSUNS, UNICORNS, PRICKLY PEARS, CACTUS COWBOYS, EAGER BEAVERS, DESERETTES, FABLES, SINNERS, DUST DEVILS, THUNDERBELTERS, ARIZONIACS, POOBAHS, DOMINATORS, MERRY MEN, BASKETEERS, BOYS, MULESKINNERS, TIPINEERS, BABY STATERS, LARIATS, BOX CARS, HOT SHOTS, PACKRATS and the PRIDE. Phoenix itself is nobly named after a beautiful, lone bird which tradition says lived in the Arabian desert for 500 or 600 years and then consumed itself in fire, rising renewed from the ashes to start another long life, becoming a symbol of immortality.

Nicknames: The Purple Gang, Sunderella Suns (1975-76 playoffs)

PORTLAND TRAIL BLAZERS

In 1970, the National Basketball Association granted expansion franchises to Buffalo, Cleveland, and Portland. Within a month a contest was held in the west coast city, asking Oregonians to submit nominations for the new team's name. The contest attracted more than 10,000 entries, and TRAIL BLAZERS was identified by many as synonymous with the rugged individualism, exploration, and pioneering spirit of Oregon and of the Pacific Northwest corner of the United States. The term TRAIL BLAZING comes from the act of chopping BLAZE type notches in tree trunks at eye level with axes to mark new TRAILS made through the wilderness. Hence, TRAIL BLAZERS was recognized as a perfect fit for a basketball team from Oregon finding a successful path for itself in major league basketball. Local media support for the selected name was strong for several reasons, not the least of them that it was easily shortened to BLAZERS, making it fit nicely into headlines.

Nickname: Blazers

SACRAMENTO KINGS

The Sacramento KINGS began their lives as an original team in the National Basketball Association, but as the Rochester ROYALS. They played in Rochester from 1946 to 1957, when they moved to Cincinnati. The last NBA Championship the ROYALS of Rochester won before leaving town was in 1950-51, when they defeated the New York KNICKS 4-3. The Cincinnati ROYALS played for fourteen years in Ohio before packing their bags for Kansas City. But they didn't bring the nickname with them. They became the Kansas City-Omaha KINGS — intentionally maintaining a royal-like moniker, but one with more alliteration for Kansas. The name changed to the Kansas City KINGS in 1975-76, and stayed that way until 1986. Then the team moved to the capital of California, becoming the Sacramento KINGS.

SAN ANTONIO SPURS

In 1967-68 the Dallas CHAPPARALS (a roadrunner-type bird) joined the American Basketball League. They changed their name in 1970-71 to the Texas CHAPPARALS, to help the CHAPS draw more fans statewide. For some reason, in 1972 they went back to the Dallas CHAPPARALS. It was announced late in this season that the team would be sold to New Jersey. That didn't happen. In 1973-74 the team moved to San Antonio, picking up a new nickname, the SPURS. This was in reference to the famous western horseback riding accessory — and its kick-butt, get-up-and-go connotation. The dictionary defines "spur" as anything that can urge, incite, or stimulate to action and a greater effort. In 1976-77 the SPURS changed leagues, joining the National Basketball Association, winning the Central Division Title in its first year. Teams that played alongside the SPURS in the ABL that were not invited to join the NBA in 1976 were the Pittsburgh CONDORS, Florida FLORIDIANS, Kentucky COLONELS, Baltimore CLAWS, SPIRITS of St. Louis, Utah STARS, Virginia SQUIRES, and San Diego SAILS.

SEATTLE SUPERSONICS

After poring over about 25,000 entries in a week-long name-the-team contest, franchise General Manager Don Richman announced that Seattle's new National Basketball Association club would be called the SUPERSONICS. "We think the name best expresses Seattle's people and its present and future," Richman said. The winning entry was submitted by Howard E. Schmidt, an economics and history teacher of Seattle. The nickname was suggested by Boeing's proposal to build a Concorde-style commercial airplane during the late 1960s. The new plane was to be known as the SST, for SuperSonic Transport. Although the transport never got off the ground, the name had a lasting effect, as the Schmidt's entry (with son, Brent, 10) was one of many using a variation of SUPER or SONIC. The father and son team's contribution to Seattle history won them a weekend trip to Palm Springs and two season tickets for the 1967-68 season. G.M. Richman said 162 other persons also entered the name SUPERSONICS and 278 entries listed either SUPERS or SONICS. All received two tickets to a SONICS game.

Nicknames: Sonics, Supes

TORONTO RAPTORS

This franchise, which took to the court for the 1995-96 season, was the second Toronto entry in professional basketball. The HUSKIES played in the pre-NBA Basketball Association of America League,

for only one season in 1946. HUSKIES became the most enthusiastically suggested nickname when word first got out about the new
franchise. But concern over the difficulty finding a logo that didn't
look like that of the TIMBERWOLVES in Minnesota provoked a
name search. The entire Canadian nation was invited to suggest
franchise names, and over 40,000 were received — the record in
all of professional sports. The top ten names were culled from a
reduced list of 189 by a panel of celebrity judges, including two-
time Lillehammer Olympic gold medal biathlete Myriam Bédard,
and hockey great Wayne Gretzky. This list of potential names was
made up entirely of animals: DRAGONS, BEAVERS, HOGS,
TERRIERS, RAPTORS, SCORPIONS, TARANTULAS,
TORONTOSAURUS-REX (T-REX), GRIZZLIES, AND BOB-
CATS. The finalists were the BOBCATS, the DRAGONS, and the
eventual winner, RAPTORS — which was chosen by team ownership. Marketing the dinosaur had much to do with the final decision. In 1995, NBA merchandising pulled in 75 million dollars in
Canada alone, and 1.4 billion worldwide. The top sellers worldwide
are the Chicago BULLS, Charlotte HORNETS, and Orlando
MAGIC, giving RAPTOR president John Bitove Jr. two out of
three good reasons to pick an animal as his team's logo.

UTAH JAZZ

Pro ball existed in Utah once before the JAZZ came to town. In
1967-68 a team called the Anaheim AMIGOS entered the American Basketball Association. The following year the name changed to
the Los Angeles STARS — a reference to all of Hollywood's
STARS. In 1970-71 that ABA team moved to Utah, but kept the
STARS nickname. It's generally believed that a professional sports
team is defined by its nickname and logo, because both are chosen
at a team's inception. A bad nickname could mean bad PR. That's
why, while a team's home city might change, the logo most likely
will not. It made perfect sense to name the New Orleans basketball
team the JAZZ and the Minneapolis team the LAKERS. But when
these teams moved to another city (as both eventually did), the
nickname and the logo followed, even though it didn't make much

sense. Fans just had to get used to it. It was in 1974 that a National Basketball Association team took to the court in New Orleans. A public contest brought the very appropriate JAZZ moniker to the attention of team ownership — in appreciation for the famous musical element of the city's heritage. When the franchise moved to Salt Lake City, Utah, in 1979, it was somewhat mysteriously decided to bring the nickname along.

VANCOUVER GRIZZLIES

In 1994, during the NBA All-Star Weekend in Minneapolis, Vancouver Basketball Management Inc. had its Vancouver MOUNTIES bid unanimously endorsed. By April, the Royal Canadian Mounted Police had informed the Vancouver club that using their famous Mounties moniker was not an option. So the ownership of Arthur R. Griffiths and John E. McCaw Jr. went looking for a new name that would include something powerful to reflect the nature of the team and of basketball, a cultural or geographical association with Canada, especially British Columbia, an indigenous species or spirit, longevity and durability, and a positive emotional appeal with fans and players. The trend in pro sports was towards team identities based on animate subjects, such as living people or animals, so it was not surprising that a name such as GRIZZLIES was a front runner from the beginning, along with DRAGONS, ORCAS, and RAVENS. It was decided that the franchise would adopt the name and identity associated with the Grizzly Bear, which was highly prominent in northwestern native culture and mythology and was a leading icon of Canadiana. Team colors include Naismith Red, in honor of Dr. James A. Naismith, the Canadian who invented basketball in 1891 while studying at the YMCA International Training School in Springfield, Mass. The GRIZZLIES joined the Toronto RAPTORS, their first Canadian expansion cousins, in memorializing the Naismith legacy — the RAPTORS carry Naismith Silver in their dinosaur moniker. On May 16, 1995, the National Basketball Association officially made the Vancouver GRIZZLIES and Toronto RAPTORS their 28th and 29th teams.

WASHINGTON WIZARDS

The Washington BULLETS have changed cities and nicknames many times since their Baltimore beginnings as one of the original National Basketball Association teams in 1946. The Baltimore BULLETS received their moniker because the team practised near the Old Shot Tower, a munitions factory, and also played some of their games near an armory. Owner Stan Behrend said his nickname reasoning was hope that the BULLETS would utilize their "significant explosive talents and speed in humbling the opposition." These BULLETS folded in 1954, then were reborn as an expansion team in 1961 — the Chicago PACKERS. In 1962 they changed the nickname to the ZEPHYRS. When this franchise packed its bags back to Baltimore, they resurrected the old Baltimore BULLETS name. In 1973-74 the BULLETS took to the road once again, this time to Washington. By the way, an American Basketball Association franchise moved into this Baltimore vacancy quickly. This club had started its life as the New Orleans BUCCANEERS in 1967, moved to Memphis becoming the Memphis PROS, the Memphis TAMS, then the Memphis SOUNDS. Then they made that move to Baltimore after the BULLETS left, calling themselves the Baltimore CLAWS, as in crabs, a popular Chesapeake Bay dish. They folded in 1975. Meanwhile, the NBA Baltimore club that had moved to Washington called themselves the Capital BULLETS for one season, then became the Washington BULLETS. In November of 1995, Abe Pollin, who'd owned the team since 1964, decided to change the nickname because of its street-violence connotation. "I've thought about it for 31 years," he said, "because bullets connote killing, violence, death. Our slogan used to be 'Faster than a speeding bullet,' but that is no longer appropriate." On February 22, 1996, it was announced that the team would be called the WIZARDS, the result of a fan phone contest which attracted 500,000 suggestions, including 2,996 different names. From ACCELERATORS to ZULUS, other considered monikers included DRAGONS, EXPRESS, SEADOGS, STALLIONS, MONUMENTS, WOLVERINES, AURA, COBRAS, COURT MARSHALLS, CUCKOOS, DEAL MAKERS,

DODECAHEDRONS, DUNKIN' DONKEYS, ENCHANT-
ERS, FURY, GLORY, JUSTICE, RAVENS, JAM-A-RAMAS,
LIGHT OF FLOWERS, POWER, POWER CATS, RIVER
DAWGS, SAVAGE, and WIPEOUTS.

FOOTBALL
ARGOS
DOLPHINS
BUCCANEERS
VIKINGS
PACKERS
BENGALS
CHARGERS
RAMS
CARDS
JETS
OILERS
LIONS
EAGLES
COLTS
CHIEFS
BROWNS
SAINTS

NATIONAL FOOTBALL LEAGUE

Arizona Cardinals
Atlanta Falcons
Baltimore Ravens
Buffalo Bills
Carolina Panthers
Chicago Bears
Cincinnati Bengals
Cleveland Browns
Dallas Cowboys
Denver Broncos
Detroit Lions
Green Bay Packers
Houston Oilers
Indianapolis Colts
Jacksonville Jaguars
Kansas City Chiefs

Miami Dolphins
Minnesota Vikings
New England Patriots
New Orleans Saints
New York Giants
New York Jets
Oakland Raiders
Philadelphia Eagles
Pittsburgh Steelers
St. Louis Rams
San Diego Chargers
San Francisco 49ers
Seattle Seahawks
Tampa Bay Buccaneers
Washington Redskins

CANADIAN FOOTBALL LEAGUE

British Columbia Lions
Calgary Stampeders
Edmonton Eskimos
Hamilton Tiger-Cats
Montreal Alouettes

Ottawa Rough Riders
Saskatchewan Roughriders
Toronto Argonauts
Winnipeg Blue Bombers

NATIONAL FOOTBALL LEAGUE

ARIZONA CARDINALS

The CARDINALS, a charter member of the National Football League, boast the distinction of being the oldest continuously run pro football franchise in the nation. Founded in 1898, the team began as a neighborhood group which gathered to play football in a predominantly Irish area of Chicago's south side, playing under the name MORGAN ATHLETIC CLUB. When its playing site changed to nearby Normal Field, so did the nickname — to the NORMALS. In 1901, team owner Chris O'Brien bought used jerseys from the University of Chicago. When attempting to fade them to a maroon color, O'Brien declared, "That's not maroon, it's CARDINAL red!" The club's permanent nickname was born. The jersey color and the location of the field, on a Chicago street called Racine, led to a new name, the RACINE CARDINALS. Two years after joining the American Football League in 1920, a team from Racine, Wis. joined the National Football League, forcing the CARDINALS to change their name to the CHICAGO CARDINALS. In 1944 the CARDINALS and Pittsburgh STEELERS combined to form one team, called CARD-PITT (nicknamed the CARPETS). In 1960 the team moved and became the St. Louis CARDINALS. After 18 years in St. Louis, the CARDINALS relocated to Arizona in the spring of 1988 and made Sun Devil Stadium on the campus of Arizona State University their new home. Now they were the Phoenix CARDINALS. On March 17, 1994, team president Bidwill announced his intention to broaden the team's horizons, and changed the name from the Phoenix to the Arizona CARDINALS.

Nickname: The Big Red

ATLANTA FALCONS

As fast as the flight of a FALCON, the new National Football League team got its name. On June 30, 1965, the NFL won a battle with the American Football League to place a pro football franchise in Atlanta and play at the Atlanta Stadium, the new home of the Atlanta BRAVES (from Milwaukee). Local radio station WSB began a name-the-team campaign with a deadline of August 15 for entries. Fans were asked to give them a name and a reason in 25 words or less. As thousands of entries poured in, a panel of five persons was selected to choose the winner. Fan submissions included such monikers as PEACHES, REBELS, CONFEDERATES, GEORGIANS, CRACKERS, BOMBERS, KNIGHTS, FIREBIRDS, LANCERS, THRASHERS, WILDCATS, and many more. More than 40 entries offered the FAL-CONS. The winner, high-school teacher Julia Elliot, wrote, "The falcon is proud and dignified with great courage and fight. It never drops its prey. It is deadly and has a great sporting tradition." The Atlanta FALCONS celebrated their 30th anniversary season in 1995, still with the same owner, still in the same city, still with the same nickname.

BALTIMORE RAVENS

In 1995 Cleveland Browns' owner Art Modell announced he was moving his team to Baltimore to fill the void left by the Colts, who had departed in 1984. Quarterback Vinny Testaverde started the rumor that the new team in Baltimore would be called the MUS-TANGS. But twelve years to the day that the COLTS bolted from Baltimore in the dark of night and left a gaping hole in the hearts of area football fans, the name RAVENS was picked for the city's new National Football League team. Modell announced the name before a crowd of officials and fans huddled under umbrellas at Baltimore's Inner Harbor. RAVENS, named after the famous poem by Edgar Allan Poe who died in 1849 and is buried in Baltimore, beat out AMERICANS and MARAUDERS in a phone-in poll fans used to choose the team's name. Modell's team was temporarily nameless after he agreed to leave the BROWNS' moniker and colors behind in Cleveland — which intends to land an expansion team by 1999.

BUFFALO BILLS

Bob Curran of the *Buffalo News* had to do some digging to get this one. He discovered that Jim Breuil, the owner of the Buffalo franchise in the All-American Football Conference, had organized a contest for fans who would be interested in trying to pick a name for the new club that would start playing in 1946. The impetus behind the contest was the desire to break away from "the unimaginative Buffalo BISONS name that all prior or existing professional teams were named." Breuil's company was called the Frontier Oil Company, and a young employee of that organization had it in the front of his mind when he was thinking of a name for the new team. An entrant had to accompany his proposed name with a 25-word explanation of his choice. Jimmy Dyson wrote about Buffalo Bill, the famous Western hero, being part of the American frontier and the new team that was being supported by Frontier Oil was opening a new frontier in sports in Western New York. Hence the name, the Buffalo BILLS. The officials liked the name, so Jimmy won the contest. No one was more pleased than Jimmy, who passed away in 1975, when Buffalo kept the moniker even after it changed leagues in 1959. Owner Ralph Wilson said of his new National Football League BILLS, "The old team was a proud team. Its fans had been very loyal. I could not see any reason why we should change the name, and so a change was never considered."

CAROLINA PANTHERS

The Richardson family of Charlotte, Carolina had been contacted about possibly buying the New England PATRIOTS, Seattle SEAHAWKS and—before Jerry Jones emerged—the Dallas COWBOYS. "But we always came back to one simple thing," said Mark Richardson, director of business operations, "We were only interested in a National Football League team in the Carolinas." It was Mark who first suggested the PANTHERS nickname and the team colors of black, blue, and silver. "I told my father (Jerry Richardson, whose sons Mark and Jon call the "Boss") I thought it needed to all work together. There needed to be a synergy between the name, the color scheme, the logo, and the image the team portrays." Mark suggested the power colors, and he had always liked the PANTHER animal. It wasn't a cinch, though. Mark and his father discussed the nickname COUGARS, and NFL Properties offered for consideration COBRAS and RHINOS, and the color purple. PANTHERS stuck as did the colors — a nod in the direction of Mark's favorite childhood teams, the Oakland RAIDERS and Pittsburgh STEELERS. In the long history of the NFL, only one other team has had the nickname PANTHERS — the Detroit PANTHERS of 1925-26. Detroit fans had their interest centered on the Michigan WOLVERINES in nearby Ann Arbor, and failed to support the team — they moved, becoming the Providence STEAM ROLLER. In 1995 the Carolina PANTHERS made NFL history, becoming the first expansion team ever to beat the reigning Superbowl champs (San Francisco 49ERS) while in their inaugural season.

CHICAGO BEARS

On September 17, 1920, George S. Halas met with representatives from 12 other football teams in Canton, Ohio and formed the American Professional Football Association, which later became the National Football League. He originally named the team the Decatur STALEYS, after A.E. Staley, a starch manufacturer and enthusiastic sports fan who sponsored a semi-pro baseball team and commissioned Halas to organize the team. In 1920 the Decatur STALEYS moved to Chicago where they played in Wrigley Field, the same park as the Chicago CUBS. George Halas decided that he wanted to keep his club's nickname in the same family as the baseball CUBS, so he chose BEARS. The Chicago BEARS and Green Bay PACKERS enjoy the oldest rivalry in pro football. The jersey colors have always been blue and orange, the same colors as the University of Illinois.

Nickname: Monsters of the Midway

CINCINNATI BENGALS

Why BENGALS? Paul Brown picked the name BENGALS for Cincinnati's football team "to give it a link with past professional football in Cincinnati." From 1937 through 1941 the BENGALS were a famous unit in the Cincinnati area. In 1938 they played three teams from the National Football League. They beat the Chicago BEARS 17-14, and the Pittsburgh STEELERS 38-0, and tied the Chicago CARDINALS 7-7. "If we can pick up a thread of tradition, we think it's good," said Brown when he named the team. Hundreds of names were suggested by fans in an effort to name the new Cincinnati team and the most popular was BUCKEYES, but they kept searching for the obvious reason. "The owners rejected it because we didn't want it to be confused with the Ohio State BUCKEYES and wanted something to embody four states rather than just the one. We feel at home with the name BENGALS."

CLEVELAND BROWNS

In 1996 mayor Michael White lost his Cleveland franchise to Baltimore, but learned that his city would be keeping the nickname and colors for a new NFL club to arrive in 1999. The storied franchise was originally named after a boxer. In 1945 the Cleveland RAMS shocked the National Football League by winning the championship. But they did it in a near-empty Cleveland Stadium, and the team owner decided he'd had enough of the town. On January 12, 1946, the RAMS moved to Los Angeles and suddenly Cleveland's new team in the All-American Conference had the town to itself. But it didn't have a name. Team owner Mickey McBride offered a $1,000 war bond to the fan who could pick an appropriate nickname. The winner, PANTHERS, came from a Navy sailor named John J. Hartnett. PANTHERS was fine with McBride and Coach Paul Brown, both of whom wanted a name that "could be animated for promotional use and around which a symbol could be forged." But soon after, McBride received a visitor in his office claiming the name PANTHERS had a prior owner. Brown ordered some inquiries and discovered that it was the name of a semi-pro football team near Cleveland, a franchise that was apparently a chronic loser. This provoked another contest, one that was actively to pursue names of championship calibre. "Joe Louis was the best known champion at the time, and we received a lot of entries suggesting we name the team after him," Brown said. Everyone liked the idea. So the Cleveland franchise was named the BROWN BOMBERS after the heavyweight champion of the world, Joe Louis. Soon after, the name was shortened to the BROWNS. Of course it didn't go unnoticed that the name also coincided with that of its coach-general manager and chief architect, but there weren't many who blamed Paul Brown if he might want a familiar name close by. In 1995, after 50 years of NFL tradition in Cleveland, owner Modell signed a 30-year lease to play in Baltimore, with the RAVENS.

DALLAS COWBOYS

When the Dallas expansion team was looking for a nickname in 1960, the job fell to General Manager Texas E. Schramm. Some of the first names considered were RANGERS, LONGHORNS, and STEERS. The RANGERS name at that time had been associated with minor league baseball. The University of Texas had a lock on LONGHORNS. When STEERS was brought up, Tex Schramm tossed it aside commenting that when you consider what a steer is, that's not a very macho image for a pro football team. So, Tex began asking people what they thought of when the state of Texas was mentioned. The word COWBOYS kept coming back to him. The COWBOYS "Star" emblem was just a logical extension of the COWBOYS name, since Texas is the Lone Star State. Schramm must have made the right choices — the COWBOYS have a vast world-wide following, the COWBOYS Star is recognized everywhere, and Schramm was the first General Manager inducted into the Pro Football Hall of Fame.

Nicknames: America's Team, Cowpokes, Boys

DENVER BRONCOS

The Denver BRONCOS arrived on the scene in 1960, and the search for a nickname went public. Fans were invited to submit names, with the suggestion that any new moniker would have to be symbolic of the region. But Denver is an area with many personalities. Remember, this is the city that sports the National Hockey League's Colorado AVALANCHE and Denver NUGGETS. The original name for the franchise still playing in its original location was the Denver BRONCOS — a nod in the direction of the wild horses once associated with the wild west. These wild broncos, an English word derived from the Mexican word for "rough," had a reputation for being tough to break.

Nickname: The Broncs

DETROIT LIONS

Detroit welcomed the LIONS in 1934, but it was not the area's first look at professional football. In 1920, the Detroit HERALDS were a charter member of the American Professional Football Association. They folded after two years as did their replacements, the Detroit PANTHERS. In 1928 the Detroit WOLVERINES were formed, but they failed after just one year. In 1930, the then ten-year-old National Football League added a franchise from Portsmouth, Ohio, called the SPARTANS. After four seasons, the team was purchased by Detroit radio executive George A. Richards and moved to the Motor City. A 1934 *Detroit Times* article announced the team's new nickname. "Inspired by the spirited fight the Detroit TIGERS are making for the American League baseball championship, sponsors of the Detroit professional football team have decided to call their entry in the National Football League the Detroit LIONS. They would call this team the TIGERS, but that might create confusion." Cy Huston, team GM, explained that the lion is monarch of the jungle, and he hoped to be monarch of the league. "It is our ambition to make the LION as famous as the Detroit ball club has made the TIGER." The blue and silver LIONS won the NFL Championship in 1935, their second year.

Nickname: The Pride

GREEN BAY PACKERS

On the evening of August 11, 1919, a score or more of husky young athletes, called together by Curly Lambeau and George Calhoun, gathered in the dingy editorial room of the old Green Bay Press-Gazette building on Cherry Street and organized a football team. They didn't know it, but that was the beginning of the Green Bay PACKERS. First they talked Lambeau's employer at the Indian Packing Company into putting up some money for equipment. Because the team's jerseys had been provided by the packing company, which also permitted the use of its athletic field for practice, the club was identified in its early publicity as a project of the company. With this tie-in the name PACKERS was a natural, and PACKERS they have been ever since, although the corporation had practically faded out of the picture before that first season was half over. After two years of "passing the hat," the team was so successful that Lambeau was backed by two officials of the packing plant in obtaining a franchise in the new national pro league that had been formed in 1920. But it wasn't until the Green Bay Football Corporation was formed in support of the team that the PACKERS overcame their enormous financial troubles. From those modest and somewhat tenuous beginnings, the PACKERS have gone on to earn national stature and virtual world-wide recognition by winning more championships (11) over the intervening 70-plus years than any other team in professional football. The fact that these achievements have come while representing a city of only 96,000 inhabitants in competition with the country's population giants has endeared them to all fans of the David versus Goliath concept. The Green Bay PACKERS/Chicago BEARS rivalry is the oldest in pro football.

Nickname: The Pack

HOUSTON OILERS

"Houston's First Pro Sports Team," the posters used to say. K.S. "Bud" Adams parleyed a 1946 chance stop in Houston, resulting from fog which grounded his plane, into a highly successful business empire. He incorporated the ADA Oil Company, and built his ADA OILERS into a perennial power in the National Industrial Basketball League in the 1950s. And it was Adams who finally brought professional sports to the Gulf Coast when he founded the Houston OILERS football team. On August 3, 1959, the OILERS and the Dallas TEXANS became the first two major league sports franchises in the state of Texas. The American Football League had been organized at that time with four other cities — Los Angeles, New York, Denver, and Minneapolis-St. Paul. It was on Halloween of 1959 that Adams, who had lettered in football with the Kansas JAYHAWKS, named the team the OILERS for obvious "sentimental and social reasons." The OILERS lost their first pre-season game to the Dallas TEXANS, but went on to win the first AFL Championship in 1961, defeating the Los Angeles CHARGERS 24-16. It was announced on April 29, 1996, that the OILERS would be moving to Nashville for the 1998 season, and they had been promised the staggering sum of $292 million for a stadium and an eight-million-dollar subsidy for 30 years for owner Bud Adams.

INDIANAPOLIS COLTS

Follow the bouncing ball. The roots of the franchise go back to December 28, 1946, when the bankrupt Miami SEAHAWKS of the All-American Football Conference were purchased and relocated in Baltimore. As a result of a contest in Baltimore won by Charles Evans, the team was renamed the COLTS. The AAFC and the National Football League merged in 1950 and after being a member of the NFL for two years, the franchise was dissolved because of its failing financial condition. Now, rewind. In 1943, a man named Ted Collins was granted a National Football League franchise he called the Boston YANKS. In 1944, Boston and the

Brooklyn DODGERS merged into a team that played home games in both cities and was known simply as the YANKS. When the Brooklyn franchise withdrew from the NFL, the YANKS went back to Boston. In 1949, the Boston YANKS moved, becoming the New York BULLDOGS, and shared the Polo Grounds with the GIANTS. In 1950, they became the New York YANKS. Ted Collins sold the team to the NFL in 1952, and a group from Dallas purchased the assets. But those Dallas TEXANS were not to be, and the franchise cancelled at the end of that season was the last time an NFL team failed. But in 1953, a Baltimore group headed by Carroll Rosenbloom was granted a franchise and was awarded the holdings of the defunct Dallas organization. So it was this Dallas team that became the second NFL franchise in Baltimore where, keeping the COLTS nickname, the Texas team colors of blue and white were inherited. Thirty years later the franchise left Baltimore for the Hoosier Dome in Indianapolis. And that's how the Miami SEAHAWKS, Dallas TEXANS, Boston YANKS, and original Baltimore COLTS ended up the Indianapolis COLTS in 1984.

JACKSONVILLE JAGUARS

In 1995, a new breed of cat pounced onto the National Football League playing field, although the name wasn't chosen because the animal is indigenous to the area. In the U.S., jaguars are found mainly in the Southwest, but mostly they are found in Central and South America. "We liked JAGUARS because no other professional sports team has it," said Rick Catlett, the executive vice-president of Touchdown Jacksonville! Ltd. "Plus, we do have the oldest living jaguar in North America at the Jacksonville Zoo — it's a 24-year-old female." Three other names were finalists in the contest: SHARKS, PANTHERS, and STINGRAYS. Ownership liked the animal's rep; the jaguar is considered by many to be more dangerous than the lion (sorry Detroit) or leopard. Maya Indians worshipped it as a god, a symbol of strength and courage. They believed it was a sacred animal and that the sun hid inside the jaguar at night. And maybe most important for Jacksonville fans — considering the movement of franchises of late — the jaguar is not known to migrate. Pete Prisco of the *Florida Times Union* suggested that if the team lived up to its nickname, the NFL should look out, because "The *Encyclopedia Americana* says a jaguar is the most powerful, most feared carnivorous animal in Latin America."

Nickname: Jags

KANSAS CITY CHIEFS

Lamar Hunt did more than bring the Dallas TEXANS into the big leagues in 1959. He established and organized the whole American Football League with six original cities — Dallas, New York, Houston, Denver, Los Angeles, and Minneapolis (Buffalo and Boston were added later and Oakland replaced Minneapolis). "Without him," said Boston's Billy Sullivan, "there would have been no AFL." In 1961 the AFL Dallas TEXANS and NFL Dallas COWBOYS both drafted E.J. Holub, described by many scouts at the time as "the best football player in America." Holub, much to the benefit of the fledgling league, went with the TEXANS and a Hall-of-Fame career. On May 14, 1963, Hunt announced he was moving the franchise to Kansas City and renaming it the CHIEFS. Kansas City mayor H. Roe Bartle had promised to enlarge Municipal Stadium and guaranteed Hunt three times as many season ticket sales as the TEXANS had in Dallas. The Mayor's nickname? The Chief.

MIAMI DOLPHINS

MARINERS, MARAUDERS, MUSTANGS, MISSILES, MOONS, SHARKS, SUNS — none of these other names suggested to the American Football League expansion franchise in 1965 could raise a fin to the runaway winner. DOLPHINS was submitted by 622 entrants in a contest which attracted 19,843 entries and more than a thousand different names. The dozen finalists were delivered to a seven-member screening committee of local media. The beloved dolphin has inspired wonder for centuries. Plutarch observed 1,900 years ago that the dolphin "is the only creature who loves man for his own sake." Every trainer will have a tale of the dolphin's cleverness and ingenuity, and scientists are fascinated by a dolphin's natural equipment which far surpasses the range of Navy sonar equipment. "The dolphin is one of the fastest and smartest creatures of the sea," Joe Robbie said in announcing the team name on October 8, 1965. "Dolphins will attack and kill a shark or whale. Sailors say bad luck will come to anyone who harms one of them." Mrs. Robert Swanson of West Miami was selected from the six hundred winning entries, and won two lifetime passes to Dolphin games. The tiebreaker was naming the winner and score of the 1905 game between the University of Miami and Notre Dame — it ended in a scoreless tie.

Nickname: The Fish

MINNESOTA VIKINGS

Minnesota was granted a National Football League franchise in 1960 and fielded a team in 1961. When Bert Rose was selected General Manager in 1961, one of the first steps he took was to recommend to the Board of Directors that the club be nicknamed the VIKINGS. A nickname should serve a dual purpose, he said. First, it should represent an aggressive person or animal imbued with the will to win. Secondly, if possible, it is desirable to have it connote the region that the particular team represents. The VIKINGS score well on both points. Certainly, the Nordic Vikings were a fearless race. Following many years of victories against the British Isles and France, under Erik the Red they sailed in open boats across the North Atlantic, seeking new peoples to conquer. Their entire history is punctuated with the aggressive desire to will and win. While Minnesota is populated by the descendants of settlers from many nations, the area has a rich Nordic lore, perhaps due to the mythology of Paul Bunyan and his Blue Ox, perhaps due to the preponderance of the "sons" and "sens" in the phone book. Karl Hubenthal, sports cartoonist for the *Los Angeles Times*, did the original drawing of the VIKING logo. Marking the entrance to Winter Park — home of the Minnesota VIKINGS — is an authentic replica of a Viking coastal raider ship, patterned after relics that have been discovered in Scandinavian countries.

Nickname: Vikes

NEW ENGLAND PATRIOTS ——————

In the late 1950s, the National Football League's Chicago CARDI-
NALS were looking for a new home and Boston opened its doors.
But that franchise decided on Missouri and became the St. Louis
CARDINALS. William Sullivan, who had pursued the CARDI-
NALS for Boston, decided then to join the fledgling American
Football League in 1959. The first promotion was to name the club.
A contest was held and the various names were submitted to a panel
of sportswriters. Seventy-four fans suggested the name PATRI-
OTS, which the panel agreed best personified the New England
region. So the PATRIOTS were born in 1960, as were their colors
of red, blue, and white. The original Patriot logo was designed by
local cartoonist Phil Bissel — it was in the *Boston Globe* where
William Sullivan saw it, and Pat PATRIOT was born. They started
playing the game as the Boston PATRIOTS, changing finally to the
New England PATRIOTS to help attract a broader fan base. For a
team without any change of locale in 35 years, the PATRIOTS sure
have called a lot of stadiums their home field. The PATRIOTS have
played home games on five different gridirons, including: Boston
University Field in 1960-62, Fenway Park in Boston in 1963-68,
Boston College Alumni Stadium in Chestnut Hill in 1969, Harvard
Stadium in Cambridge in 1970, before leaving the Hub for perma-
nent residence in Schaefer (1971-82)/Sullivan (1983-89)/Foxboro
Stadium (1990-present) in Foxboro from 1970 to the present.

Nickname: The Pats

NEW ORLEANS SAINTS ——————

The merging of the American Football League with the National
Football League allowed for expansion into New Orleans. Art
dealer Dave Dixon, one of the visionaries who brought the fran-
chise to town, said, "My wife and I were sitting in a little cafe in
Paris in 1961, and all of a sudden this three-piece band played
'When the Saints Go Marching In'. I was flabbergasted and realized
that this song had universal appeal. I said to my wife 'By God, the
SAINTS would be a perfect name for the New Orleans football

team,' but later when it came to decision time, some people felt that the name might have an improper religious connotation. That was dispelled by Archbishop Phillip Hannan when he first arrived in town. I asked him what he thought of the name SAINTS for the football team. He replied, 'I think it would be wonderful. Besides, I have a premonition we are going to need a 12th man on our side for several years to come.'" Plus, ownership at the time didn't consider it a coincidence when New Orleans received news of their franchise on November 1, 1966. It was All Saints Day, a holiday significant to the religious history of the city. There was a name-the-team contest, but it was only a formality. New Orleans had an NFL football team with a heavenly nickname. So it was September 17, 1967, opening day in the NFL, and a throng of 80,879 fans witnessed rookie John Gilliam take the opening kickoff and return in 94 yards for a touchdown against the Los Angeles RAMS. That's how the SAINTS came marching in.

NEW YORK GIANTS

Tim Mara purchased a National Football League franchise in 1925 for $500. And it was Mara, as owner and founder, who picked the GIANTS nickname. The GIANTS originally played their games at the Polo Grounds which was also home to the very successful Major League Baseball's GIANTS. The football team felt that they might be able to attract some attention by sharing the name. Therefore they were named the GIANTS in the year of their inception, with no other nicknames considered at that time. According to the football GIANTS information, the baseball GIANTS got their name from the large buildings that compose New York City. But the baseball GIANTS claim their name was changed from the New York GOTHAMS in 1886 when Jim Mutrie, the Manager at the time, shouted at his players after a victory, "My big fellows! My giants! We are the people!" The baseball GIANTS left for San Francisco in 1957, leaving the NFL GIANTS alone to carry on their name in New York.

Nicknames: The Big Blue Wrecking Crew, Mara Tech

NEW YORK JETS

On March 28, 1963, a five-man syndicate composed of David A. (Sonny) Werblin, Leon Hess, Townsend B. Martin, Donald C. Lillis, and Philip H. Iselin purchased the New York TITANS of the American Football League for the price of one million dollars. Less than a month later, on April 15, Warblin, the team's president and CEO, renamed the club the JETS. The reasons, he said, were two-fold. At the time, the United States was entering the "space" or "Jet Age." Commercial airlines were filling the air and soon there would be men walking on the moon. Also, the JETS new facility, Shea Stadium, would be located in Flushing Meadows, New York, between the LaGuardia and Idlewild (later renamed John F. Kennedy) Airports. Hence the name, the New York JETS.

OAKLAND RAIDERS

The RAIDERS were added to the American Football League as an afterthought and subsequently had to draft from the other teams' rejects. At first, they were named the SENORS, the name picked by a raffle winner. After throwing a celebration for the winner, team officials quietly changed the name from SENORS to RAIDERS the following day! The new nickname was a tip of the pirate's hat to Oakland's proximity to the Pacific and its rich history of sea robbers — much like the Spanish who terrorized the east coast, and are remembered by the Tampa Bay BUCCANEERS. It was probably the Dutch raiders on the West Coast, however. In 1963, Al Davis left his assistant coaching job in San Diego to become head coach of the RAIDERS. He changed the team colors from orange and black to silver and black and lead the club to their first-ever winning season. In 1982 the franchise moved, becoming for the next 12 years the Los Angeles RAIDERS. They returned to Oakland for the 1995 season.

PHILADELPHIA EAGLES

In 1902, baseball's Philadelphia ATHLETICS and Philadelphia PHILLIES formed football teams. It was the first attempt at a pro gridiron league, and was named the National Football League. The first World Series of pro football was played with a team made up of players from both the ATHLETICS and the PHILLIES, but for some reason named NEW YORK! They lost to the Syracuse ATHLETIC CLUB, and soon the league itself failed. In 1922 another league started up with the same NFL name, and it soon included a club from a section of Philly called Frankford. When the Frankford YELLOWJACKETS won the NFL Championship in 1926, no one in the 22-team league had played more games — and that included the Philadelphia QUAKERS playing in the renegade American Football League. When the YELLOWJACKETS went into bankruptcy, a syndicate bought it from the NFL. The new owners named their team the EAGLES in honor of President Franklin Roosevelt's New Deal, whose symbol was the American Eagle. Roosevelt's "thunderbird" was meant to symbolize the nation's industrial rebirth. At first blue and yellow were adopted because they were Philadelphia's city colors, but owner Bert Bell decided to use Kelly Green, a hue that survived until the Midnight Green used since '95. In 1943, because of the World War Two manpower shortage, Philadelphia and Pittsburgh were granted permission to merge for one season. The Phil-Pitt STEAGLES were dissolved after the last day of the season.

Nickname: The Birds

PITTSBURGH STEELERS

The fifth oldest franchise in the National Football League (behind the Chicago (Arizona) CARDINALS, Green Bay PACKERS, Chicago BEARS, and New York GIANTS), the Pittsburgh football team was founded in 1933 by Art Rooney. The gridiron club has experienced a number of name changes, including the MAJESTIC RADIOS ATHLETIC CLUB pre-1933 and Pittsburgh PIRATES from 1933-39. But the STEELERS nickname in 1940 was the result of a name-the-team contest, and was in tribute to the livelihood of the town that hosted it. The name was suggested by the wife of Joe Carr, who was the ticket manager. In 1943, because of the World War Two manpower shortage, the Philadelphia EAGLES and Pittsburgh STEELERS were granted permission to merge for one season. The Phil-Pitt STEAGLES were dissolved after the last day of the season — the same season the National Football League made the wearing of helmets mandatory. In 1944 the STEELERS merged with the Chicago CARDINALS. The CARDS-PITTS (or, CARPETS as they were known), didn't win a single game. In 1945 they were once again the Pittsburgh STEELERS. The colors on the hypercycloid — the extruded diamond shape found on the STEELERS helmet — represent the three materials used to make steel: yellow for coal, orange for ore, and blue for scrap steel. In 1952 the men from Steel City became the last club to move from the single wing to the T-Formation we now recognize as the standard in football. In 1962, Republic Steel of Cleveland, Ohio suggested that the STEELERS use the national Steel Industry's logo because of their long association with the industry. The STEELERS accepted, and the Steel logo is now worn on the right side of the helmet only.

Nickname: Steel City

ST. LOUIS RAMS

This franchise is responsible for a number of interesting firsts in pro sports. They were the first and probably the only pro club ever to take its name from a college football team! It was 1937, Cleveland. The football team's first General Manager, Buzz Wetzel, admired a college team known as the Fordham University RAMS. The pro squad's first owner, Horner Marshman, also liked the name and baptized their NFL team the Cleveland RAMS. In 1946, new owner Dan Reeves, heir to a 600-store grocery chain that was sold to Safeway for $11 million in 1940, felt the future of his franchise was in the West. The RAMS became the first major professional sports team on the Pacific Coast, forging the way west for the National Football League. Another first: in 1947 halfback Fred Gehrke, an art major in college, made a pen-and-ink sketch of a ram's horns. Head Coach Bob Snyder could not visualize the art work on a helmet till Gehrke transferred the design onto his teammate's leather headgear. The following season, the RAMS became the first pro team with a helmet insignia. Ironically, of the 28 NFL clubs playing today only the team that took root back in Ohio after the Rams left, the Cleveland BROWNS, does not have helmet insignia. In the 1995-96 season, the team packed its bags and moved back east to become the St. Louis RAMS. Also, the RAMS win hands-down for most cleverly nicknamed cheerleading squad — those Embraceable Ewes.

SAN DIEGO CHARGERS _____

No sooner had the American Football League been formed than on October 14, 1959, Frank Leahy, former Notre Dame University football coach, was named General Manager of the Los Angeles-based team. The club held its own name-the-club contest and received a number of considered monikers, including FRONTIERSMEN, CABALLEROS, CHALLENGERS, RANCHEROS, JETS, TOWNSMEN, BRACEROS. Frank Leahy liked the sound of a name submitted by Gerald Courtney of Hollywood, the CHARGERS. The AFL club shared the Coliseum with the college football USC TROJANS until the Greater San Diego Sports Association made an offer the CHARGERS couldn't refuse. In 1961 construction finished to enlarge Balboa Stadium, and the CHARGERS took to their own homefield. It was in 1960 and while still in Los Angeles that owner Barron Hilton unveiled the CHARGERS uniform, blue and gold with lightning bolts on sides of helmets and trousers. It was at his Santa Monica residence, and one of the players who modelled the new nickname and uniform was none other than Republican Jack Kemp.

Nicknames: The Lightning Bolts, The Bolts

SAN FRANCISCO 49ERS

The San Francisco 49ERS have the distinction of being the first major league professional sports franchise on the West Coast. Beginning play in 1946 as a member of the All-American Football Conference, the 49ERS were also the first professional sports team to "originate" on the West Coast, later to be joined by the National Football League's Los Angeles RAMS, who moved from Cleveland (and left L.A. for St. Louis in 1995), and Major League Baseball's Los Angeles DODGERS and San Francisco GIANTS, who migrated from Brooklyn and New York, respectively — bringing their East Coast nicknames along with them. The San Francisco 49ERS franchise was founded in 1946, which was very close to the one hundredth anniversary of the Gold Rush of 1849. In 1849, San Francisco experienced an influx of settlers, adventurers, risk-takers and hell-raisers from all over America. These newcomers brought with them a spirit that defines Frisco to this day. The team's 49ER nickname is in honor of those gold-miners of San Francisco legend, as is the gold helmet they have always worn. The 49ERS is the only name the team has been affiliated with and San Francisco is the only city in which it has resided.

Nickname: Miners

SEATTLE SEAHAWKS

In 1975 team management selected the nickname SEAHAWKS following a fan competition that attracted 20,365 entries and 1,741 different names. "Our new name shows aggressiveness, reflects our soaring Northwest heritage, and belongs to no other major league team," said John Thompson, SEAHAWKS General Manager. Other fan suggestions included the Seattle ASPARAGUS, SWARTHY SWANS, Washattle WHOPPERS, and Milltown MAULERS. Popular suggestions included the MARINERS, SKIPPERS, PIONEERS, LUMBERJACKS, SPACERS, SOCKEYES, SEAGULLS, and SPINNAKERS. Listen to some fans' reasons for selecting their names: "The UFOs. People will come from everywhere to see a UFO." "The Seattle SEPTICS is easy to say, and has a certain air about it." "Seattle SEMANON. That's NO-NAMES spelled backwards." "Seattle SAMS, from SOUND and MOUNTAINS and SEA. Play it again, Sam." And how about "The Seattle FIRE, because fire leaves total destruction in its path, boys have a 'burning desire' to become pro football players, and most of us girls carry a 'torch' for a pro football player," offered Sue Simon of Coupeville.

Nickname: Hawks

TAMPA BAY BUCCANEERS ⸺

The BUCCANEERS was originally the nickname of a local Florida semi-pro football team. Tampa Bay was granted their National Football League franchise in 1974, and played their first game in the Fall of 1976. It was February of 1975 that the club got its moniker. They were nicknamed by a panel of local newspaper sportswriters and members of the new NFL organization. There had been a local name-the-team competition, which was non-binding. That is to say the authorities were not obligated to use the winning name. But, coincidentally, BUCCANEERS was the unanimous choice of the panel as well as the winning entry. The nickname is a nod in the direction of the Florida coastline and its history. It was the buccaneers, the pirates or sea robbers, who raided the Spanish coasts of America in the 17th century.

Nickname: The Bucs

WASHINGTON REDSKINS ⸺

The Washington REDSKINS were originally located in Boston and were named the Boston BRAVES by team owner George Preston Marshall. They were renamed in 1933 to differentiate between the Boston BRAVES of the National League and the Boston BRAVES of the National Football League. The team retained the name when it relocated to Washington in 1937. Over the long history of the Washington REDSKINS, the name has reflected positive attributes of the American Indian such as dedication, courage, and pride. The REDSKINS have become an institution in the Nation's Capital and the team's popularity brings the community together. Because of the respect that goes with the name REDSKINS, the team has never been referred to by any other name. In the 1970s, when Head Coach George Allen brought in a plethora of veterans, the team became known as the OVER THE HILL GANG. During the 1980s, when the REDSKINS went to three Super Bowls, several nicknames were born to describe certain aspects of the team. The team's offensive line became known as the HOGS, a moniker that remains today and is well known by all NFL fans.

Nicknames: *'Skins, Over the Hill Gang, Hogs*

CANADIAN FOOTBALL LEAGUE

BRITISH COLUMBIA LIONS

The remarkable Annis Stukus took my call and held me spellbound with his wonderful anecdotes. Among other responsibilities Stukus was the coach, general manager, and publicity manager of the British Columbia LIONS from the team's inception ("Started something from nothing.") in 1953 until 1955. When he retired after his three-year contract, they had to hire five men to take his place. The LIONS nickname was the product of a fan contest held in all local media. Twin mountain peaks can be seen just north of the city of Vancouver, and legend has it they look like lions guarding over British property. They are actually called the LION Peaks. Stukus rejected the Vancouver LIONS because he wanted the team to embrace all of B.C. The only other name he remembered from that time was the Vancouver ELECTRICS, after the B.C. Electric company, because, as a fan suggested, "They're big and strong and powerful and never get beaten." Stukus was responsible for financing and came up with a novel approach for getting funds. He sold memberships to the club for twenty dollars apiece. He announced that it was his intention to sell only three thousand memberships, and after that it didn't matter if you knew the King of England, you couldn't get one. He sold five thousand, including memberships to Bob Hope and Bing Crosby! Stukus' contribution to the second year ad campaign was the line "The Lions Will Roar in '54." They only roared at the box office, winning only one game on the field. The fans went crazy, tearing down the wooden goalposts. They sold pieces of this "authentic" wood door-to-door for two dollars apiece. Stukus laughed, "If we got all that sold wood back we could've built goalposts from here to the clouds."

Nickname: Leos

CALGARY STAMPEDERS

Records show the cities of Calgary and Edmonton playing a home and home series in 1891, but there is no mention of nicknames. In 1908, the Alberta city formed the Calgary TIGERS. The club was disbanded for the war years, then reformed as the 50th BATTAL-ION, then later the Calgary ALTOMAS. The Calgary BRONKS were formed in 1935. During World War Two Calgary had been entertained by several North Hill BLIZZARDS and East End STAMPEDERS games. In 1945 these teams combined to become the Calgary STAMPEDERS, adopting blue and black outfits. Their first game they won 12-0 over the Regina ROUGHRIDERS. In 1948 the STAMPEDERS won the Grey Cup and turned the annual fall classic into a national festival — Canada's national drunk as it is called today. The 55-year-old franchise has played in eight Grey Cups, won three, and retired four jerseys of gridiron stars who have "given the club the shirts off their back."

Nickname: Stamps

EDMONTON ESKIMOS

In 1892 the city of Edmonton assembled a rugby club. This and other such rugby squads were what would become the football teams we now know. The Edmonton ESQUIMAUX claimed their second Alberta Rugby Football Championship in 1908. In 1910 the ESQUIMAUX became the ESKIMOS, playing until 1924 when the franchise folded. In 1930 a new Western Rugby League was formed, and the Edmonton BOOSTERS represented the city. It wasn't until 1938 that a team from Edmonton calling itself the ESKIMOS joined the Western Interprovincial Football Union, adopting the colors blue and white. The moniker is an alliterative reference to the city's northernmost Canadian Football League location.

Nickname: Esks

HAMILTON TIGER-CATS —————————

On Wednesday, November 3, 1869, in a room above George Lee's Fruit Store, the Hamilton Football Club was formed. Hamilton clubs have captured the Canadian Football League's Grey Cup in every decade of the 20th century, a feat matched in pro sport by only one other franchise, the National Hockey League's Montreal CANADIENS. Prior to World War Two, the football team of the City of Hamilton was known as the TIGERS. The colors of yellow and black were well represented and the present philosophy of tough football was established in those early days. The only time that football was interrupted in Hamilton as a spectator sport was during the First and Second World wars. After World War Two the TIGER Football Team started competition once again. At the same time a new group in the city was formed and they became known as the Hamilton WILDCATS. The TIGER and WILDCAT competition for fan participation was so great that both teams were unable to operate on a sound financial basis. It was decided that the two Clubs should amalgamate and form one representative team for Hamilton. The present name, TIGER-CATS, and what is known as the modern era of football, started in 1950. And contrary to popular belief, the move toward U.S. expansion dates back before World War One when the *New York Herald* published an invitation for two Canadian teams to strut their stuff at an exhibition game. And so it was on December 11, 1909, that 15,000 curious Americans at Van Cortlandt Park watched the Hamilton TIGERS beat the Ottawa ROUGH RIDERS 11-6.

Nicknames: Ti-Cats, the Tabbys, Steel City

MONTREAL ALOUETTES —————————

Following tours as the HORNETS, INDIANS, and WINGED WHEELERS, in 1946 the Montreal ALOUETTES joined the Canadian Football League. After winning championships and luring top-flight American talent away from the National Football League, including Heisman winner Johnny Rodgers, the franchise folded due to bankruptcy in 1981, then was reborn under new ownership as the CONCORDES in 1982. Other names considered at this time were the OLYMPICS and the VANDOOS, named after the world famous Montreal regiment. In 1985 they returned to the ALOUETTES moniker, actually a lark, but also a fictionalized red bird made popular in a French-Canadian children's song. Legend has it that original co-owners Leo Dandurand and Lew Hayman heard and loved the folk tune. Another story has the ALOUETTES being named after a World War One army squadron. But again the team was forced to fold in June of 1987. When the South (American) Division of the CFL folded in 1996, the Grey Cup Champion Baltimore STALLIONS moved their franchise up to Montreal, resurrecting the ALOUETTES nickname by popular demand once more.

Nicknames: Als, Red Birds

OTTAWA ROUGH RIDERS

The roots of Canadian football can be traced to an 1876 rugby football team called the OTTAWAS. But it is in revisiting the city of Ottawa's connection to the lumber trade that we find the CFL team's reason for adopting its name. Hardworking individuals, riding and directing logs as they would pass through the waterways on the way to the lumber mills, were referred to as rough riders. Creating this personality called for a "rugged, handsome, proud, ready for action" image that would translate itself clearly onto a football helmet and capture the essence of what a rough rider in his prime would resemble. The logo—a fur hat, a bandanna, a handle bar moustache and incorporation of the logger's gaff, the principle tool of the trade, further connects the meaning of what a rough rider was to Ottawa. The ROUGH RIDERS' uniform now features the traditional RIDER'S colors of red and midnight blue, the same as those worn at the birth of the Ottawa ROUGH RIDERS Football Club in 1876. In 1924, the club changed its name from the ROUGH RIDERS to the SENATORS following a merger with the St. Brigit's Club and ironically won its first Grey Cup in 1925 as the

Ottawa SENATORS. It was this name-changing decision that prompted the team from Saskatchewan to snatch up the abandoned ROUGH RIDER nickname. The SENATORS repeated their Grey Cup victory in 1926. In 1927, Ottawa returned to its original name—the ROUGH RIDERS. The Frank Clair Stadium is sometimes referred to as The ROUGH HOUSE, and the players as ROUGH RAGE.

Nicknames: the Riders, the Ruffies

SASKATCHEWAN ROUGHRIDERS ———

Saskatchewan football began on the night of Tuesday, September 6, 1910, with the formation of the Regina RUGBY CLUB, which initially had been intended to be a rowing club. The original colors were old gold and purple. They went to blue and white the following year, and in 1912 turned red and black — a combination that would remain for the next 36 years. In 1924 the Regina RUGBY CLUB became the Regina ROUGHRIDERS. Ottawa's rugby club had been called the ROUGH RIDERS since the 1890s, but dropped it in favor of calling themselves the SENATORS in 1924, and the Saskatchewan RUGBY CLUB jumped at the chance to adopt ROUGHRIDERS as their new nickname. There are two versions of where the name ROUGHRIDERS came from. One states that Saskatchewan got it from the history of the North West Mounted Police who were called roughriders because they broke the wild horses used by the force, while Ottawa's ROUGH RIDERS supposedly were Ottawa Valley lumberjacks who rode log booms down the Ottawa River. The other, which is just as speculative, states there was a Canadian volunteer contingent that once fought with Teddy Roosevelt in the Spanish-American War. His troops became known as Roughriders, and following the war, the Canadian volunteers returned to Canada, part of the group settling around Ottawa, the others moving west. Apparently the colors of the infantry unit were red and black. Some of these men became involved in the organization and running of the Ottawa and Regina RUGBY CLUBS, and thus the romance for the ROUGHRIDER nickname — and why both had black and red as their team colors. Ottawa still is black and red. In 1948 the Regina ROUGHRIDERS became a provincially owned and operated club, prompting the name change from Regina to the Saskatchewan ROUGHRIDERS.

Nicknames: the Roughies, Green Riders

TORONTO ARGONAUTS

The Canadian Football League's oldest team is also its winningest with 12 Grey Cup Championships. The ARGONAUT storybook began in 1872 when a man named Harry O'Brien gathered crews of oarsmen, decked them out in Oxford and Cambridge blues and formed the ARGONAUT Rowing Club. The original intent was to give the oarsmen an alternative way of keeping fit. In these early days they were an amateur club, playing a few games a year. In 1873, the first ARGONAUT football club was formed under the guidance of Head Coach H.T. Glazebrook. The ARGO footballers played one game that year and lost 3-0 to their cross-town rival, the University of Toronto. But still the game played second fiddle to the water sport. In fact, in 1879 the ARGONAUTS didn't play a single football game because many of the players were suffering from stretched stomach muscles sustained in rowing competitions. The sport became more organized when the Ontario Rugby Football Union was formed in 1883. In 1907 the ARGONAUTS, along with the Hamilton TIGERS of the ORFU, joined the Ottawa ROUGH RIDERS and Montreal WINGED WHEELERS of the Quebec Rugby Football Union to form the Interprovincial Rugby Football Union — or the Big Four. It wasn't until 1956 that the Canadian Football Council was formed, which two years later withdrew from the Rugby Union to become the Canadian Football League. The ARGONAUTS have the distinction of once being owned by former Los Angeles KINGS owner Bruce McNall, hockey superstar Wayne Gretzky, and the much missed comedian John Candy.

Nicknames: the Boatmen, the Argos

WINNIPEG BLUE BOMBERS

This Canadian Football League team was the second franchise in pro sports to be named after popular world heavyweight boxing champion, Joe Louis. The first was the Cleveland BROWN BOMBERS (later the BROWNS), a reference to the boxer's nickname, the Brown Bomber. The second franchise was the boys in blue from Winnipeg. It was during the 1936 season that the WINNIPEGS were playing an exhibition game against the University of North Dakota, when a young reporter named Vince Leah remarked "These are the blue bombers of Western Football." He was coining the phrase from a Grantland Rice description of Joe Louis, and with a nod toward the attending American press familiar with it. And from that day in 1936, the team has always been known as the Winnipeg BLUE BOMBERS. Founded on June 30, 1930, the team then known as the WINNIPEGS became the first team west of Ontario to win the coveted Grey Cup Trophy. Considering the American connection to the club's nickname, it is perhaps fitting that in 1993 the Winnipeg BLUE BOMBERS hosted the Sacramento GOLD MINERS in the first-ever Canada-U.S. game in the Canadian Football League.

Nickname: Bombers

HOCKEY
BLACKHAWKS
LEAFS
FLYERS
RED WINGS
OILERS
ISLANDERS
CANADIENS
RANGERS
SENATORS
FLAMES
GO TEAM
3:08
DUCKS
KINGS
CANUCKS
PENGUINS
SABRES
BRUINS
AVALANCHE
BLUES
COYOTES

NATIONAL HOCKEY LEAGUE

Anaheim Mighty Ducks
Boston Bruins
Buffalo Sabres
Calgary Flames
Chicago Blackhawks
Colorado Avalanche
Dallas Stars
Detroit Red Wings
Edmonton Oilers
Florida Panthers
Hartford Whalers
Los Angeles Kings
Montreal Canadiens

New Jersey Devils
New York Islanders
New York Rangers
Ottawa Senators
Philadelphia Flyers
Phoenix Coyotes
Pittsburgh Penguins
St. Louis Blues
San Jose Sharks
Tampa Bay Lightning
Toronto Maple Leafs
Vancouver Canucks
Washington Capitals

MIGHTY DUCKS OF ANAHEIM

The film that became a hockey club! *The Mighty Ducks* was a successful feature film released by the Walt Disney Studios in 1992. This film was followed by an equally successful sequel, *Mighty Ducks 2* in 1994. In between these two pictures Disney released a National Hockey League club which they called the MIGHTY DUCKS of Anaheim. Early in the 1992 movie hit we are introduced to the main character, played by actor Emilio Estevez. The character's name? Ducksworth. You got it. The ragamuffin bunch of inner-city kids he leads to national hockey prominence were named the Mighty Ducks — after himself. When it was learned that Disney had purchased itself an NHL team, word quickly spread that the film moniker was being considered as the franchise nickname. Fans of the rough and tumble sport held their collective breath, for good reason — MIGHTY DUCKS they became. It was Disney CEO Michael Eisner who named the team. The DUCKS team colors are purple, yellow, white, and green. The mascot is named Wild Wing. Between period entertainment is supplied by the NHL's first ice-skating cheerleaders, an all-female squad called the "Decoys"!

Nickname: Ducks

BOSTON BRUINS

After Charles F. Adams acquired the National Hockey League franchise for Boston and hired Art Ross as the first general manager and coach, it became necessary to acquire an appropriate name for the new entry into the hockey wars. Adams' ground rules for the selection of a name at that time were: The team's basic colors should be brown with yellow trim (brown eventually became black). This color scheme was selected primarily because Adams was then president of Brookside Stores and all said stores had a color combination of brown and a yellow trim. The name chosen should preferably relate to an untamed animal whose name was synonymous with size, strength, agility, ferocity and cunning, and in the color brown category. Dozens of names were submitted from various sources like news media, sportsmen, and fans, none of which proved entirely satisfactory. It remained for Ross's secretary — Ross ran a sporting goods store part time in Montreal — to submit the name BRUINS. The team's bear-like nickname was accepted by owner Charles F. Adams, who appreciated the animal's combined qualities of speed, strength, agility, ferocity, and animal cunning. The bear logo was replaced by the letter "B" in a wheel, which comes from the city's nickname "The Hub."

Nicknames: Big Bad Bruins, The B's, Beantowners

BUFFALO SABRES

Awarded its National Hockey League expansion franchise on December 2, 1969, Buffalo SABRES management worked on the matter of getting a name by sponsoring a contest. There were 13,000 entries submitted, suggesting 1,047 different names. Some of the nicknames that didn't reach the finals included the FLYING ZEPPELINS, MUGWUMPS, MOGULS, BUZZING BEES, BANDITS, BORDER WEAVERS, FLASHES, JESTERS, EAGER BEAVERS, and STREAKS. Five people came up with SABRES, and Robert Sonnelitter, Jr. of Williamsville won a drawing of those five for a pair of season tickets. It's probably a good thing the club's management didn't go with one of the other nickname suggestions: the Buffalo BABOONS. The Knox brothers, owners of the team, explained that the sabre is a symbol of authority, a weapon carried by a leader. Team colors were taken from the polo club where the Knox brother's father was a member.

Nickname: Sabes

CALGARY FLAMES

The Calgary FLAMES nickname comes from the team's original home, Atlanta, and the infamous burning of that southern city during the Civil War — remember that thrilling scene from *Gone With the Wind?* The team played in Georgia beginning with the 1972-73 season and up until 1979-80. They arrived in Alberta for the 1980-81 season. Despite fans wanting to change the nickname when the franchise moved north into Canada, a media panel decided that the FLAMES moniker would still be appropriate for an oil town like Calgary, with its population hovering around half a million. The red and gold trim on the uniforms was also retained after the move, while a new flaming red "C" replaced Atlanta's "A".

CHICAGO BLACKHAWKS

The man behind the creation of the name for this Chicago club was Major Frederick McLaughlin, the first owner of the team. When Major McLaughlin initially purchased the NHL franchise from Portland (Oregon) in 1926, it was known as the Portland Rosebuds. The name BLACKHAWK was adopted by McLaughlin in memory of the Blackhawk Field Gun Battalion, a unit that the Major served with during World War One. The battalion was named after a famous Indian Chief who headed the Sauk tribe in the early 1800s. And it is Chief Blackhawk himself who rides proudly on every team jersey. It is believed that the colors red, white, and black also have some military connection. The uniform was designed in 1954 by then-GM Tommy Ivan's wife. Tomahawks were added to the shoulders and the Indian head was made more prominent. By the way, Major McLaughlin's pride in his battalion reached beyond the ice surface. He also owned an eatery in Chicago called the BLACK HAWK, and for some time it was believed the team was named after it. In 1988, the two words were officially merged into one, the BLACKHAWKS.

Nickname: Hawks

COLORADO AVALANCHE

The National Hockey League was founded on a chill November day in 1917, inheriting six teams from a seven-year-old circuit, the National Hockey Association, where the Quebec BULLDOGS were two-time Stanley Cup winners. The team was formally renamed the Quebec ATHLETICS, but the BULLDOG name remained popular with the club's fans, and though 1919-20 proved to be the franchise's final season in Quebec — they became the Hamilton TIGERS in 1920-21, folding in 1925 — the fact that the club was called the ATHLETICS has been almost entirely forgotten. With the formation of the NHL's rival World Hockey Association in 1971 came the rebirth of pro hockey in Quebec. The name NORDIQUES was chosen from 1500 contest entries, illustrating the team's geographical location as the most northerly franchise in professional sports. The NORDS were swallowed by the NHL, and then the team moved to Denver for the 1995-96 season, becoming the Colorado AVALANCHE. Even the location name was contested in-house; Denver, Rocky Mountain, or Colorado? Selected by the team's new owners, COMSAT, rejected names included the ROCKY MOUNTAIN EXTREME, the ICE, the STORM, RAPIDS, OUTLAWS, COUGARS, RENEGADES, WRANGLERS and briefly, the ROCKY MOUNTAIN AVALANCHE. COMSAT even filed copyright protection for the name BLACK BEARS. Why AVALANCHE? A press release mentioned Colorado's Rocky Mountains, and the strength required to succeed in the NHL. Also, the AVALANCHE on a puck logo represents the power and speed of the skating, passing and shooting in the game. It's not the first local use of the moniker, however. In the late 1970s and early 80s, the Denver AVALANCHE played in the Major Indoor Soccer League. The AVALANCHE are not the first NHL team in Colorado, either. In 1976 the Kansas City SCOUTS moved to Denver to become the Colorado ROCKIES. In 1982 the ROCKIES left Denver, becoming the New Jersey DEVILS and winning their first Stanley Cup in 1994-95. In 1996, the first-year AVALANCHE won the Cup.

Nicknames: 'Lanche, Av's

DALLAS STARS

Three months into their inaugural 1967 season, the California SEALS were renamed the Oakland SEALS. In 1970 they became the California GOLDEN SEALS, then were re-christened with their original name in 1975, the California SEALS. In 1976 the

SEALS left the coast for Cleveland. In 1978 the Cleveland BARONS merged with the Minnesota NORTH STARS — Star of the North is the Minnesota State nickname, and fans chose it in a contest — becoming the Minnesota NORTH STARS. The team color of green came from Dartmouth College in New Hampshire, where Walter Bush, Jr., a club founder, attended college. In 1993, after 26 seasons, the Minnesota NORTH STARS moved to Dallas, and had their moniker shortened to the STARS — a nod in the direction of the Lone Star State, along with the rich Texas history of lawmen, wearers of the sheriff's Star. Under the new ownership of Norman N. Green, the uniform and team logo were redesigned. Team colors became blue, yellow, red, and white.

DETROIT RED WINGS

Pro hockey arrived in Detroit on September 25, 1926, when a group of Detroit businessmen purchased a National Hockey League franchise and stocked it with players from the Victoria COUGARS of the Western Hockey League. The club was called the Detroit COUGARS but played its inaugural season across the Detroit River in Canada at Windsor's Border Cities Arena. In 1930, the Detroit COUGARS were getting blitzed by the fans and media, who wanted to see some changes. The team missed the playoffs in 1929-30, and had only made the playoffs once in their four-year existence — a rather unimpressive record, considering there were only six teams in the league. The owners renamed the team the Detroit FALCONS, hoping a facelift would give the club new life. Unfortunately, the FALCONS — like the COUGARS — missed the playoffs in their first year. In 1932, with the nation still recovering from the Great Depression, James Norris bought the FALCONS. In 1933 the team's new president changed the FALCON nickname to the RED WINGS in memory of the Winged Wheelers, the amateur Montreal Athletic Association team he'd played on in the 1890s. Of course it isn't a coincidence that the red jersey insignia has a wing protruding out of an automobile wheel, a nod in the direction of Motown's car industry.

Nicknames: Wings, Red Army (1996 team with 10 Russian players)

EDMONTON OILERS

The Edmonton OILERS was a charter member of the World
Hockey Association when the league was formed in 1972-73. During that first season the team was called the Alberta OILERS. The
name was changed to Edmonton OILERS in 1973-74, and has remained that way ever since. In 1979-80, the OILERS, along with
three other WHA teams, merged with the National Hockey League.
The team nickname is derived from the City of Edmonton's long
history with the discovery of oil in the area. In 1949 a major oilfield
was discovered just south of Edmonton and the oil industry has
been vital to the economic well-being of both the city and province
since that time. The selection of the nickname OILERS was a decision
made by the team owner Dr. Charles Allard, and the first General
Manager, Bill Hunter — with Edmonton fans agreeing overwhelm-
ingly. The OILER'S logo employs a script-style in which the letters
appear to be sitting in a pool of oil. This is to symbolize depth of
talent, and the flame is to demonstrate the eternal nature of the
team. The teams that came and went with the WHA were the Los
Angeles SHARKS, which became the Michigan STAGS, which
became the Baltimore BLADES; the Minnesota FIGHTING
SAINTS, which became the NEW FIGHTING SAINTS; the New
Jersey KNIGHTS, which became the San Diego MARINERS; and
the New York RAIDERS, which became the NEW JERSEY
GOLDEN BLADES.

Nickname: Oils

FLORIDA PANTHERS

Felis Concolor Coryi, a subspecies of the North American cougar
discovered in 1896 by naturalist Charles B. Cory, can be found only
in Florida. Given that the protection efforts on the Florida Panther's
behalf are somewhat recent developments, and the population
growth of Florida in the latter half of the 20th century severely en-
croached on the animal's natural habitat, the panther is one of the
most endangered mammals on Earth. In fact, it's estimated that only

between 30-50 of these animals remain in the wild. Shortly after being granted an NHL expansion franchise, team owner H.Wayne
Huizenga held a "name-the-team" contest. The organization received
thousands of responses in little more than a week, and the overwhelming favorite was PANTHERS. Because of the alarming problems which surround this beautiful animal, the Florida PANTHERS
Hockey Club has made the commitment to raise to a higher plateau
the awareness level of this animal's plight. To accomplish this goal, the
entire hockey organization is committed to working with the groups
and individuals who dedicate themselves to sharing the common desire to help sustain and replenish the population of the Florida Panther. The hockey club's "PANTHERS Saves help Save the Panther"
program enlists individuals and corporations to help the creature's
cause. The team and various support groups solicit pledges from
people wishing to help: they may make a financial contribution for
every save a PANTHER'S goaltender makes at home games. Due to
the high visibility of a professional sports team, it is hoped that this
program will receive widespread exposure throughout North
America and thusly generate significant financial contributions to
help save *Felis Concolor Coryi,* the Florida Panther.

Nickname: Cats

HARTFORD WHALERS

This name is a nod in the direction of the league that introduced
Hartford to professional hockey, the World Hockey Association.
WHALERS was suggested by Virginia Kelly, wife of the New England team's general manager, because the first three letters were the
initials of the league in which the team played — the WHA. Also,
the club started in Boston where they played two seasons, and there
was a whaling industry in Beantown. Originating as the New England WHALERS, the team played in Boston from 1972-74, in West
Springfield from 1974-75, Hartford from 1975-78, then Springfield
in 1979. The team moved back to Hartford when it joined the National Hockey League in 1979-80. The team logo was changed when
the franchise moved to Hartford, with the whale's tail put atop the
"W" forming an "H" for Hartford. Other teams that played in the

defunct WHA included the Ottawa NATIONALS, who moved to Toronto; the Ottawa CIVICS; the Philadelphia BLAZERS, who moved to Vancouver and stayed the BLAZERS; the Phoenix ROADRUNNERS; the Quebec NORDIQUES (now the NHL's Colorado AVALANCHE); the Toronto TOROS, who moved to Birmingham and became the BULLS; and the Winnipeg JETS, now the Phoenix COYOTES.

Nicknames: The Whale, The Fish

LOS ANGELES KINGS

This Southern California-based team's first owner, Jack Kent Cooke, named the team the KINGS himself. It was Cooke's idea to give his franchise a jump start by connecting it with established concepts, including naming his rink the Great Western Forum — a show of respect and appreciation for what the Russians call the Shrine of Hockey, the Montreal Forum. The crown is a natural logo and the original colors of purple and gold represented the traditional hues of royalty. With the addition of former Edmonton OILER superstar Wayne Gretzky to the lineup in 1988, then-owner Bruce McNall wanted his team to stand on its own and not look like hockey's version of the Los Angeles LAKERS, owned by a former KINGS owner, Dr. Jerry Buss. New team colors were introduced as silver and black — similar to National Football League RAIDERS, who were Los Angeles-based at the time.

MONTREAL CANADIENS

The storied Montreal CANADIENS are the most successful franchise in professional sports. When *The Sporting News* compiled a book entitled "Dynasty — The 12 Most Dominant Teams in Sports History," the Montreal CANADIANS were there among basketball CELTICS, football PACKERS, college SOONERS, and baseball's YANKEES. NOS GLORIEUX, French for OUR GLORY, hold the hockey record for most consecutive championships — five. When J. Ambrose O'Brien founded the team on December 4, 1909, it was known as the CLUB CANADIEN, and for its first game at Jubilee Rink the players wore jerseys of red, white, and blue which were, at that time, the colors of the Canadian flag. In 1911-12 a "CAC" was placed in the center of the sweater, and the team was called the CANADIAN ATHLETIC CLUB. The CANADIANS introduced the famed CH sweater now in use in 1916 en route to their first Stanley Cup. The French influence has given LES CANADIEN their most endearing nickname, with partial credit going to American Tex Rickard who had picked up a false rumor about the "H" (for Hockey) on the club's uniform. Camille Desroches recalled, "This guy told Tex that the French-speaking players were "farmers," and therefore HABITANTS." And HABS is derived from HABITANT, meaning "person of the land." Other clubs that have played out of Montreal for the Stanley Cup and won included the Montreal WANDERERS (nicknamed the REDBANDS), the SHAMROCKS, the VICTORIAS, and the first-ever winner of Lord Stanley's trophy, the Montreal AMATEUR ATHLETIC ASSOCIATION. And a franchise that survived across town from the CANADIENS until 1938 — the Montreal MAROONS. Another Montreal club, the CRYSTALS, never won the Cup.

Nicknames: The Canucks (Pre-Vancouver Canucks), Les Habitants, The Habs, Nos Glorieux, Les Boys, bleu-blanc-rouge (blue, white, and red)

NEW JERSEY DEVILS ———————

New Jersey DEVILS named after a baby? Well, this wasn't just any kid. Starting out as the Kansas City SCOUTS, the club moved to Colorado to become the ROCKIES, in pre-baseball days. The New Jersey DEVILS were christened at the Byrne Meadowlands Arena June 30, 1982. The question at hand however, is whether that date comes within two centuries of the actual birth of the Jersey Devil. It was 1735, or so the legend goes, that a farm woman named Mrs. Leeds gave birth to her thirteenth child — the Jersey Devil, itself. In and out of hiding, the Devil seems to have appeared just often enough to remain a permanent fixture in the minds of area inhabitants. He became so ingrained in people's thoughts that in 1939 the Devil was appointed the "official state demon." In statewide, name-the-team newspaper contests, familiar handles such as BLADES, LIGHTNING, COLONIALS, MEADOWLANDERS, GENERALS, and AMERICANS found widespread support. But local folklore was steeped so high that DEVILS couldn't miss. Team owner John McMullen agreed, saying "Webster's Dictionary defines devil as a person of notable energy, recklessness and dashing spirit — an excellent way to describe what we're going to have with this new franchise." It's said that Mrs. Leeds went into labor in the midst of a violent thunderstorm, fuelling rumors that the mother-to-be was involved in sorcery. That uneasiness was transformed into horror as the child was born. With features described as those of a bat, a kangaroo and a serpent, the newborn creature flew right out the window, destroying crops, ravaging livestock, cutting the throats of hogs, cattle, sheep, and people! The Devil has been "sighted" over the years by luminaries no less than politicians, military men, clergymen, and policemen. It has been exorcised, hunted, shot at by posses, and traced with electronic equipment. Or so they say.

Nickname: The Devs

NEW YORK ISLANDERS

The team is based in Uniondale, Long Island, New York. The New York ISLANDERS nickname came about from a suggestion made by co-owner Roy Boe's wife. Instead of naming the team the LONG ISLANDERS, she suggested calling the team the New York ISLANDERS, in an effort to win over some unhappy New York RANGER fans, a team that had not won the Stanley Cup in fifty years. The ISLANDERS colors of orange and blue are also the colors of Nassau County. Mrs. Boe, a dress designer, recommended the use of the map of Long Island as part of the logo. Long Island is in southeast New York, between Long Island Sound and the Atlantic. It is 1,411 square miles and has a population of over seven million.

Nickname: Isles

NEW YORK RANGERS

In 1926 the New York AMERICANS took to the ice in spectacular "stars and stripes." They lasted seventeen mostly uneventful seasons, their last in 1941 as the BROOKLYN AMERICANS. The 1926 birth of the RANGERS was something of a team effort that involved team president Lester Patrick, a successful hockey man from Toronto named Conn Smythe, and Madison Square Garden fight promoter Tex Rickard. Rickard, a Texan, had become fascinated with hockey, and was convinced the game would be enthusiastically supported in the Garden, the world's premier sports arena that had opened its doors just a year earlier. As a nod to Rickard's home state and the famed police force that existed there, the team was jocularly called TEX'S RANGERS. As displaced as this moniker may have appeared in geography and tone, the latter part of the name stuck. The club soon became the toast of New York, attracting a formal "dinner-jacket" crowd to the games. These fans were headed to "the classiest team in hockey" by no less a personage than the Mayor himself, the Honorable Jimmy Walker. The RANGERS have the distinction of ending one of the longest droughts in professional sports when they won the Stanley Cup in 1994. Not since 1940 had hockey's most prestigious banner been hung from the Garden rafters. The colors of blue, red, and white had nothing to do with the AMERICANS. Today the words "New York" are on the sweaters for road games while the home jerseys sport the nickname "RANGERS."

Nicknames: Broadway Blues, Blueshirts

OTTAWA SENATORS

As far back as the 1880s Ottawa fielded a team to contest the Stanley Cup named the CAPITALS. A lack of success drove them away, but the team returned at the turn of the century called the SILVER SEVEN, so named when Manager Bob Shillington handed over a silver nugget to each player in recognition of their winning season. The SEVEN was in reference to the fact that teams played seven aside then, not the six used now. In their three-year reign as Cup champions they turned back the challenges of seven now long gone teams: the Rat Portage (the city later changed its name to Kenora, thankfully), THISTLES, the Winnipeg ROWING CLUB, the Toronto MARLBOROUGHS, the Brandon WHEAT KINGS, and the fabled Dawson City KLONDIKERS. The SILVER SEVEN were the sport's first legitimate heroes, finally defeated in 1906 by the Montreal WANDERERS. Team nicknames were employed much more casually in the early days of hockey than they are today, and so it was in the season following the Ottawa club's defeat in Montreal that SILVER SEVEN began to be replaced by SENATORS, a reference to the Canadian capital city. In 1934, seven years after winning their last Cup, the SENATORS were gone. The team was gutted, the owners broke, the fans no longer supportive. The remnants moved to St. Louis, becoming the EAGLES — a team which folded in 1935. Incredibly, the man who scored the first goal of the game in which the Ottawa SENATORS won their last Stanley Cup in 1927, Frank Finnigan, lived long enough to be on hand when the Ottawa SENATORS were awarded their new NHL franchise in 1991. He died a hockey legend just after learning his old sweater, number eight, would be retired with glory. The team logo represents a SENATOR from Roman times, and the colors are red, black, and gold.

Nickname: The Sens

PHILADELPHIA FLYERS

The earliest Philadelphia hockey team arrived in 1930 by way of Pittsburgh. The PIRATES, the first franchise granted to Philadelphia, had its name changed to the QUAKERS. They played only one season, in 1930-31. The FLYERS nickname was selected from a public contest which attracted 25,000 entries. Actually, the new team moniker had been reduced to two choices: the FLYERS and re-introducing the QUAKERS (some sources claim one entry, seriously considered, had the spelling PHLYERS). The idea of the FLYERS came down from Philadelphia's first General Manager,

Bud Poile, who once ran a pro team in Edmonton called the FLY-ERS. Many thought the QUAKERS represented losing, which the original team did quite often, holding the second-worst record in league history (4-36-4). Thus, the FLYERS were born. The winged "P" was designed by a local artist. Orange and black were chosen as team colors. Among the other contest entries were names such as PIPERS and MOHAWKS.

Nicknames: Broad Street Bullies, Philly

PHOENIX COYOTES

In 1896 the Winnipeg VICTORIAS played the Montreal VICTORIAS (imagination!) for the Stanley Cup. The Winnipeg goaltender put on a pair of goalie pads, the first ever, and shut out the club from the east. Winnipeg returned to the big leagues in 1972 with the formation of the World Hockey Association. Team owners attracted one of the biggest names in the National Hockey League at the time, Bobby Hull, from the Chicago Black Hawks, to help bolster the new league. The Golden JET, which was his nickname, signed the first million-dollar contract in pro hockey, and though it sounds like he lent his nickname to the club from Winnipeg, that's not the official story. The team name was developed by team owner Ben Hatskin. He originally picked the name to mirror Sonny Werblin's New York JETS of the National Football League fame. Hatskin also said the nickname was chosen because of the city's growing air transport business. The Winnipeg JETS was one of four WHA clubs to be welcomed into the NHL when the upstart league folded in 1979. Other clubs that came and went in the WHA included the Baltimore BLADES; Birmingham BULLS; Calgary COWBOYS; Chicago COUGARS; Cincinnati STINGERS; Cleveland CRUSADERS, who moved to Minnesota; Denver SPURS, who moved to Ottawa; Houston AEROS; Indianapolis RACERS. After a deal to move the franchise to Minnesota fell apart, an arrangement was struck with Jerry Colangelo, who owns the Phoenix SUNS of the National Basketball Association. A name-the-team contest attracted 10,000 entries, with the front-runners including SCORPIONS, MUSTANGS, POSSE, OUTLAWS, JETS, and DRY ICE. But COYOTES beat the other finalist, the Phoenix PHREEZE. The word coyote is Spanish, and comes from the Aztec, coyotlinoult. The wily coyote can be found in most of North and South America.

PITTSBURGH PENGUINS

Pittsburgh iced a team in 1925 called the PIRATES, built around an amateur club called the Pittsburgh YELLOW JACKETS. In 1930, this club moved to Philadelphia where it played one season as the Philadelphia QUAKERS, folding in 1931. The latest Pittsburgh franchise held a contest in 1967 to find a name and chose PENGUINS, partly because the first three letters match those in PENnsylvania. The winning entry was submitted by Milton Roberts, a steelworker who won a pair of season's tickets and a color television. Pennsylvania State Senator Jack MacGregor's wife also recommended the name. When the General Manager of the time, Jack Riley, heard the decision of the judges his response was to the point, "You're kidding." He then proceeded to design uniforms that did not contain the team nickname. Perhaps more upset than G.M. Riley was The Hornet Booster Club. One member called it a sacrilege to drop the name that other Pittsburgh hockey teams had carried for 25 years. Coach Red Sullivan remarked at the time, "Detroit has a team called the RED WINGS. What's a RED WING, anyway? Is it a bird? Is it a flower? At least we have something that people recognize." Right. "A little fat man in a tuxedo," commented *Pittsburgh Press* journalist Roy McHugh. When looking for a connection between PENGUINS and Pittsburgh, fans were reminded that the Civic Arena where the home team would play was known as the Big Igloo. But when G.M. Riley and Coach Sullivan were asked what the team should have been called they answered together, "The SHAMROCKS." Riley and Sullivan? It figured. The team color was originally light blue, but was changed to a black and gold combination when the STEELERS and PIRATES were in the midst of winning six world titles in the 1970s.

Nickname: The Pens

ST. LOUIS BLUES

In 1934 the Ottawa SENATORS, after winning six Stanley Cups, moved to St. Louis. The St. Louis EAGLES played one season in the National Hockey League, in 1934-35, then folded. The city of St. Louis had to wait until 1967-68 for the birth of the BLUES. The name came unchallenged from Sid Saloman III, part-owner of the team, who drew his inspiration from the famous song written by W.C. Handy. Saloman also authorized use of the musical note for the logo. Team colors are blue, yellow, red, and white. In 1983 Harry Ornest saved the BLUES from deportation to Saskatoon, which would have certainly required a nickname change.

Nickname: Blue Notes

SAN JOSE SHARKS

Suggestions for the team name came in the form of sea creatures, fictional characters, and computer components. They included BLADES, BREAKERS, BREEZE, CONDORS, FOG, GOLD, GOLDEN GATERS, GOLDEN SKATERS, GRIZZLIES, ICE-BREAKERS, KNIGHTS, REDWOODS, SEA LIONS, SHARKS, and WAVES. Although the most popular name submitted by San Jose fans was BLADES, management felt the word had too many negative connotations — as in weapons — and went with the second most popular suggestion. Good choice. The neighboring Pacific Ocean is home to seven different varieties of sharks including the Great White, Leopard, Mako, Seven-gill, Blue, Soupfin, and Spiny Dog. A specific area of the Pacific in the Bay Area is called the "Red Triangle" because of its shark population. And, as stated by the team's vice-president at the time, "Sharks are relentless, determined, swift, agile, bright and fearless. We plan to build an organization that has all these qualities." In its first year the San Jose SHARKS took a 40 percent share of all NHL hockey merchandising sales. This was no accident. Many merchandising organizations believe that the SHARKS created the blueprint for sports merchandising later used successfully in all sports from basketball (Toronto RAPTORS) to football (Jacksonville JAGUARS and Carolina PANTHERS). The question asked in-house was, how aggressive could the moniker be and still be acceptable? Pretty aggressive it turns out, because this extensive research also gave the SHARKS their motto, "If looks could kill."

TAMPA BAY LIGHTNING _____

Over the years professional sports team names have been determined through some rather unusual circumstances and procedures. But to the Tampa Bay hockey franchise's first General Manager Phil Esposito the answer came to him like a lightning bolt out of the sky. Make that exactly like a lightning bolt. "I never expected to decide on the team name in the manner we did," said Esposito. "The story behind it is unique. When I first came to Tampa, everyone mentioned the frequent lightning storms that would hit the area. I didn't actually believe it until we were out on a deck that overlooks the bay one afternoon and a lightning storm hit." Too close for comfort, it turned out. Running for cover... "Someone said that LIGHTNING would be a great name for the hockey team, and I knew it was the perfect name." The Tampa Bay area is known as the lightning capital of the world as storms occur frequently throughout the year. Plus, the name relates closely to the sport. In fact, the theme line for the NHL's 75th anniversary season (1991-92) was "Lightning on Ice." The LIGHTNING colors of black, blue, silver, and white are unique within the league. They are considered powerful, dynamic and exciting, matching the approach and image of the team.

Nickname: Bolts

TORONTO MAPLE LEAFS _____

Toronto teams that played for the Cup before and after the turn of the century included the BLUESHIRTS, the MARLBOROUGHS, and the WELLINGTONS, a Toronto railway powerhouse nicknamed the IRON DUKES. But the true bloodline to the MAPLE LEAFS started with the Toronto ARENAS, which then became the

ST. PATRICKS. In 1926 Conn Smythe bought the club for $160,000. Smythe was not a follower. He was the sort of man to leave his imprint in the hardest of pavement, and it would not do to have the new team continue as the ST. PATRICKS. Among the teams he scouted for talent were a group of young men who called themselves the East Toronto MAPLE LEAFS — grammatically incorrect, but effective just the same. Smythe liked the name. He liked the fact that the maple leaf was something of a Canadian symbol, and that it was the logo of the 1924 Olympic team, the Toronto GRANITES. Smythe had also worn the symbol proudly as a soldier in the Great War. It would be the symbol of his proud new team. Smythe designed new uniforms for the squad, but he kept the green color for one more season, as a sign of respect for the loyal supporters of the SAINT PATS team. So, on February 14, 1927, the Toronto MAPLE LEAFS were born wearing the blue color of the great Canadian skies, and white, representing the color of snow.

Nickname: Leafs

VANCOUVER CANUCKS

Like many pro hockey cities, Vancouver had a team before the turn of the century, then lost it, only to return again to the National Hockey League decades later. The CREAMERY KINGS became the MILLIONAIRES, then the MAROONS. The inspiration for the latest Vancouver franchise nickname came from "Johnny Canuck," a term used to describe Canadian soldiers in World War Two — and many Americans still believe it was meant as a putdown. Not true. Legend has it that the moniker Johnny Canuck was taken from a Canadian folk hero; a great logger who was a skater and hockey player in his spare time. The moniker actually began its professional life as the nickname for the Montreal CANADIANS hockey club. The Vancouver CANUCKS have gone through a number of changes since their 1970 debut, but all to do with costume. The original team color was Pacific Ocean blue. The logo was a hockey stick jutting into a rink. Known throughout the hockey world as the Vancouver UGLY SWEATERS, the club has worn an array of vulgar colors and uninspired designs on their jerseys. The CANUCKS made a radical change in 1978, introducing new team colors of yellow, red, and black with a stylized skate as their logo. So the team that played for the 1993-94 Stanley Cup looked good doing it.

WASHINGTON CAPITALS

We ALL know that Washington D.C. is the capital of the U.S., so here's some history. Before the National Basketball Association's GOLDEN STATE WARRIORS came to the Bay Area, Oakland had played host to another pro basketball club, the Oakland OAKS of the American Basketball Association. That franchise left town in 1970, however, becoming the Washington CAPITALS, which later folded. Management of the expansion National Hockey League Washington franchise knew this when they went looking for a nickname that would best represent the prominence of the region they played in. When Abe Pollin was awarded the NHL franchise in 1974, a contest was held in which the name CAPITALS was chosen. The team plays in the USAIR Arena in Landover, Maryland, approximately 20 minutes from downtown Washington, DC.

Nickname: Caps

COLLEGE

CORNHUSKERS RAINBOW WARRIORS

HURRICANES HOOSIERS

TERRAPINS

GOLDEN GOPHERS

WOLVERINES CHIPPEWAS

GOLDEN FLASHES

GATORS

YOUNG COUGARS ZIPS

SUN DEVILS

JAYHAWKS

MIDSHIPMEN

SEMINOLES RAZORBACKS GREEN FALCONS

AMERICAN TEAMS

Air Force Falcons
Akron Zips
Alabama-Birmingham
 Blazers
Alabama Crimson Tide
Arizona State Sun Devils
Arizona Wildcats
Arkansas Razorbacks
Arkansas State Indians
Auburn Tigers
Ball State Cardinals
Baylor Bear
Boise State Broncos
Boston College Eagles
Bowling Green Falcons
Brigham Young Cougars
California Golden Bears
Central Florida Knights
 of Pegasus
Central Michigan
 Chippewas
Cincinnati Bearcats
Clemson Tigers
Colorado Buffaloes
Colorado State Rams
Duke Blue Devils
East Carolina Pirates
Eastern Michigan Eagles
Florida Gators

Florida State Seminoles
Fresno State Bulldogs
Georgia Bulldogs
Georgia Tech Yellowjackets
Hawaii Rainbow Warriors
Houston Cougars
Idaho Vandals
Illinois Fighting Illini
Indiana Hoosiers
Iowa Hawkeyes
Iowa State Cyclones
Kansas Jayhawks
Kansas Wildcats
Kent Golden Flashes
Kentucky Wildcats
Louisiana State Fighting
 Tigers
Louisiana Tech Bulldogs
Louisville Cardinals
Maryland Terrapins
Memphis Tigers
Miami (Ohio) Redskins
Miami Hurricanes
Michigan State Spartans
Michigan Wolverines
Minnesota Golden Gophers
Mississippi Rebels
Mississippi State Bulldogs
Missouri Tigers

Navy Midshipmen
Nebraska Cornhuskers
Nevada Las Vegas Runnin'
   Rebels
Nevada Wolf Pack
New Mexico Lobos
New Mexico State Aggies
North Carolina State
   Wolfpack
North Carolina Tar Heels
North Texas Eagles
Northeast Louisiana Indians
Northern Illinois Huskies
Northwestern Wildcats
Notre Dame Fighting Irish
Ohio Bobcats
Ohio State Buckeyes
Oklahoma Sooners
Oklahoma State Cowboys
Oregon Ducks
Oregon State Beavers
Penn State Nittany Lions
Pittsburgh Panthers
Purdue Boilermakers
Rice Owls
Rutgers Scarlet Knights
San Diego State Aztecs
San Jose State Spartans
South Carolina Fighting
   Gamecocks
Southern California Trojans
Southern Methodist
   University Mustangs

Southern Mississippi
   Golden Eagles
Southwestern Louisiana
   Ragin' Cajuns
Stanford Cardinal
Syracuse Orangemen
Temple Owls
Tennessee Volunteers
Texas A&M Aggies
Texas Christian Horned
   Frogs
Texas El Paso Miners
Texas Longhorns
Texas Tech Red Raiders
Toledo Green Wave
Toledo Rockets
Tulane Golden Hurricane
UCLA Bruins
Utah State Aggies
Utah Utes
Vanderbilt Commodores
Virginia Cavaliers
Virginia Tech Hokies
Wake Forest Demon
   Deacons
Washington Huskies
Washington State Cougars
West Point Black Knights
West Virginia Mountaineers
Western Michigan Broncos
Wisconsin Badgers
Wyoming Cowboys

CANADIAN TEAMS

Acadia Axemen
Alberta Golden Bears
Bishop Gaiters
Brandon Bobcats
British Columbia
  Thunderbirds
Calgary Dinosaurs
Carleton Ravens
Concordia Stingers
The Blue of Dawson
Grant MacEwan Griffins
Guelph Gryphons
Laval Rouge et Or
Lethbridge College
  Kodiaks
Lethbridge Pronghorns
Manitoba Bisons
McGill Redmen
McMaster Marauders
Medicine Hat Rattlers
Memorial Sea-Hawks

Mount Allison Mounties
New Brunswick Varsity
  Reds
Northern Alberta Ooks
Ottawa Gee-Gees
Prince Edward Island
  Panthers
Queen's Golden Gaels
Regina Cougars
Ryerson Rams
St. Francis Xavier
  X-Men
Saint Mary's Huskies
Saskatchewan Huskies
Simon Fraser Clansmen
Toronto Varsity Blues
Trent Excalibur
Waterloo Warriors
Western Mustangs
Winnipeg Wesmen
York Yeomen

AMERICAN TEAMS

AIR FORCE FALCONS

The Class of 1959, the first cadets to enter the Academy, selected FALCONS as the nickname and mascot of the Cadet Wing. The falcon's characteristics were believed to typify the Air Force as a combat service, including "high speed flight, powerful and graceful flight maneuvers, great courage, keen eyesight, alertness and noble bearing, and noble tradition." The Academy's first falcon was named Mach 1 in October 1955, and this has been retained as the official name through the years, even though there usually are six to eight falcons in the mews at the Academy at any one time. They are cared for, trained, and flown by cadet handlers who volunteer their spare time to practice the ancient sport of falconry. The flying falcon mascot can reach speeds exceeding 100 mph during dives upon their prey. Experts said falcons could not be trained to perform before large audiences, but Guinevere, the bird's pet name, has flown before more than 50,000 spectators at intercollegiate football games, soaring and diving throughout the stadium just above the crowd — the only demonstration of its type in college sports.

AKRON ZIPS

The association of the ZIPS with varsity sports began in 1925 when a University of Akron freshman, Margaret Hamlin, tried on a pair of Zippers. At the time, the University athletic teams were without a name and a contest was conducted on campus. Hamlin submitted her entry after trying on a $6 pair of rubber overshoes called Zippers — a brand name of the BF Goodrich Company — and the word went out to all concerned. She received a $10 prize when her name was chosen on January 15, 1926. On September 13, 1950, Athletic Director Kenneth "Red" Cochrane shortened the nickname to ZIPS. Some say this happened because of the opportunity for puns when the zipper became a popular addition to men's trousers. Others say the shorter name was easier to use. Whatever the case, the nickname ZIPS has stuck. On May 1, 1953, ZIPPY the kangaroo was declared official mascot.

ALABAMA-BIRMINGHAM BLAZERS

The University of Alabama-Birmingham became a full-fledged university in the late 1960s and began its athletic program in 1977. At that time a name-the-team contest was held in the *Kaleidoscope,* UAB's student newspaper. Among the thousands of entries received from students, faculty, and employees, nicknames such as BARONS — a tribute to the city's industrial heritage and the name of Birmingham's AA baseball team — TITANS, and WARRIORS were finalists, as was the name BLAZERS. Whether it was a reference to the school's "trailblazing" in the medical field (UAB has a world-class medical center and is the home of one of the nation's top medical schools), the fact that UAB was blazing a new trail in the field of athletics, or the recent success of the Portland TRAIL-BLAZERS, who had won the NBA title in 1977, BLAZERS won the contest and became the official nickname. The question "what is a BLAZER?" was a tricky one, however, and the question of how to represent the BLAZER concept would pose difficulties for many years. The original BLAZER mascot was a dragon, who was soon replaced by "Beauregard T. Rooster," who bore a striking resemblance to the famous San Diego Chicken. The Rooster character lasted until the advent of "Blaze," a fierce-looking Nordic Warrior, who lasted less than a year before succumbing to complaints about his violent image. In 1995 UAB unveiled the dragon again, still named "Blaze." In 1996, the BLAZERS gridiron team was invited to join Division 1-A.

ALABAMA CRIMSON TIDE

Alabama's first game was played in Birmingham on Friday afternoon, November 11, 1892, at the old Lakeview Park. They beat opposition furnished by Professor Taylor's school and Birmingham high schools 56-0. In early newspaper accounts of Alabama football, the team was simply listed as the VARSITY or the CRIMSON WHITE, after the school colors. The first nickname to become popular and used by the headline writers was the THIN RED LINE. This moniker was used until 1906. The name CRIMSON TIDE is supposed to have first been used by Hugh Roberts, former sports editor of the *Birmingham Age-Herald*. He used "crimson tide" in describing an Alabama-Auburn game played in Birmingham in 1907, the last football contest between the two schools until 1948 when the series was resumed. The game was played in a sea of mud and Auburn was a heavy favorite to win. But, evidently, the THIN RED LINE played a great game in the red mud and held Auburn to a 6-6 tie, thus establishing the name CRIMSON TIDE. Zipp Newman, former sports editor of the *Birmingham News*, probably popularized the name more than any other writer. Around 1930, an unusually large group of Alabama linemen earned the nickname the RED ELEPHANTS, a reference to their size and jersey color.

Nicknames: Red Elephants, The Tide, 'Bama

ARIZONA WILDCATS

Before 1914 the University of Arizona's teams were called the VARSITY or Arizona RED AND BLUE. In 1914 a student correspondent for the *Los Angeles Times,* covering the Arizona-Occidental football game on the Occidental campus, penned the following phrase: "The Arizona men showed the fight of wild cats..." Back in Tucson, when the student body read the dispatch of the game, a resolution was passed that henceforth, Arizona athletic teams would be called the WILDCATS. The L.A. writer, the late Bill Henry, was then a senior at Occidental and his reputation grew as did the WILDCATS'. He later became a columnist for the Times and a war correspondent and news analyst for N.B.C. Henry was honored as the "Father of the Arizona WILDCATS" at the 50th Homecoming in 1964, when Arizona defeated Idaho, 14-7. Until the University fielded its first football team in 1899, the school colors were sage green and silver. However, the student manager that year, Quintus

J. Anderson, was able to strike a particularly good deal with a local merchant for game sweaters of solid blue with red trim. He then wrote a request that the school colors be changed, which was approved quickly. It's been cardinal red and navy blue ever since.

Nickname: Desert Swarm

ARIZONA STATE SUN DEVILS

It was the summer of 1946 when someone uttered those words for the first time. But who? That question has haunted Arizona State University historians for years. The nickname SUN DEVILS is the third in the school's 110-year history. When the second Tempe Normal football team opened play in 1889, the student body chose OWLS for its moniker. And when Tempe Normal became Arizona State Teachers College, OWLS became BULLDOGS. The *State Press*, the student newspaper, ran frequent appeals during the fall of 1946, urging the BULLDOG be replaced by the new SUN DEVIL. And on November 20, 1946, the student body voted 819 to 196 to make the change. On November 20, says *The Arizona Republic*, the student council made it official. The following day, the first Arizona State team played as SUN DEVILS. The problem of drawing a Sun Devil was handed over to the late Bert Anthony, an artist for Walt Disney. Anthony, creator of the defunct Stanford Indian symbol, designed the current SUN DEVIL imp, Sparky. It is rumored that Sparky was modeled after Walt Disney himself.

ARKANSAS RAZORBACKS

The history of Arkansas' athletic appearance began in 1894 when a contest was held on the University of Arkansas campus to select school colors 23 years after classes were first held. Cardinal, a shade of deep red, was voted in over heliotrope, a shade of moderate purple. The school athletic teams carried the name of CARDINALS into battle for the next 15 years until the close of the 1909 season.

Arkansas Coach Hogo Bezdek referred to his team as "a wild band of Razorback hogs" at a post season rally following an unbeaten season. The name RAZORBACKS quickly caught on and the famous yell, "Whooo, Pig! Sooie!" was added in the 1920s. Arkansas didn't have a live mascot until the mid-1960s when some fans donated a pig which was named Big Red I. That pig, and a second, Big Red II, were duroc hogs which died of heart attacks. The Little Rock Zoo secured an Australian wild boar in 1975. Christened Big Red III, it served at games until it escaped from an animal exhibit near Eureka Springs in the summer of 1977. An irate farmer in Carroll County shot and killed Big Red III as it broke into an animal pen. Ragnar, a wild hog captured in South Arkansas by Leola farmer Bill Robinson, served as mascot in 1977. During Ragnar's reign it killed a coyote, a 450-pound domestic duroc, and seven rattlesnakes. Ragnar died 1978 of unknown causes although no autopsy was performed. Big Red X currently serves as Arkansas' number one Razorback. He makes the rounds before the games but no longer remains in the stadiums after kick-off.

ARKANSAS STATE INDIANS

The term INDIANS officially became the school's athletic nickname in 1931. The first nickname in 1911 was the AGGIES, since Arkansas State University was the only agricultural school in Eastern Arkansas. For the same reason, FARMERS was also sometimes used as a moniker. In 1925 it was changed to GORILLAS, but that one wasn't too readily accepted. WARRIORS was adopted in 1930, and it evolved to INDIANS one year later. INDIANS is taken from the heritage of the state of Arkansas — from the Osage tribe which roamed Northern Arkansas before the settlers arrived. During the 18th century the Osage were at war with practically all other tribes of the plains, as well as with the woodland tribes. For that reason, ASUers look with pride to the fighting spirit which dwelled among the Indians of Northern Arkansas.

Nickname: The Tribe

AUBURN TIGERS

Through the years, Auburn teams have been known as both the WAR EAGLES and TIGERS. The news media often refers to an Auburn team as the WAR EAGLES or an Auburn player as a WAR EAGLE. In fact, when the TIGERS play a game on the road, there is often an article written in the local paper wondering why Auburn has three nicknames — the Auburn TIGERS, the Auburn WAR EAGLES, and the Auburn PLAINSMEN. Officially, Auburn has one nickname, the TIGERS. WAR EAGLE is a battle cry, used by Auburn fans in the same manner Alabama fans yell "Roll TIDE!" and Arkansas fans yell "Sooie Pig!" According to legend, a spectator at the first Auburn-Georgia game in 1892 had with him a golden eagle which had been his pet for 20 years. The eagle broke free and began circling the field. As the eagle soared, the Auburn team began a steady march down the field, and the fans took on its presence as an omen for success. At the game's end, the eagle fell to the field and died! The nickname TIGERS comes from a line in Oliver Goldsmith's poem, "The Deserted Village," published in May 1770, "where crouching tigers wait their hapless prey..." The term PLAINSMEN comes from a line in the same Goldsmith poem, "Sweet Auburn! loveliest village of the plain..." Since Auburn athletes were, in the early days, men from the plains, it was only natural for newspaper headline writers to shorten that to PLAINSMEN. Confused? Add this — WAR EAGLE VI, Auburn's golden eagle mascot, is named TIGER. And if he could read English, we're told that standing at one end of a football field, an eagle can read the date on a penny at the other end of the field.

BALL STATE CARDINALS

In November of 1927 discontent emerged among the Ball Teachers College HOOSIEROONS about their nickname. Quickly, BTC's weekly newspaper sponsored a contest to decide a new name with the award of a $5 prize in gold (in 1927!) going to the winner. Some of the names considered included INDIANS, BALL PLAYERS, FLYING CRIMSON, THE EASTERNERS, BTC BRAVES, SCRAPPIN' TEACHERS, and BALL BULLETS. It was Professor Billy Williams, a loyal fan of the St. Louis CARDINALS baseball team, who commented that the "Cardinal" on Rogers Hornby's sweatshirt was "distinctive." The name was submitted, and in a student election, CARDINALS became the new nickname for Ball Teachers College athletics over other finalists INDIANS, DELAWARES, and HOOSIEROONS. Since 1927 the name CARDINALS has remained synonymous with teams from Ball Teachers College, Ball State Teachers College, and finally Ball State University.

Nickname: Cards

BAYLOR BEARS

It was almost San Jacinto University, and then Milam University, but Baylor University finally won out. When the Texas Baptist Education Society petitioned the Congress of the Republic of Texas for a charter to start a university, the first name suggested was San Jacinto to recognize the victory which enabled the Texans to become an independent nation. Then it was changed to honor revolutionary hero Ben Milam. Just before the final vote of the Congress, the petitioners requested the university be named in honor of Judge R.E.B. Baylor. Republic of Texas president Anson Jones signed the Act of Congress on February 1, 1845, officially chartering it as Baylor University. The nickname could have been the BUFFALO, ANTELOPE, FROG, FERRET, or BOOKWORM, but after seventy years without an official mascot, students in 1914 voted to name the BEAR the official "Patron Saint of all Baylordom," two-to-one over the BUFFALO. School colors green and gold were selected in 1897 when a student riding a train admired the passing wild spring dandelions. *Pro Ecclesia, pro Texana* (For Church, for Texas) became the school motto in 1851.

BOISE STATE BRONCOS

At the time, it didn't seem like a momentous decision...just a handful of athletes choosing the school colors and mascot for their tiny 80-student junior college. Little did they know that decades later 20,000 football fans would be wearing all forms of blue and orange, and that the BRONCO symbol could have been seen everywhere from corporate offices to neighborhood bars. In 1932 the junior college was preparing to play more established teams like Gooding College and the College of Idaho, and students like Preston Hale decided Boise needed a mascot and colors. Hale says he and his fellow students picked blue and orange because they wanted to come up with something different than their rivals' colors. "Boise Junior College was pretty small then. We didn't realize the impact it (the decision) would have," he says. "We were just eager to get a team together and start playing somebody." BRONCO was selected because in those days Boise was surrounded by ranches, cattle country, and many of the students rode horses. Hale owns one priceless piece of memorabilia — the college's first BRONCO jacket. He'd bought a suede jacket, and art teacher Frances Westfall drew a Bronco on it. "It's about the same symbol you (Boise) use now," Hale says. Boise was named by French Canadian explorers in the 1800s — Les Bois means trees. It is now known as the city of trees.

BOSTON COLLEGE EAGLES

One Rev. Edward McLaughlin, incensed at a Boston newspaper cartoon depicting the champion Boston College track team as a cat licking clean a plate of its rivals, penned a passionate letter to the student newspaper, *The Heights*, in 1920. "It is important that we adopt a mascot to preside at our pow-wows and triumphant feats. And why not the eagle, symbolic of majesty, power, and freedom? Its natural habitat is high places. Surely the Heights is made to order for such a selection." And so it was. The EAGLE was adopted as mascot and nickname that same year. The national attention that followed brought gifts of two live mascots, but one escaped and the other was injured attempting to. After a 40-year hiatus, another live bird named Margo — a combination of the first letters of the school colors maroon and gold — began attending home games. When she died in 1966, the status of the eagle as an endangered species made it undesirable for B.C. to replace Margo, and a costumed human has been cavorting along the sidelines ever since.

BOWLING GREEN FALCONS

The 1996-97 athletic year marks the 70th anniversary of Bowling Green State University's nickname, the FALCONS. Before 1927, BG teams were called the NORMALS or TEACHERS. Ivan Lake, Class of '23 suggested the nickname after reading an article on falconry. Lake, managing editor and sports editor of the *Sentinel Tribune* in Bowling Green at the time, proposed the name change because it fit headline space and because falcons were "the most powerful bird for their size and often attacked birds two or three times their size." Burnt orange and seal brown have been the school colors since the first year of classes — 1914. Former Cleveland BROWNS head coach liked the combination as well. Following a trip to Bowling Green in the 1940s, Brown used the same colors for his All-American Conference team. "Ay Ziggy Zoomba" is BG's unofficial fight song. Gil Fox, an Air Force bombardier in World War Two stationed in Italy with other Allied troops, brought a loose translation of a Zulu war chant back with him, and it has been in campus spirit history since its introduction in 1946.

BRIGHAM YOUNG COUGARS

Brigham Young University, founded in 1875, is part of the Church of Jesus Christ of Latter-Day Saints Educational System, serving over a million people worldwide in education. The university traces its roots to Utah's rich pioneer heritage. The original school, Brigham Young Academy, was established on October 16, 1875, on a little over one acre of land in what is today downtown Provo. At that time, Brigham Young, the second president of the LDS Church, charged that all secular learning at the institution should be fused with teachings from the scriptures. The academy's high school and college curriculum improved and strengthened, and on October 23, 1903, the name was officially changed to Brigham Young University. In the search for a school mascot in 1923, the native Utah cougar was looked on favorably, primarily for its grace, agility, and great strength. It was felt the mountain lion combined the qualities of its symbolic relatives, embodying the strength and majesty of the lion, the symbol of kings; the speed of a cheetah, the symbol of pharaoh; the beauty of the leopard, and the cunning of a panther. In 1923, David Rust, an alumnus of BYU and guide on the Colorado River, captured a mother cougar and her three kittens. Two of these kittens were brought to Provo and kept as University mascots, fixing the COUGARS nickname for athletic teams forever. The COUGARS won the national football championship in 1984, going 13-0.

CALIFORNIA GOLDEN BEARS

It was Charles Mills Gayley, a Professor of English at the University of California at Berkeley, who suggested the school's nickname. Originally called the BLUE AND GOLD in the 1860s, after the school colors, Gayley saw an opportunity for a name change when the track team travelled back east for an event with a blue banner (made of silk). On the banner was a gold-colored bear. Shortly thereafter, Gayley wrote a song entitled "Our Sturdy Golden Bear," based on the banner, and the name stuck. This was in 1895, and they have been called the GOLDEN BEARS ever since. The team was also known as the BRUINS, sort of a sub-nickname, until UCLA's adoption of that moniker in the 1920s.

Nickname: Go-Bears

CENTRAL FLORIDA
KNIGHTS OF PEGASUS

In 1970 at the University of Central Florida, "Operation Mascot" yielded the name "KNIGHTS" OF PEGASUS, a link to the University Seal which features the winged horse of Greek mythology. Other schools in the Trans America Athletic Conference include Southeastern Louisiana University and their LIONS, a name provided by a center on the football team in the 1930s; the Mercer University BEARS, borrowed from a bemused spectator who asked "Whence cometh that bear?" while watching a brawny Mercer lineman, with long hair and handlebar moustache, charge onto the field; the Jacksonville State football team chose the new nickname GAMECOCKS in the early 1970s, in honor of the bird's fighting spirit, and replacing EAGLE OWLS; formerly known as the SUNBLAZERS, the Florida International University GOLDEN PANTHER nickname was adopted in 1987, with its golden color distinguishing it from other similar mascots; and the College of Charleston adopted the alliterative COUGARS nickname in 1970.

CENTRAL MICHIGAN CHIPPEWAS

The nickname CHIPPEWAS reflects the rich heritage of the Mid-Michigan region, but has not always been applied to Central Michigan University athletes. The first official nickname was the DRAGONS, which appeared in 1925. The student newspaper began calling the Central athletes BEARCATS three years later and this lasted until 1942 when student and faculty dissent led to CHIPPEWAS. The nickname actually has changed fewer times than the school name. Central opened its doors in 1892 as Central Michigan Normal and Business Institute. Central Michigan Normal School was initiated in 1896 along with the first football team and the unofficial nickname NORMALITIES for all the students. The school offered its first four-year degree program in 1919. Subsequent name changes include Central State Teachers College (1927), Central Michigan College of Education (1941), Central Michigan College (1955) and the present CMU (1959).

CINCINNATI BEARCATS

There are at least three stories as to how University of Cincinnati teams earned their nickname. One version has the moniker a result

of a 1913 cartoon of UC lineman Leonard K. "Teddy" Baehr standing on the field next to a Stutz Bearcat automobile. Another theory
traces the nickname's origin to another sports cartoon which followed
the 1914 UC-Kentucky game which showed a bear-like, cat-like animal harassing a wildcat. A third holds that in a 1912 newspaper account of a UC game, *Cincinnati Enquirer* sports editor Jack Ryder
stated that "the team played like bearcats." Beyond that speculation,
it is known that the bearcat is a native animal of Southeast Asia, a carnivorous mammal known to be ferocious if provoked. The bearcat,
also known as a binturong, is a relative to the mongoose. UC's athletic teams sport a logo in which the letter "C" has been converted
into a paw.

CLEMSON TIGERS

In Thomas Green Clemson's will he bequeathed the Fort Hill plan-
tation and a considerable sum from his personal assets for the establishment of the Clemson Agricultural College of South Carolina.
Opened in 1893, after Clemson's death, the college was an all-male
military school until 1955 when the change was made to "civilian"
status. In 1964 the college was renamed Clemson University. William
J. Latimer, 1904 Clemson grad, suggested that Professor Walter
Merritt Riggs, who coached Clemson's first football team in 1895,
planted the TIGER nickname seed, saying this about his players,
"Due to the lack of helmets and head protection they wore long hair.
These long manes might have gained them the name of LIONS had
it not been for the orange and purple striped jerseys and stockings
that resembled TIGERS. The latter nickname seemed to stick."
Latimer's findings are substantiated by the fact Coach Riggs had
played football at Auburn (nicknamed TIGERS) whose colors were
orange and blue.

COLORADO BUFFALOES

Prior to 1934, Colorado University athletic teams usually were referred to as the SILVER AND GOLD, but other nicknames teams

were sometimes called included SILVER HELMETS, YELLOW JACKETS, HORNETS, ARAPAHOS, BIG HORNS, GRIZZLIES, and FRONTIERSMEN. The campus newspaper announced the contest in the fall of 1934, with a $5 prize to go to the author of the winning selection. Claude Bates of New Madrid, Mo., and James Proffitt of Cincinnati, Ohio, were co-winners for the prize as both submitted BUFFALOES as their entry. Athletic Director Harry Carlson, graduate manager Walter Franklin and Kenneth Bundy of the SILVER AND GOLD were the judges. Through the years, synonyms which quickly came into use included BISONS, BUFFS, THUNDERING HERD, STAMPEDING HERD, GOLDEN AVALANCHE, and GOLDEN BUFFALOES. The University of Colorado possesses perhaps the most unusual mascot in all of intercollegiate athletics — an actual buffalo named Ralphie. The buffalo first appeared in 1943, three weeks after the contest to select an official nickname was completed. It is truly one of the special sights that exists anywhere in college or professional sports, especially for opposing teams, who often stop in their tracks watching the massive buffalo round the end zone and head directly at their sideline.

Nickname: The Buffs

COLORADO STATE RAMS

Unknown even to many Colorado State University fans is that CAM, the live ram mascot's nickname since 1946, is an abbreviated acronym for Colorado State College of Agricultural and Mechanical Arts, the school's original name. At that time, the university athletic teams were called the AGGIES, an agricultural reference. While the AGGIES, team mascots included "Peanuts," a homely little English bulldog. The unfortunate animal was poisoned in 1917, and was replaced by a second mascot in 1919. This black bear marched proudly in parades and was a regular attendant at football games. His job was over in the late 20s, and it wasn't until "Buck" arrived in 1946 that CSU had another mascot. This ram provoked a slight nickname change to AGGIE RAMS, eventually shortened to simply RAMS. Historical records do not indicate exactly how many rams have preceded the present mascot, but all save the first has been named CAM.

DUKE BLUE DEVILS

What would have been different about Princeton had the university accepted an endowment from the tobacco baron James Buchanan Duke? It's name! All Princeton needed to do to get the tobacco dough was change its name to Duke. Not surprisingly, the regents turned down the offer and Duke took his business to Durham, North Carolina, where a small institution called Trinity College was transformed into Duke University. Only then did the issue of a team nickname come up BLUE DEVILS. First used *by The Chronicle* in 1922-23, the nickname BLUE DEVILS was derived from the French Blue Devils. This originated with the nickname given the French Infantry in World War One. Then the name was applied to a French crack alpine team which wore a striking blue uniform with a blue beret. Fight songs include Fight BLUE DEVIL, Dear Old Duke, and Blue and White — a song in honor of the school colors.

Nickname: Devils

EAST CAROLINA PIRATES

The PIRATE, a symbol of East Carolina university and its athletic teams, was adopted from the legend and lore of coastal North Carolina and was a natural choice for the nickname when intercollegiate athletics began at the school almost 60 years ago. Pirates, fearful and colorful, were prominent in North Carolina's colonial period. The state's Outer Banks which jut far out into the Atlantic were ideal hide-outs for these legendary gangsters of the high seas. Many had homes and families in small villages along the Carolina coast. East Carolina University's interest in pirates and sea lore began in 1934. That year, *The Tecoan*, the yearbook for what was then East Carolina Teachers College, carried PIRATES as its theme. The pages were filled with paintings and sketches of patched-eye figures, tall ships, and buried treasure. The book referred to the tales of the infamous "Teachy the Pirate" often told by natives in the nearby historic town of Bath. The bigger-than-life pirate cartoon figure enjoyed by East Carolina University fans today is a 1983 creation. At first this swaggering, tough-guy creation was called Pee Dee, named after a river that extends through parts of North and South Carolina. In the mid-seventies, the defensive players on the PIRATES' football team were called the WILD DOGS because the players performed like a vicious pack of them. A live wildcat was the mascot in 1930-31!

EASTERN MICHIGAN EAGLES

The EAGLES name was officially adopted on May 22, 1991, when the Eastern Michigan University Board of Regents voted to replace the existing HURON nickname and logo with the new one. EMU originally went by the nicknames NORMALITES and MEN FROM YPSI and various other titles down through the years before HURONS was adopted in 1929. The HURONS first came into being as the result of a contest sponsored by the Men's Union in 1929. The name was submitted by two students, Gretchen Borst and George Hanner. Hanner was working at the Huron Hotel at the time and was no doubt as much influenced by his place of employment as by the Huron Indian tribe. The runner-up in that contest was PIONEERS. EMU began investigating the appropriateness of its HURON Indian logo after the Michigan Department of Civil Rights issued a report in 1988 suggesting that all schools using such logos drop them, indicating that the use of Native American names, logos, and mascots for athletic teams promoted racial stereotypes. At that time, four colleges, 62 high schools and 33 junior high/middle schools in Michigan used Indian names. The EMU Board of regents voted to replace the HURON name with EAGLES, taken from three recommendations from a committee charged with supplying a new name. The other two finalists were GREEN HORNETS and EXPRESS.

FLORIDA GATORS

Austin Miller, a native of Gainesville, was enrolled in the University of Virginia in the fall of 1907, and was visited by his father, Phillip. The elder Miller then owned a combination drug and stationery store in Gainesville, a popular rendezvous for university students. While in Charlottesville the father decided to order some college pennants and banners for his Florida shop from the Michie Company, which was engaged in the manufacture of such items — but found the University of Florida had no emblem! The name ALLIGATORS occurred to young Austin as a suitable nickname, both because the Mitchie Manager said no other school had adopted it and because the alligator was native to Florida. Problem was, the Mitchie Manager had never seen an alligator so didn't believe he could design one. Austin volunteered to find a suitable picture of a "gator," and located one in the library of the University of Virginia. So it was that the first appearance of the alligator emblem was in the Miller store in 1908. In 1965 researchers at the University of Florida used the school's football team as guinea pigs to test a special beverage they had developed to combat dehydration and enhance athletic performance. The players liked the stuff, which was christened Gatorade after the university's mascot.

FLORIDA STATE SEMINOLES

The SEMINOLE nickname was chosen by students in 1947, when Florida State College for Women became Florida State University. The brand new football team played its first game without benefit of a symbol. So, a contest was held on campus, and numerous nicknames poured in, including the FLEAS, TALLYWHACKERS, GOLD DIGGERS, and PINHEADS. According to FSU history professor James P. Jones, the name SEMINOLES was selected from a final list of six that included the GOLDEN FALCONS, STATESMEN, SENATORS, CRACKERS, and INDIANS. But writer Bill McGrotha's account states that the other finalists were CRACKERS, FIGHTING WARRIORS, REBELS, STATESMEN, and TARPONS. The SEMINOLE are a tribe of North American Indians who left their traditional homeland in Georgia after separating from the Creek during the 18th century to live independently in Florida. Many escaped black slaves took refuge with the Seminole. When the Seminole obstructed the advance of white land-seekers and refused to return slaves, Andrew Jackson pushed them farther south in the First Seminole War (1817-18). In 1819 the United States purchased Florida from Spain, and pressure from whites increased. The treaty of Payne's Landing (1832) called for the removal of the Seminole, but the tribe resisted in the Second Seminole War (1835-42) under the leadership of Osceola, Wildcat, and Halek. At last, beaten and destitute, 4000 of the 4300 Seminole moved west to Indian Territory. They became one of the so-called Five Civilized Tribes, and many tribespeople gradually lost their Indian identity. Those who stayed in Florida, however, living on three reservations near Lake Okeechobee, retained many of their traditional ways. In the late 1980s about 1500 Seminole lived in Florida and about 4000 in Oklahoma. Florida State, founded in 1857, wears the SEMINOLE nickname with pride, as well as its garnet and gold colors, and the symbols of Chief Osceola and his horse Renegade.

Nickname: '*Noles*

FRESNO STATE BULLDOGS

Late in the 1921 season, student body president Warren Moody and friends were continually greeted outside the main campus building by a white bulldog. The dog adopted the group and they decided to make him the mascot. Arids Walker made the motion to adopt BULLDOGS as the official nickname in a student body meeting. It was November 21, 1921, that the *Morning Republican* first referred to Fresno State as the BULLDOGS. The colors evolved out of an argument by women from Fresno Normal School and men from Fresno Junior College. The women were seeking blue and white to the men's red and white. A compromise was struck with the school adopting red and blue with the red later changed to Cardinal. Fresno State's fan following is commonly referred to as the RED WAVE, which was coined by *Fresno Bee* sportswriter Ron Orozco in the early '80s.

GEORGIA BULLDOGS

The University of Georgia's first mascot for its first football game against Auburn, on February 22, 1892, in Atlanta was a goat. Old newspaper clippings say the goat wore a black coat with red U.G. letters on each side. He also had a hat with ribbons all down his high horns, and the Auburn fans yelled throughout the game "Shoot the billy-goat!" Two years later, in 1894, the BULLDOGS' mascot was a solid white female bull terrier owned by a student, the late Charles Black of Atlanta. Then came the bulldog mascots, beginning with a couple of brindled English Bulldogs. Butch served from 1947 till 1951, and was succeeded from 1951 till 1956 by Mike. Then came the famous "Uga" lineage. The solid white English Bulldogs have served as faithful mascots since 1955, and have now reached "Uga V." The BULLDOG moniker was adopted for its reputation and characteristics of "stubbornness and strong-jawed, unrelenting commitment."

Nickname: The Dogs

GEORGIA TECH YELLOWJACKETS

The YELLOW JACKET nickname and mascot are two of the most beloved trademarks of Georgia Tech athletic teams, but many conflicting accounts exist as to the origins and beginnings of the YELLOW JACKET. One thing that is clear however, is that the nickname did not grow out of the familiar six-legged insect, but the insect mascot, known as "Buzz," grew out of the nickname. As far as can be determined, the first reference to Tech students as YELLOWJACKETS appeared in the *Atlanta Constitution* in 1905 and came into common usage at the time. Historians say the name, spelled as one word, was first used to describe supporters who attended Tech athletic events, dressed in yellow coats and jackets. The actual mascot was conceived at a later date, still undetermined. Other common nicknames which have applied to Georgia Tech teams include ENGINEERS, which is still used by some writers; the TECHS, the first known nickname which was phased out sometime around 1910; and the BLACKSMITHS, which was common between 1902 and 1904 and is thought to be an invention of sportswriters at the time. The GOLDEN TORNADO is another former nickname thought to be created by sportswriters when Coach John Heisman led Tech to its first national championship in football in 1917. Tech was the first team from the South to earn the honor bestowed by the International News Service, and any team thereafter which approached the same level of excellence was referred to as the GOLDEN TORNADO. The nickname was used as late as 1929, when Tech defeated California in the Rose Bowl. And it was in 1891, two years before Georgia Tech fielded its first football team, that the colors white and gold were voted on at a mass student meeting.

Nickname: Rambling Wreck

HAWAII RAINBOW WARRIORS ———

Before 1923, University of Hawaii teams were nicknamed the DEANS. Then, in the final game of the 1923 season, UH Head Coach "Otto" Klum's squad upset Oregon State 7-0 at Moiliili Field. During the game, a rainbow appeared over the field. Reporters started calling UH teams the RAINBOWS, and the tradition began that Hawaii would not lose a game if a rainbow appeared. Rainbows, however, had magical powers long before football came to the islands. Hawaiian chiefs considered them sacred and used them as signs of a chief's presence. A rainbow hovering over a newborn child indicated that he was of a god-like rank. The warrior holds an honored place in Hawaiian history for it was Kamehameha I, the great warrior and his armies, that united the Hawaiian Islands. The Hawaiians expected the warrior to display great strength, courage, skill, and a fighting spirit. Although it wasn't until 1974 that the UH football team adopted the nickname RAINBOW WARRIORS, the university's use of the name goes back a number of years. Only the football team is dubbed the RAINBOW WARRIORS. All other men's teams are the RAINBOWS.

HOUSTON COUGARS

Athletic teams at the University of Houston have been called the COUGARS since 1927, the year the school was founded as a junior college. One of the original faculty members, John R. Bender, tutored a volunteer football squad and named them the COUGARS. Bender came to Houston after serving as the head football coach at Washington State University, which also had the nickname of COUGARS. The name must've been contagious, because he brought it to Houston saying he liked the mountain lion as a symbol of courage and tenacity. The school became a four-year university in 1932. The student newspaper adopted the name in 1935 and when the University of Houston began sponsoring intercollegiate athletics in 1946, COUGARS was adopted as the name for athletic teams. Houston has not used a live mascot since 1988, when the mountain lion Shasta V (shortened form of she-has-to) reigned over COUGAR athletic events. The cougar's name beat out finalists Spiritana and Raguoc — cougar spelled backwards. Scarlet and white, the colors on General Sam Houston's family shield, were adopted in 1938.

IDAHO VANDALS

The silver and gold VANDALS first took to the court around 1918 when the University of Idaho basketball team had the reputation of destroying their opponents. The press in the Northwest took up the cause, initially referring to the team as the WRECKING CREW. Vandals was the name of an East Germanic tribe that ravaged Gaul, Spain, and North Africa, and sacked Rome in 455 A.D. So effective were these Vandals, their name became a word in the dictionary describing a person who destroys with malice! It was in 1921, with the encouragement of College of Liberal Arts Dean Edward M. Hulme and school sports editor Lloyd McCarty, that VANDALS became the official nickname of all University athletic teams. The mascot is nicknamed Joe Vandal. A large silver and gold VANDAL head graces the front of Student Union in glowing neon lights and the burly, be-whiskered individual can be seen throughout the campus. Members of the Idaho rodeo team are called the VANDAL RIDERS. In 1996, the VANDALS fielded their first football team in Division 1-A.

ILLINOIS FIGHTING ILLINI

The symbol of Chief Illiniwek, originally dressed in an authentic outfit made by a Sioux woman, has stirred pride and respect at the University of Illinois since 1926. Illiniwek (pronounced "ill-EYE-nih-wek") was the name of the loose confederation of Algonquin tribes that once lived in the region. The French changed the ending to "ois" in naming what became the state of Illinois. Illiniwek means "they are men" and former Illinois football Coach Robert Zappke is believed to have suggested calling the UI symbol Chief Illiniwek. According to Sports Information at Illinois, the term ILLINI is simply a shorter form of Illiniwek, and FIGHTING ILLINI implies an aggressive behaviour on the field. In 1930, an Indian trader helped the school make contact with an old Sioux woman who created an authentic Chief Illiniwek outfit to be worn by the mascot.

INDIANA HOOSIERS

Ask a HOOSIER what one looks like or from where the name sprung and you're likely to draw a blank stare. Historians have un-earthed many theories but find agreement in few of them. One which seems to have more validity than most cites a Samuel Hoosier, who in 1825 was a contractor on the Louisville & Portland (Ohio Falls) Canal. He appreciated the "better workers" from the Indiana side of the river, and these men later brought home a proud new moniker, the hoosiers, named after their boss. Another, less-authentic version was that of Col. Jacob Lehmanoski. This Polish officer, who had served with Napoleon before settling in Indiana, delivered a series of stirring lectures in which he extolled the courage and endurance of the Hussars, which he pronounced as Hoosier. According to the story, the natives adopted it for them-selves. There are others who say it originated from the habit of travellers hailing a cabin for a night's lodging as they approached. The cautious pioneer would, before unlatching the door, call out, "Who's there?" It's only a step through frontier enunciation from there to "hoosier." And there's that lighthearted explanation stemming from the rowdy, brawling nature of the early settlers. It is credited to Indiana's James Whitcomb Riley and no doubt was Riley's whimsy. He claimed there were vicious fighters who not only gouged and scratched but frequently bit off noses and ears. "Whose ear?" was not an uncommon remark when sweeping up afterward. Others? Indiana Governor Joseph Wright claimed the term derived from "hoosa," an Indian word for corn. The dictionary tells us that "hoojee" means tramp, but no HOOSIER would buy that. "hoosier" was an English dialect word meaning "anything unusually great." Historian Jacob P. Dunn wrote that the word was a term common in the South applied to uncouth persons. Regardless, HOOSIERS can take comfort in the fact that it carries a very positive and inspirational connotation these days — thanks to the storied teams from Indiana.

IOWA HAWKEYES

The University of Iowa borrowed its athletic nickname from the state of Iowa many years ago. The name Hawkeye was originally applied to a hero in a fictional novel, "The Last of the Mohicans," written by James Fenimore Cooper. Author Cooper had the Delaware Indians bestow the name on a white scout who lived and hunted with them. In 1838, 12 years after the book was published, people in the territory of Iowa acquired the nickname, chiefly through the efforts of Judge David Rorer of Burlington and James G. Edwards of Fort Madison. Edwards, editor of the *Fort Madison Patriot*, moved his paper to Burlington in 1843 and renamed it the *Burlington Hawk-Eye*. The two men continued their campaign to popularize the name and were rewarded when territorial officials gave it their formal approval. The HAWKEYE nickname gained a tangible symbol in 1948 when a cartoon character, later to be named Herky the Hawk, was hatched. The creator was Richard Spencer III, instructor of journalism. The impish hawk was an immediate hit and he acquired a name through a statewide contest staged by the athletic department. John Franklin, a Belle Plain alumnus, was the man who suggested Herky. Since his birth more than 30 years ago, Herky has symbolized Iowa athletics and epitomized University life. He even donned a military uniform during the Korean War and became the insignia of the 124th Fighter Squadron. During the mid-1950s Herky came to life at a football game as the Iowa mascot with a black leather head and gold felt feathers. Since then Herky has become a familiar figure at HAWKEYE athletic events.

IOWA STATE CYCLONES

On September 28 of 1895 the Iowa State Agricultural College swept into Illinois to play a tough Northwestern football squad. The next day a *Chicago Tribune* headline proclaimed "Iowa Cyclone Devastates Northwestern, 36-0." According to Iowa State historian Earle D. Ross in his 1943 book, "History of Iowa State College," a *Chicago Tribune* sportswriter reported: "Northwestern might as well have tried to play football with an Iowa cyclone as with the Iowa team it met yesterday. At the end of fifty minutes play the big husky farmers from Iowa's Agricultural College had rolled up 36 points, while the 15-yard line was the nearest Northwestern got to Iowa's goal." The nickname penned by the Chicago sportswriter stuck and eventually became the official nickname for all Iowa State sports teams.

KANSAS JAYHAWKS

The word JAYHAWK was first used in present-day Kansas about 1858. The name combines two birds; the blue jay, a noisy, quarrelsome thing known to rob nests, and the sparrow hawk, a stealthy hunter. The message here: Do not turn your back on this bird. JAYHAWK was originally associated with robbing, looting, and general lawlessness in the Kansas Territory. During the Civil War it took on new meaning. In 1861 surgeon Dr. Charles R. Jennison used it when he was commissioned as a colonel by Kansas Governor

Charles Robinson and charged with raising a regiment of cavalry. Jennison called his regiment the Independent Mounted Kansas Jayhawkers, although it was officially the First Kansas Cavalry and later the Seventh Kansas Regiment. During the Civil War the word JAYHAWK became associated with the spirit of comradeship associated with efforts to keep Kansas a free state. And following the war, most Kansans were proud to be called JAYHAWKERS. By 1886, the University of Kansas had adopted the mythical bird as part of the KU yell.

KANSAS STATE WILDCATS

Prior to 1915, Kansas State Agricultural College teams had been known as the AGGIES. But the nickname WILDCATS was given to the football team in 1915 by Head Coach Chief Bender because of what he called the squad's "fighting spirit." The moniker was changed to FARMERS in 1916, but Head Coach Charles Bachman switched back to the WILDCAT nickname in 1920. Kansas State itself is referred to in many different shortened versions. The most popular is K-STATE, which is used by alums, friends, and journalists from coast to coast. Fans are called CATBACKERS, or PURPLE PRIDE, in reference to the team's only official color. The tradition of Touchdown the bobcat mascot began in 1922, but the creature no longer attends the games. Touchdown XII resides at Manhattan's Sunset Zoo.

Nickname: Cats

KENT GOLDEN FLASHES

Originally Kent Normal School, the Kent State University origin of the nickname GOLDEN FLASHES has been a topic of debate. According to documentation in Phillip Shriver's book, "The Years of Youth," widely regarded as historically correct, it is noted that in a letter to Linda Baughman, dated August 6, 1959, Merle Wagoner recalled that the change in the name of Kent athletics teams from

SILVER FOXES to GOLDEN FLASHES occurred in 1926 after the dismissal of President John E. McGilvrey for whose silver fox farm east of the campus the teams had first been named. With acting President T. Howard Winters providing the impetus, a contest was held to select the new name. GOLDEN FLASHES, a subtle nod in the direction of the school color, was used first in 1927 by the basketball team after it had been introduced. Also laying partial claim to the origin was Oliver Wolcott, one-time Kent grid great who played center on the 1921 and 1922 teams. As former sports editor of the *Kent Courier Tribune*, the local newspaper, the name SILVER FOXES seemed pretty frail to him. So, during the 1927 football season, he began referring to the team as GOLDEN FLASHES. By the way, Kent's school colors are blue and gold — purely by accident. In the 1910 State Charter, Kent's school colors were orange and purple. However, a local laundry changed the colors. The basketball uniforms, orange and purple when they went into the hot water, came back gold and blue-black. Word has it that the team and student body liked the new colors so well they adopted them as the new school colors!

KENTUCKY WILDCATS

The official nickname for the University of Kentucky's athletics teams is WILDCATS. The nickname became synonymous with UK shortly after a 6-2 football victory over Illinois on October 9, 1909, on the road. Commandant Carbusier, then head of the military department at old State University, told a group of students in a chapel service following the game that the Kentucky football team had "fought like wildcats." Later the name WILDCATS became more and more popular among UK followers as well as with members of the media. As a result, the nickname was adopted by the University. Blue was added to white as official colors in 1892 when a student pulled off his blue necktie and tossed it into the selection process. In April 1994 WILDCAT Brent Claiborne finished eighth nationally in the mascot division of the Universal Cheerleaders Association competition.

Nickname: Big Blue

LOUISIANA STATE FIGHTING TIGERS

In the fall of 1896, Coach A.W. Jeardeau's Louisiana State University football team posted a perfect 6-0-0 record, and it was in that pigskin campaign that LSU first adopted the TIGER nickname. TIGERS seemed a logical choice as most collegiate teams were adopting the names of ferocious animals that year, but the underlying reason for the nickname dates back to the Civil War. During the "War Between the States," a battalion of Confederate soldiers comprised of New Orleans Zouaves and Donaldson Cannoneers distinguished themselves at the Battle of Shenandoah. These Louisiana rebels had been known by their contemporaries as the fighting band of Louisiana Tigers. Thus when LSU football teams entered the gridiron battlefields in their fourth year of intercollegiate competition, they tagged themselves the TIGERS. It was the 1955 LSU "fourth-quarter ball club" that helped the TIGER moniker grow into the nickname FIGHTING TIGERS. Just to the north of TIGER Stadium is the home of Mike V, LSU's Bengal TIGER mascot. The Tiger Cage, constructed for the first Mike in 1937, was renovated in 1981 to include a grassy area, a tiger-sized wooden scratching post, a pool, a climbing platform, and an indoor area for use in inclement weather.

Nickname: Bayou Bengals

LOUISIANA TECH BULLDOGS

In 1899, five Tech students were returning home from school and came upon an old, hungry bulldog sitting under a tree. The boys fed it, and upon arriving home found the dog had followed. They sought permission for it to stay the night, and the landlord agreed — but the dog had to stay in the kitchen. That night the house caught fire. The dog awakened first, and ran from room to room until all occupants were alerted to the danger. The homeless dog re-entered the burning house when it was discovered that one boy remained inside. When the fire was extinguished and the smoke cleared, the lifeless bulldog was found in an unburned corner of one room — dead from the smoke and heat. The shaken students buried the dog where they'd found him, wrapped in two jackets — one red, the other blue, now the school's colors. The whole campus mourned the death of the dog with no name, and two years later when Tech organized a football team, the choice of mascot was unanimous. They were named the BULLDOGS, after the first hero of Tech.

Nickname: Tech

LOUISVILLE CARDINALS

The University of Louisville's athletic symbol, chosen sometime after 1913, is a CARDINAL. The Cardinal bird was chosen to give Louisville statewide identification, since the Cardinal is the state bird of Kentucky. The school colors — cardinal red, black, and white — were adopted at the suggestion of Mrs. John L. Patterson. This nickname for UL atheletes is also an acronym for the following areas: Commitment, Academics, Respect, Discipline, Integrity, No! to Drugs, Achievement, Leadership, and Service. The bright-red, crested American songbird is the nickname of a number of college and pro teams, but not Stanford, whose CARDINAL moniker actually refers to the color — to which, of course, there is no plural ("Don't call us the Cardinals!"). The CARDINALS namesake, *richmondena cardinalis,* is related to the finch.

Nickname: The Cards

MARYLAND TERRAPINS

Dr. H.C. Bird, a football coach who later became University President, recommended the Diamondback TERRAPIN as the school nickname and mascot in 1932 in response to the student newspaper's search for an "official" leader. Byrd's childhood in Crisfield, Md., apparently included skirmishes with this brand of snapping turtle, indigenous to Chesapeake Bay, and with a reputation for intimidation and unpredictability. The mascot is nicknamed Testudo — derived from a Latin word meaning a shelter held over the head of Roman soldiers, like a tortoise shell. Earlier, Maryland had been referring to itself as OLD LINERS. Historians are in a scrimmage over whether that nickname is a reference to a Revolutionary War troop of Maryland soldiers who distinguished themselves on the field of battle, or they feel it could refer to a squabble with Pennsylvanians over just where the border between the two states should be. Further turtleization came when the student yearbook, *The Reveille*, became *The TERRAPIN* in 1935. Then local newspapers took to shortening TERRAPIN to TERP for headline writing ease.

Nickname: Terps

MEMPHIS TIGERS

1912 references to the football team had them tabbed as the BLUE AND GRAY WARRIORS of West Tennessee Normal School. They became West Tennessee State Teachers College in 1925, Memphis State College in 1941, Memphis State University in 1957, and finally the University of Memphis in 1994. After the final game of the 1914 season, there was a student parade where several Normal students shouted "We fight like tigers!" Campus publications loved the new nickname, but the newspapers downtown stuck with NORMALS and BLUE AND GRAY. Under Coach Laster Barnard in 1922, the team adopted the motto "Every man a tiger!" In the late 1920s, student publications and downtown newspapers began referring to the football team as the TEACHERS or TUTORS. But the TIGER moniker would return, and in 1939 was finally adopted as the school's official nickname. For nearly a quarter century the mascot has been a Bengal Tiger! This naming-contest attracted 2,500 entries, including Spook, Sampson, Goliath, Bengo, Sultan, Sahib, Big Cat, Ptah, Touchdown, Sonny, Shiloh, and Bengie Wougie Bengal Boy from Tennessee. The winner was TOM, for Tigers Of Memphis.

MIAMI HURRICANES

Why HURRICANES? Because on opening day of the University of Miami's 1926 football season a real-life hurricane hit the field! The event was postponed. Even the birth of the nickname began in storm-like conditions. Some reports say the 1927 football club held a team meeting to select HURRICANES, hoping they would sweep away opponents just as the devastating storm did on September 16, 1926. Another version holds that *Miami News* columnist Jack Bell asked end Porter Norris of the 1926 squad what the team should be called. Told that the local dignitaries and University officials wanted to name the team for a local flora or fauna, Norris said the players wouldn't stand for it and suggested HURRICANES as a nod to that opening game. From time to time, opposition has arisen to the name that would "reinforce Miami's negative reputation as a weather-beaten community living constantly under the threat of destruction." But as one University of Miami official rationalized in the '60s, "Does anyone think Chicago is overrun by BEARS just because the town has a football team by that name?" The school colors address the local flora and fauna, however. Ruth Bryan Owens, daughter of famed attorney William Jennings Bryan, while a member of the board of regents suggested the colors of the Florida orange tree. Orange symbolizes the fruit of the tree, green represents the leaves and white is the blossom. Folklore maintains that the ibis, a symbol of knowledge found in the Everglades and Egypt, is the last sign of wildlife to take shelter before a hurricane, and the first to reappear after a storm. The local marsh bird was first considered the school's mascot in 1926, and through the years has become one of the most recognizable in the United States.

Nickname: 'Canes

MIAMI (OHIO) REDSKINS ——

Use of the nickname REDSKINS for Miami athletic teams dates back to the 1930-31 school year when the Miami alumni magazine, then edited by the school's lone publicity man, Ralph McGinnis, announced the new nickname as successor to BIG RED, which had caused confusion with Denison University teams. A similar tag had popped up in a 1928 story in the *Miami Student* that referred to Big Red-Skinned Warriors, but the transition wasn't made for another three years. For a time in 1931, REDSKIN and BIG RED were used interchangeably in *The Student*. Throughout the sports world,

Miami University has the unique reputation as the "Cradle of the Coaches." At last count, more than one hundred Miami graduates were active in coaching or administrative work at the pro and collegiate levels.

Nickname: The 'Skins

MICHIGAN WOLVERINES

Since the earliest recorded moment of Michigan sports history in 1861, students of the University of Michigan have been calling themselves WOLVERINES. The reason for this nickname probably comes from the fact that Michigan has been called the Wolverine State, but the creation of that moniker is an interesting story. Wolverines are the largest members of the weasel family, measuring about three feet long and weighing about 26 pounds. Other members of this family include the otter, skunk, mink, weasel, and the wolverine's closest relative, the badger. Wolverines are crafty and destructive, and enjoy killing just for the sake of killing, even members of their own kind. Wolverines have very poor eyesight, but were despised by the Indians and early pioneers because of the wolverine's ability to find and consume vast amounts of stored food. Wolverines also were hated because of their fondness for eating the catch out of traps before the trapper himself had the opportunity to retrieve it. Early reports indicated that hunters would rather stumble into the den of a mother bear than come in contact with a mother wolverine, because "she is a tigress of ferocity, absolutely fearless, and so strong and quick that a man, even armed with a gun, is taking risks if he gets too near." The nickname of WOLVERINES probably arose during the Michigan-Ohio border dispute of 1803, but it is unclear whether Ohioans pinned this name on Michigan natives or Michiganders chose it as a symbol of tenacity. However, it is a certainty that wolverines have never been abundant in the state of Michigan and would not be the reason for the nickname. The University of Michigan originally started in Detroit but was transferred to Ann Arbor after local citizens donated a 40-acre plot of land to entice the University to come to Ann Arbor in 1837. A very loose nickname for Michigan's team is the MAIZE AND BLUE. In 1879, the new football team was automatically called the WOLVERINES.

MICHIGAN STATE SPARTANS

Starting life as the Michigan Agricultural College and nicknamed the AGGIES, the exact origin of the SPARTANS nickname came from *a Lansing State Journal* sportswriter who detested another former nickname, Michigan STATERS. He commented that the old nickname was too long to write in articles. So he searched through old entries from a contest that had been held to pick the nickname and found SPARTANS as one of the entries. The person who made the SPARTAN suggestion is unfortunately unknown. The writer liked the name and began using it in his articles on April 5, 1926. No administrators or alumni protested, and the name stuck. The SPARTAN nickname is shared with about a dozen other college teams, including the University of Tampa, Manchester College, and the University of Dubuque. When World War Two ended, a new campus fixture greeted the returning GIs — the SPARTAN statue. The statue, fondly known as SPARTY, is the largest freestanding ceramic sculpture in the world. Designed by faculty member Leonard D. Jungwirth, it is symbolic of the spirited warriors of ancient Sparta, designed in the ideal classical form, reinterpreted in the Art Deco style popular in the 1940s, and has incised figures on the base of the statue representing various campus sports. The SPARTAN helmet shows the image of Gruff, created in 1955.

MINNESOTA GOLDEN GOPHERS

Over the years there has been a good deal of bantering about regarding the University of Minnesota's nickname, but history shows that the name goes way back to 1857. First it must be realized that Minnesota was tabbed the "Gopher State" as the result of a cartoon satirizing the "Five Million Loan Bill" which appeared in the legislature on February 24, 1858. That bill, providing a loan for the building of railroads in Minnesota, was bitterly opposed, and in order to bring the subject into perspective, a cartoon was circulated showing the "Gopher Train" drawn by nine striped Gophers with human heads. It permanently fastened upon Minnesota the nickname "Gopher State." In the early 1930s, the Minnesota football teams, under the direction of Coach Bernie Bierman, were establishing themselves as national champions. During those championships, the local press described the GOPHER teams as the GOLDEN-SHIRTED HORDE and the GOLDEN SWARM. These descriptions were simultaneous with the team's change to golden colored jerseys, bringing the name GOLDEN GOPHERS.

MISSISSIPPI REBELS

The University of Mississippi, informally known as Ole Miss (suggested by Elma Meek in 1896), was chartered on February 24, 1844. For a while referred to as the FLOOD, and the RED AND BLUE, in 1936 it was decided by the Coach Ed Walker that Ole Miss needed a new nickname. The school newspaper received 600 entries from its name-the-team contest, but it took till the following year to select one from the final five: RAIDERS, CONFEDERATES, STONEWALLS, OLE MISS, and REBELS. Ole Miss alumnus Ben Guider suggested REBELS with these comments: "The name is short, musical, inspiring, simple for publication purposes, and should catch the eye of the sports public. In addition, the name recalls to mind the glories of the Old South and that historic struggle of the Civil War in which the State of Mississippi took so noble and outstanding a part, and for which every Mississippian should feel proud. Inasmuch as so many sections of our state are rich in tradition and memory of classic battles of that famous war, this name seems to me to be closely and peculiarly identified with the State of Mississippi, just as much so as the CAVALIERS of Virginia, GATORS of Florida, or the GAMECOCKS of South Carolina."

Nickname: Rebs

MISSISSIPPI STATE BULLDOGS

As with many universities, State teams answered to different nicknames through the years. The first squads representing Mississippi A&M College were proud to be called AGGIES, and when the school officially became Mississippi State College in 1932 the nick-name MAROONS, for State's uniform color, gained prominence. BULLDOGS became the official title for State teams in 1961, not long after State College was granted university status. Yet references to school teams as BULLDOGS go back to early in the century, and this name was used almost interchangeably with both AGGIES and MAROONS since at least 1905, when, after a victory, the ca-dets held a mock funeral parade for the losers. *The Reflector* campus newspaper reported, "A coffin was secured, decorated with Univer-sity colors and a bulldog pup placed on top." Other reports of the victory commented on the "bulldog" style of play, and the BULL-DOG was soon publicly accepted as a school athletic symbol. The official mascot is an American Kennel Club registered English Bull-dog, given the inherited title of "Bully."

MISSOURI TIGERS

The nickname TIGERS, given to Missouri University's athletic teams, traces its origin to the Civil War period. At that time, plun-dering guerilla bands habitually raided small towns, and Columbia people constantly feared an attack. Such organizations as tempo-rary "home guards" and vigilance companies banded together to fight off any possible forays. The town's preparedness discouraged any guerilla activity and the protecting organization began to dis-band in 1854. However, it was rumored that a guerilla band, led by notorious Bill Anderson, intended to sack the town. Quickly organ-ized was an armed guard of Columbia citizens, who built a block-house and fortified the old courthouse in the center of town. This company was called "The Missouri Tigers." The marauders never came. The reputation of the intrepid TIGERS presumably traveled abroad, and Anderson's gang detoured around Columbia. Soon af-ter Missouri's first football team was organized in 1890, the athletic committee adopted the nickname TIGERS in official recognition of those Civil War defenders. The MU mascot "Truman the Tiger" is named for the Missouri-bred President of the United States, Harry S. Truman.

NAVY MIDSHIPMEN

The Naval Academy athletic teams from Annapolis use the nickname MIDSHIPMEN. The name is derived from the Navy term "midshipman." The word first appeared in English in the seventeenth century in the form of the word "midshipsman" (note the extra "s") to designate those men who were stationed "amidships," i.e., in the waist or middle portion of the vessel, while on duty. By 1687, however, the second "s" had been dropped to give the current form of the word. Midshipmen were originally boys, sometimes as young as seven or eight, who were apprenticed to sea captains to learn the sailor's trade. In the early days of the American navy, midshipmen trained aboard ship until they were eventually commissioned as ensigns. With the founding of the Naval Academy in 1845, it became possible, as it still does today, for a midshipmen to enter the Navy directly from civilian life. The name of students at the naval Academy changed several times between 1870 and 1902, when Congress restored the original title of Midshipman and it has remained unchanged since. Since the term Midshipman is considered a rank, both the men's and women's athletic teams at the Naval Academy are known as the MIDSHIPMEN. The term MIDDIES is considered inappropriate.

Nickname: Mids

NEBRASKA CORNHUSKERS

A newspaper account reported that fans celebrated by waving banners of old gold. The date was November 27, 1890, and the State University of Nebraska had just won its first game. In the early years, Nebraska's football team had several nicknames, including the BLACK KNIGHTS (probably the most common), RATTLESNAKE BOYS, ANTELOPES, OLD GOLD, and BUGEATERS. The team was first called CORNHUSKERS in 1900. Cy Sherman, a sportswriter for the *Lincoln Daily Star* newspaper, assigned the name in reference to the expansive cornfields of the team's home state. When Edward O. "Jumbo" Stiehm was hired as coach in 1911, the team's unofficial moniker became the STIEHM ROLLERS. A similar aside occurred in 1915 when a tough Nebraska team was referred to as the MANKILLING MASTODONS in an Eastern newspaper. Nebraska is the only state to bear a nickname based on a college football team. Football at the university is so popular with the Nebraskans that on Saturdays when there is a home game, the stadium in Lincoln becomes "the third largest city in the state" after Omaha and Lincoln.

Nickname: The Huskers

NEVADA WOLF PACK

The Nevada WOLF PACK, one of only two teams nationally to use the designation — NC State uses one word, WOLFPACK — has been using the designation since at least the early 1920s. Nevada's first athletic teams in the late 1890s and early 1900s were referred to as the SAGEBRUSHERS or even SAGE HENS after Nevada's state flowering plant, the sagebrush. There are references in print to the SAGE WARRIORS, although none of these names made official mascot. In the 1921 or 1922 athletic season, a local writer described the spirited play of a Nevada team as a "pack of wolves." The name stuck, and soon almost every reference to the athletic teams was the Nevada WOLVES. In 1923, students "officially" designated WOLVES as the school's mascot. Since all teams are a group of players, the word PACK followed quickly. In the 1928-29 Nevada student handbook under athletics, the teams are referred to as the WOLF PACK. The two "wolf packs" have met only once in athletic competition when defending national champion North Carolina State and Nevada were paired up in the first round of the 1985 NCAA Basketball Tournament, NC State winning 65-56.

Nickname: The Pack

NEVADA LAS VEGAS RUNNIN' REBELS

Men's basketball was the first sport organized at the University of Nevada, Las Vegas, opening play in 1958 under head coach and athletic director Michael "Chub" Drakulich. Baseball, also coached by Drakulich, started in 1960 and football came to campus nearly a decade later when Head Coach Bill Ireland's squad went 8-1 in 1968. Women's sports such as tennis emerged in 1960 under administrator Alice Mason but basketball became the first women's varsity sport in 1974. UNLV currently sponsors seven men's and seven women's athletic programs. The nickname REBELS was given to UNLV athletic teams because the school, emerging from the shadow of the University of Nevada, Reno, in effect "rebelled" against its bigger and older brother to the north. The name RUNNIN' REBELS, always spelled without a "g," was coined in 1974 by then-sports information director Dominic Clark but refers only to the UNLV men's basketball team. The school colors of scarlet and gray can be traced to the late-50s when UNLV adopted as mascot a wolf wearing a Confederate uniform. Scarlet and gray were traditional colors of the Confederacy with its gray uniforms and red-based flag. Initially, a Colonial-like rebel soldier was the official logo and there was talk at one time of changing UNLV's nickname to MINUTEMEN. When a group of black athletes voiced displeasure with having a mascot associated with the "wrong side" of the Civil War, authorities agreed. Former UNLV president Don Baepler explained that "UNLV was rebelling against the status quo," and the nickname actually has nothing to do with the Civil War. So, in the early 1970s, the human REBEL logo was born.

NEW MEXICO LOBOS

When the University of New Mexico began playing football in 1892, the team was simply referred to as the UNIVERSITY BOYS or VARSITIES to distinguish themselves from the prep school kids. The student body, at least as early as 1917, began to seriously explore the possibilities for both a nickname and new name for the *UNM Weekly* student newspaper. Several names were suggested, including the RATTLERS, the SAND DEVILS, the KI-YO-TE, and the CHERRY AND SILVER. But it wasn't until September 22 of 1920 that sophomore George S. Bryan suggested that the University teams be given a mascot name as at that time many universities were doing just that. Bryan suggested LOBO, the

Spanish word for wolf, and the nickname was enthusiastically received at a student council meeting. The October issue of the student newspaper said "The lobo is respected for his cunning, feared for his prowess, and is the leader of the pack. It is the ideal name for the Varsity boys who go forth to battle for the glory of the school." A captured wolf pup became the mascot, but in the late 1920s it bit a child at one of the games, and a live wolf was never used again. School colors are silver for the winding Rio Grande, and cherry, the color of the majestic Sandia Mountains' sunset.

NEW MEXICO STATE AGGIES

Here's a school with two official nicknames, one for the men, and another for the women. The New Mexico State University AGGIES nickname depicts the major area of study (agricultural) at the school. It was New Mexico A&M prior to becoming NMSU, as it is a land-grant college under the Morrill Act. After first being named Las Cruces College in 1888, the next change was New Mexico College of Agriculture and Mechanic Arts. Thus, the school has been AGGIES a long time. The women officials decided upon something indigenous to the area and the ROADRUNNER bird, also called chaparral or paisano, seemed to be a natural. It is a common sight in the southern portion of New Mexico.

NORTH CAROLINA TAR HEELS

North Carolina's principal industry for many years was the production of tar, pitch, and turpentine, and it is known as the Tar Heel State. One legend has the nickname being applied to the state's residents as long ago as the Revolutionary War. The troops of British General Charles Cornwallis were fording what is now known as the Tar River between Rocky Mount and Battleboro when they discovered that tar had been dumped into the stream to impede their crossing. Their observation that anyone who waded North Carolina rivers would acquire tar heels led to the nickname first being used. Others credit the nickname to General Robert E. Lee, who commented of those soldiers who didn't run in battle, but stuck steadfastly to their positions, with "God bless the Tar Heel boys." The TAR HEELS' mascot is a ram, named in honor of the star of the 1922 9-1 team, a bruising fullback named Jack Merritt. His nickname? The battering ram.

NORTH CAROLINA STATE
WOLFPACK

In the early days of intercollegiate competition, North Carolina Agricultural & Mechanical College teams were called the FARMERS & MECHANICS, AGGIES, TECHS, and most often, RED TERRORS. Then, in 1922, the football team received a new name from a disgruntled fan. He was unhappy with the team's 3-3-3 season, complained to athletics officials that State would never have a winning season as long as players behaved "like a WOLFPACK." Students laughed at the comparison, and then adopted the name WOLFPACK for the football team. Originally, the other sports kept the RED TERROR moniker. The label stuck for more than 20 years before Chancellor J.W. Harrelson called for a new nickname in 1946, reasoning that the WOLFPACK label put the school in an unfavorable light. "The only thing lower than a wolf is a snake in the grass," he said, even reminding students that the Nazi submarines had been called the wolfpack. Suggestions poured into the contest, including NORTH STATERS, CARDINALS (the State bird), HORNETS, CULTIVATORS, COTTON PICKERS, and PINEROOTERS — the tag given to pigs in parts of North Carolina. WOLFPACK won, with one student saying "The wolf is a scrappy, tough animal — the spittin' image of our team." So it was decided in 1947 that all NCSU varsity teams would be called WOLFPACK. In 1987, the NCSU men's and women's basketball teams were Atlantic Coast Conference champions, the only time in the conference's history that a school won both titles in one year.

Nicknames: Cardiac Pack (1983), The Pack

NORTHEAST LOUISIANA INDIANS

Northeast Louisiana University's athletic teams have been known as INDIANS since the school began as Ouachita Parish Junior

College in 1931. It is believed the nickname was taken because of the legend of the Ouachita Indians, a sub-tribe of the Caddo Indians, who supposedly roamed and raided along the Ouachita River basin. In 1974, Northeast recreated the Ouachita Indian on canvas, a profile portrait true to the legend. It is believed the Ouachita did not embrace bright war paints, instead adorning themselves with jewelry and strings of animal teeth. When Northeast became a full university in 1970, the school adopted the abbreviation of NLU for second reference, giving the university's unique identity among state schools. Other schools under the state Board of Trust with directional names use "ern" in their names, like Southwestern and Southeastern.

Nicknames: Northeast La, Northeast

NORTHERN ILLINOIS HUSKIES

In almost a century of intercollegiate competition, old NIU has been identified with several nicknames. PROFS was a moniker used in the early days, an obvious expression of the institution's mission as a teacher's college. CARDINALS stuck in the 1920s, probably due to the school's jersey colors. The EVANSMEN tag became a cognomen in the 1930s, a reverent recognition of athletic pioneer George G. "Chick" Evans. Other more direct provincial terms included NORTHERNERS and TEACHERS. In 1940, a four-man committee, all members of the Varsity Club, was appointed to search for "a term with a trifle more dash." After much debate and research, a final accord was reached as reported in the January 25, 1940, *Northern Illinois*, the student newspaper and forerunner of *The Northern Star*, "Not only does the term have color and meaning, but it is particularly apt as in regard to NI's varsity teams. From now on the word HUSKIES will be used constantly in this paper and in other papers to indicate our athletic squads." Why? The dog is "Bold. Aggressive. On the move." The HUSKIE literally represents the entire burgeoning Northern Illinois program, according to Athletic Director Gerald O'Dell: "When I look at it, the Huskie plays on the direction in which the athletic program is moving. It's coming at you. It's not static. It's always moving."

NORTH TEXAS EAGLES

The school itself has experienced six name changes since it was founded in 1890 as Texas Normal College. In 1899 they were North Texas State Normal College, North Texas State Teachers College in 1923, North Texas State College in 1949, North Texas State University in 1961, and finally the University of North Texas in 1988. In the Spring of 1922, a campus-wide election was held to choose an official nickname. Other names had been unofficially used at the time, but the ones considered were the BOYS FROM NORMAL and TEACHER'S TEAM. Neither of these projected the image the students felt they needed. So the EAGLE was chosen because of its status as both noble and majestic.

Nickname: Mean Green

NORTHWESTERN WILDCATS

These lines were written by Wallace Abbey in the *Chicago Tribune* following the memorable Northwestern-Chicago game in 1924 that heralded a new era in Northwestern football: "...football players had not come down from Evanston; wildcats would be a name better suited to Coach Thistlethwaite's boys. Once Chicago had the ball on the nine-yard line and had been stopped dead by a purple wall of wildcats." From that day on, all the Northwestern athletic teams have borne the nickname of WILDCATS. The color purple (with white) was selected by a special committee in 1894 as the official school color, not only for the athletic teams, but for the entire university. Nine years after the birth of the nickname in 1933, the Northwestern athletic department teamed up with an advertising firm to create the first caricature of Willie the WILDCAT.

Nicknames: Purple Cats, Purple Folks

NOTRE DAME FIGHTING IRISH

One story suggests the moniker was born in 1899 with Notre Dame leading Northwestern 5-0 at halftime of a game in Evanston, Ill. The

Wildcat fans supposedly began to chant, "Kill the Fighting Irish, kill the Fighting Irish," as the second half opened. Another tale has the nickname originating at halftime of the Notre Dame-Michigan game in 1909. With his team trailing, one Notre Dame player yelled to his teammates — who happened to have names like Dolan, Kelly, Glynn, Duffy, and Ryan — "What's the matter with you guys? You're all Irish and you're not fighting worth a lick." Notre Dame came back to win the game and the press, after over-hearing the remark, reported the game as a victory for the "Fighting Irish." The most generally accepted explanation is that the press coined the nickname as a characterization of Notre Dame athletic teams, their never-say-die fighting spirit and their Irish qualities of grit, determination, and tenacity. The term likely began as an abusive expression tauntingly directed toward the athletes from the small, private Catholic institution. The *Notre Dame Scholastic*, in a 1929 edition, printed, "The unkind appellation became symbolic of the struggle for supremacy on the field...The term, while given in irony, has become our heritage...So truly does it represent us that we are unwilling to part with it..." Notre Dame competed under the nickname CATHOLICS during the 1800s and became more widely known as the RAMBLERS during the early 1920s in the days of the Four Horsemen. University president Matthew Walsh officially adopted FIGHTING IRISH as the Notre Dame nickname in 1927. Other names throughout the years included PAPISTS, HORRIBLE HIBERNIANS, DUMB MICKS, DIRTY IRISH, GOLD AND BLUE, WARRIORS, NOMADS, HOOSIER HARPS, WANDERING IRISH, ROCKNE'S ROVERS, and BLUE COMETS.

Nicknames: Irish, Golden Domers, The Wonder Team (Knute Rockne's squad), University of Notre Game

OHIO BOBCATS

Until 1925 all teams representing Ohio University had been known as OHIO or the GREEN AND WHITE — named after the school colors adopted in 1896. The school's athletic board decided the team should have a nickname so the members sponsored a contest, offering a prize of $10 for the nickname that best exemplified their fighting spirit. Hundreds of names were suggested. Many animals common in the United States were mentioned. After much debate, the BOBCAT, "a sly, wily and scrappy animal," won. The BOB-CAT name had been entered by Hal. H. Rowland, a former student and a resident of Athens. The new nickname was passed by the board on December 7, 1925, and officially adopted by President E.B. Bryan. In addition to the "Bobcat" and "Bobkitten" costumes which symbolize Ohio University's mascot, a live bobcat was introduced to OU's fans in 1983, nicknamed "Sir Winsalot." "Sir Winsalot" has since been joined by a new bobcat, nicknamed "Paws," and both cats may be seen at the Columbus Zoo.

OHIO STATE BUCKEYES

The Ohio State University BUCKEYES nickname arrives by way of the state of Ohio itself. The Buckeye State nickname comes from the tree that grew so abundantly in the territory before European settlers used it for building. Native Americans supposedly gave the tree this name because the light spot in its brown seed resembled the iris in the dark eye of a buck deer. During the presidential election campaign of 1840 the name was also applied to the people of Ohio. Today, more than one fourth of Ohio's land area is still wooded. A large part of the tree stand is made up of red oak, white oak, and hard maple. Although the buckeye gave Ohio its nickname, and is the state tree, it is no longer significant in the region.

OKLAHOMA SOONERS

The University of Oklahoma fielded its first football team in 1895, 25 years after the game was started in the United States, five years after the opening of the University, and 12 years before Oklahoma became a state! Oklahoma University athletic teams were called either ROUGH RIDERS or BOOMERS for 10 years before the current SOONER nickname emerged in 1908. Historically, a Sooner was a settler who came into Oklahoma Territory before the land run officially began (having arrived sooner), but the University of Oklahoma SOONERS actually derived their name from a pep club called "The SOONER Rooters." But one of the old monikers lives on in the school mascot. The Sooner Schooner is a Conestoga, or covered wagon, reminiscent of the mode of travel of the pioneers who settled Oklahoma. The Schooner is powered by matching white ponies named Boomer and Sooner. The Schooner circles the goalposts after each Oklahoma score. Crimson and Cream (the team's colors) is also the name of a group of volunteers specially schooled on details about their football team. They will tell you that the SOONERS hold the NCAA record for the longest winning streak in the history of collegiate football. They won 47 consecutive games between 1953 and 1957.

Nickname: Big Red

OKLAHOMA STATE COWBOYS

The power of the press! When Oklahoma A&M College fielded its first athletic teams in 1901, two faculty members who were graduates of Princeton suggested TIGERS with orange and black colors. The colors remain to this day, but the nickname evolved. In 1925 there was sentiment to drop TIGERS and adopt AGGIES because it was an agricultural school. Sports editor Charles Saulsberry of the *Oklahoma City Times* began referring to the AGGIES as the A&M COWBOYS, and other papers soon took up the name. COWBOYS was firmly adopted, although AGGIES was used interchangeably until the school became Oklahoma State University in 1957. The school mascot, Pistol Pete, was patterned after an authentic Oklahoma cowboy. He fires his pistol at every OSU athletic event. A women's team mascot, Cowgirl Cale, was adopted in 1978.

OREGON DUCKS

A case of mistaken identity! Many think it was natural for the University of Oregon's original nickname, the WEBFOOTS, to evolve into DUCKS, but the meaning of the original term has been totally misinterpreted. The term "webfoots" was first used to describe fishermen off the coast of Massachusetts in the 1700s. In fact, it was the Webfoots of 1776, under the command of Gen. George Washington, that helped evacuate 10,000 troops across the East River to New York City. The Webfoots helped the colonists avoid a sure defeat and saved the war for the colonies. When Oregon's Willamette Valley was being settled in the 1840s, the name Webfoots was given to new residents — partly because of the nonstop rain and partly because so many settlers hailed from the New England area. When the university first opened in 1876, it did not take long for its athletic teams to be dubbed WEBFOOTS. In the 1890s, students voted the name in as their nickname. But as athletics got more news coverage, headline writers constantly searched for shorter names: DUCKS, thought by writers to be the same thing as WEBFOOTS, was installed by 1930 and was soon a popular name among fans. In the late 1940s, athletic director Leo Harris capitalized on his friendship with Walt Disney and received permission to use Donald Duck as the official Oregon mascot, which made it the only college in the United States to have a Disney cartoon character as its official mascot.

OREGON STATE BEAVERS

Oregon State University, like many universities in the United States, is named after its home state's official animal — Beaver. In the early days, when the school in Corvallis had a coyote named Jimmie as a mascot and was known as Oregon Agricultural College, the athletic teams were known as the AGGIES. When orange uniforms replaced the drab sweatshirt-gray and tan jerseys, the teams were referred to as the ORANGEMEN. But in 1916, when the school yearbook was renamed *The Beaver*, the name BEAVER became associated with the school. It is believed the press also had some influence in changing the name, particularly L.H. Gregory of *The Oregonian* newspaper. At any rate, the name gained instant popularity among alumni and students. Oregon State played its first football game in 1893. Reference to Benny the Beaver dates back to 1946, but the costumed beaver's first appearance was in 1952.

PENN STATE NITTANY LIONS

Penn State's athletic symbol, chosen by the student body in 1906, is the mountain lion which once roamed central Pennsylvania. H.D. "Joe" Mason, a member of the Class of 1907, conducted a one-man campaign to choose a school mascot after seeing the Princeton tiger on a trip with the Penn State baseball team to that New Jersey campus. A student publication sponsored the campaign to select a mascot and Penn State is believed to be the first college to adopt the lion as a mascot. Since Penn State is located in the Nittany Valley at the foot of Mount Nittany, the lion was designated as a Nittany Lion. In regional folklore, Nittany was a valorous Indian princess in whose honor the Great Spirit caused Mount Nittany to be formed. A later namesake, daughter of Chief O-Ko-Cho, who lived near the mouth of Penn's Creek, fell in love with Malachi Boyer, a trader. The tearful maiden and her lost lover became legend and her name was given to the stately mountain. Penn State's student-athletes are instantly identified by their blue and white uniforms — but those weren't the original school colors. The Class of 1887 was asked to select their colors from a number of options, and they chose dark pink and black in combination. Soon many students and the baseball team were sporting pink and black striped blazers and caps. However, problems arose when the pink faded to white after several weeks of exposure to the sun. The students then opted for blue, rather than black, and white. The official announcements of the new choice was made on March 18, 1890, The NITTANY LIONS and the LADY LIONS have worn them ever since.

PITTSBURGH PANTHERS

The PANTHER (*Felis concolor,* a name also embracing the puma and cougar) was adopted as the University of Pittsburgh's nickname and mascot at a meeting of students and alumni in the autumn of 1909. According to George M. P. Baird, '09, who made the suggestion, it was chosen for the following reasons: 1. the panther was the most formidable creature once indigenous to the Pittsburgh region; 2. it had ancient, heraldic standing as a noble animal; 3. the happy accident of alliteration; 4. the close approximation of its hue to the old gold of the University's colors (old gold and blue), hence its easy adaptability in decoration; and (5) the fact that no other college or university then employed it as a symbol.

Nickname: Golden Panthers

PURDUE BOILERMAKERS

Contrary to popular belief, Purdue's athletic teams are not named for a shot and a beer. The Purdue Football Media Guide tells us that BOILERMAKERS was originally meant as a term of derision and was among several terms applied to Purdue by Wabash College supporters following a lopsided (18-4) victory by Purdue in 1889. Located just 30 miles from Lafayette and bitter athletic rivals of the day, students of the liberal arts school were inclined to shun the cultural background of Purdue players who represented a school devoted to the practical arts of engineering and agriculture. BOILERMAKERS struck the fancy of the Purdue players, who were also being called the PUMPKIN SHUCKERS, BLACKSMITHS, FARMERS, CORNFIELD SAILORS, HAYSEEDS, and the RAIL SPLITTERS. There is also an unsubstantiated story that Purdue, in the late 1880s, once enrolled eight boilermakers from the shops of the Monon Railroad during the football season.

RICE OWLS

Until 1962, Rice University was known formally as the William Marsh Rice Institute of Literature, Science and Art. Rice, a Massachusetts-born businessman who made the bulk of his fortune in Houston following the Civil War, had willed the original endowment for the Institute in 1891. Death under mysterious circumstances in 1900 at age 83 provoked a legal battle over the will. Rice's valet and an attorney were later charged with Rice's death and a sensational murder trial followed. It was not until 1912 that the Rice Institute, Houston's first university, could be realized. The OWL nickname is derived from the University's heraldic shield. The designer of the crest noted that the arms of several families named Houston and Rice had both chevrons and three avian charges, and he adapted those for the Institute. In the official shield, a double chevron divides the field and the charges are the OWLS of Athena as they appear on a small ancient Greek coin. When athletic activities began at the Institute in 1912, the teams were named for the bird on the Institute's seal.

RUTGERS SCARLET KNIGHTS

When the school was still known as Queen's College, the athletic teams were referred to as the QUEENSMEN. The mascot was a Chanticleer, and though a fighting bird, to some it bore the connotation of "chicken." In fact, broadcast station WCTC had its call letters derived from the word ChanTiCleer. In the early 1950s, in the hope of spurring both the all-around good athletic promise and Rutgers University fighting spirit, a campus-wide selection process changed the mascot to that of a Knight. Meanwhile, Rutgers was a pioneer in establishing a college color, scarlet being first proposed in the campus newsletter in 1869. Scarlet was chosen because it was a striking color and because a good scarlet ribbon could be easily obtained! By 1955, the SCARLET KNIGHTS had been established, and a new mascot, riding a spirited white charger, came to represent a new era. Sports lore at Rutgers has also known terms such as "Scarlet Scourge" and the lasting "Upstream Rutgers."

Nicknames: Scarlet, Red Team

SAN DIEGO STATE AZTECS

Founded in 1897, the school was located initially above a downtown drugstore! It now has an enrollment of more than 32,000 students and occupies a sprawling 300-acre campus nicknamed Montezuma Mesa — home of the AZTECS. This unique Southwestern nickname was adopted by the school in 1926. Until then there had been no official name, although San Diego teams had been referred to as STATERS and PROFESSORS in the sports pages of their day. The nickname AZTECS was approved without dissent when proposed by Fred Osenberg and Lewis Schellbach, editors of the school newspaper and yearbook. This was announced on January 14, 1925, when the two scribes flipped a coin to decide on AZTECS. The losing name? The INCAS. At that time the AZTEC colors were purple and gold, considered too similar to other local clubs. Today the AZTECS are made easily distinguishable by their all-black uniforms.

SAN JOSE SPARTANS

In 1924, students at San Jose State University were called upon to submit names for their athletic teams. Before this time the school had no official name and had been called various things, including the DANIELS, TEACHERS, PEDAGOGUES, NORMALS, and NORMALITIES. In 1925 the SPARTANS took to the field, the new nickname just beating out the GOLDS. Historically, SPARTANS were inhabitants of the city of Sparta, a power among the states of Greece due to her warlike nature and the innovation of a strict system of physical training. The system developed the youth of the country, both boys and girls. This was done by a severe regimen of body training, and instruction in the fundamentals of physical education by which the race was improved so greatly that its warriors were feared by all other people. On December 8, 1941, San Jose State was scheduled to play the University of Hawaii, but the game was cancelled due to the Pearl Harbor bombing the previous day.

SOUTH CAROLINA
FIGHTING GAMECOCKS

The University of South Carolina is the only major college athletic program in the U.S. that uses FIGHTING GAMECOCKS as its official nickname and mascot. At the turn of the century, after struggling for more than a decade under numerous nicknames, the school's feisty and spirited football team was first referred to unofficially as the GAME COCKS. In 1903, Columbia's morning newspaper, *The State*, shortened the name to one word and South Carolina teams have been

GAMECOCKS ever since. A gamecock is a fighting rooster known for its spirit and courage. A cock fight, which was a popular sport throughout the US in the 19th century, would last until the death of one of the combatants. Cock fighting has been outlawed by most states for humanitarian reasons, but it's still held surreptitiously in many areas. The state of South Carolina has long been closely connected with the breeding and training of fighting gamecocks. General Thomas Sumter, famed guerilla fighter of the Revolutionary War, was known as The Fighting Gamecock. Introduced in 1980 as "Big Spur's" replacement, "Cocky," the garnet and black plumed gamecock, captured National Championship titles as the number one mascot in 1986 and 1994.

SOUTHERN CALIFORNIA TROJANS

Up until 1912, the University of Southern California teams were called the METHODISTS or WESLEYANS, nicknames which were not looked upon with favor by university officials. So Warren Bovard, director of athletics and son of university president Dr. George Bovard, asked *Los Angeles Times* sports editor Owen Bird to select an appropriate nickname. Bird came out with an article prior to a showdown between USC and Stanford in which he called attention to the fighting spirit of the USC athletes, calling them TROJANS for the first time. "The term TROJAN as applied to USC means to me that no matter what the situation, what the odds or what the conditions, the competition must be carried on to the end and those who strive must give all they have and never be weary in doing so." In the center of the USC campus stands one of the most famous collegiate landmarks in the country: Tommy Trojan. Unveiled in 1930 for USC's 50th jubilee, the statue of the bronzed Trojan warrior has served as a symbol of the university's fighting spirit. It has also served as the focal point in the cross-town rivalry between USC and UCLA. The pre-game tradition of the statue being painted blue and gold by UCLA pranksters was first recorded in 1941. Also, the TROJANS are in proud possession of college ball's most rabid fan. Giles Pellerin, an 88-year-old retired phone company executive has viewed in person 739 consecutive TROJAN games, home AND away! His still unbroken streak began in the 1926 season. By the way, another name change in USC TROJAN history was that of footballer Marion Morrison. He later became known to the world as movie star John Wayne. USC also has one of the most recognizable mascots in sports: Traveller, the white stallion, racing up the sidelines with its TROJAN rider.

Nicknames: Thundering Herd, Southern Cal

SOUTHERN METHODIST MUSTANGS

Originally, the football team was unofficially known as the PARSONS because of the number of theology students that were on the squad. Then Dorothy Amann, secretary to Southern Methodist University's first President, Robert H. Hyer, submitted MUSTANGS to a school contest in 1917. She said the football players looked like a bunch of wild Texas MUSTANGS when they ran onto the field. The students agreed, selecting MUSTANGS from among the other entries and making it official on October 25, 1917. Peruna, the name of a well-known elixir manufactured up until a few years ago, was the nickname given to SMU's miniature pony mascot. Of further interest, Lee Iacocca named the Ford Mustang after seeing the school's football team play Michigan. In the SMU locker room, Iacocca announced, "Gentlemen, Ford is coming out with a new sports car and we have been considering four animal nicknames. It will be light, like your team. It will be quick, like your team. It will be sporty, like your team. Today, watching Southern Methodist's MUSTANGS play with such flair, we reached a decision. We will call our new car the Mustang." SMU adopted the Ford Mustang logo, and it was agreed that the school's logo would always run facing the right, while the Ford logo would always run facing the left. Check it out.

Nicknames: The Ponies, The Hilltop (campus nickname)

SOUTHERN MISSISSIPPI
GOLDEN EAGLES

After having seen great masses of black-eyed Susans in a pine forest, Mississippi Normal College committee member Mrs. Moran

Pope suggested the colors of black and gold for the school. After being known as the SOUTHERNERS for over 60 years, the University of Southern Mississippi athletic teams underwent an identity change on November 11, 1972. More than 400 different suggestions were made during a five-month campaign to determine a new name. Suggestions were turned in to an ad hoc committee by alumni, students, and friends of the university. The committee narrowed the suggestions down to five possible nicknames — The WAR LORDS, GOLDEN RAIDERS, TIMBER WOLVES, SOUTHERNERS, and GOLDEN EAGLES. It took two votes to get the 60 percent majority needed, but GOLDEN EAGLES eventually won out the other finalist, SOUTHERNERS.

SOUTHWESTERN LOUISIANA RAGIN' CAJUNS

The University of Southwestern Louisiana has one of the most unusual nicknames in college sports with RAGIN' CAJUNS. Formerly called the BULLDOGS, the school's football teams were coined the RAGIN' CAJUNS in 1963 by the USL sports director Bob Henderson, shortly after Russ Faulkinberry was named head football coach. It resulted from the fact that at the time more than 90 percent of Faulkinberry's teams were composed of Louisiana high school players, many with French-speaking, Acadian backgrounds. The nickname stuck, and now all USL athletic teams are called the RAGIN' CAJUNS. Women's teams are called LADY CAJUNS. The mascot remained an English Bulldog, and his name is RAGIN'. A recent development, including the renaming of USL as the University of Louisiana, is the possible introduction of a new "partner" mascot and nickname — the PELICANS.

Nickname: Cajuns

STANFORD CARDINAL

What we know as Stanford is properly called Leland Stanford Junior University. The distinguished institution in Palo Alto was founded by the rail magnate Leland Stanford in 1885 as a memorial to his only son. When Stanford first accepted students in 1891, the student body actually voted for gold as the school's official color. However, another student assembly chose CARDINAL. A few days after this vote, local sportswriters picked up the CARDINAL theme after Stanford defeated Cal in the first Big Game — March 19, 1891 — i.e., "CARDINAL Triumphs O'er Blue and Gold." As for the nickname history, Stanford officially adopted the INDIAN on November 25, 1930. For years prior to the resolution, the INDIAN had been part of the Stanford athletic tradition. Perhaps it grew out of the fact that Cal's symbol was a bear, or it may have come from the large Indian population of the area, or from Indian paraphernalia in abundance in the late 1800s. Whatever the origin, it was accepted by sportswriters and gained wide recognition. The INDIAN symbol was dropped in 1972 when meetings between Stanford native American students and University president Richard Lyman concluded that the mascot and moniker were an insult to their culture and heritage. The latest incident concerning the Stanford nickname came on November 17, 1981, when University president Donald Kennedy declared that all Stanford athletic teams "will be represented and symbolized exclusively by the color CARDINAL." That's right, not the bird, but the color. "While various other mascots have been suggested and then allowed to wither, the color has continued to serve us well, as it has for 90 years. It is a rich and vivid metaphor for the very pulse of life," Kennedy said.

SYRACUSE ORANGEMEN

Things got off to a rather humbling start in 1889 when, on November 23, the Syracuse PINK-AND-BLUEMEN suffered an embarrassing 36-0 defeat at the hands of the University of Rochester in Syracuse's only game of the year. PINK-AND-BLUEMEN? That's right. SU played the game attired in white canvas uniforms trimmed with SU's school colors of pink and blue. Not only was the team much improved in 1880, finishing at 8-3, but so were the school colors. As the 1890 season began, Syracuse adopted orange as its new school color and the ORANGEMEN, and sartorial splendor, were officially born. Syracuse is far from the only institution asked to re-think its mascot. For nearly half a century the painted and befeathered Saltine Warrior, presumably named because the area was known as Salt City, tomahawked the air and whooped along the side-lines of Archbold Stadium. But when the Native American campus organization, Onkwehonweneha, protested the mascot as racist and degrading, the Warrior went the way of the Indian mascots at Dartmouth and Stanford. He was supplanted by a gladiator of inde-terminate origin, who lasted about as long as a Christian among the lions. Since then Syracuse hasn't had an official mascot. But when the ORANGE began playing both football and basketball in the Carrier Dome in 1980, a clan of dome gnomes sprang up. These included: Dome Ranger in an orange cowboy outfit; Dome Eddie, a gnatlike figure in orange tights; the Beast from the East, a splash of electric-green; and the Orange, a juiced-up, bumbling citrus fruit from which two legs encased in furry brown booties protrude. It's known on cam-pus as "the official embarrassment." If ever a mascot is chosen, a member of the Lambda Chi Alpha fraternity will portray it, as they have since the 1950s.

Nickname: The Orange

TEMPLE OWLS

The OWL is the symbol and mascot for Temple University and has been since its founding in the 1800s. Temple was the first school in the United States to adopt the owl as its symbol. Not as popular as the eagle or hawk, the owl nevertheless has special meaning for stu-dents at a dozen other four-year colleges and seven two-year colleges as well. However, Rice University in Houston, Texas, plays football at the Division 1-A level. Story has it that the owl, a nocturnal hunter, was initially adopted as a symbol because Temple University began as a night school for ambitious young people of limited means. Russell Conwell, Temple's founder, encouraged these students with the remark, "The owl of the night makes the eagle of the day." Since those modest beginnings more than a hundred years ago, the owl's role and significance have expanded along with those of the Univer-sity. The owl, in its splendid variety, inhabits all parts of the world.

The owl is accepted as a universal symbol for wisdom and knowledge and as such makes an excellent symbol and emblem for a center of learning. It must be remembered that the owl was the symbol of Athena, who was not only the goddess of wisdom, but was also the goddess of arts and skills and even warfare. Because of its other attributes, the owl also makes an appropriate mascot for the athletic teams. Besides being perceptive and resourceful, quick and courageous, the owl is really a fierce fighter.

TENNESSEE VOLUNTEERS

The University of Tennessee was founded as Blount College in 1794 in a lone two-story house. As the state's land grant university, it draws the nickname of its athletic teams from the name most associated with the state — VOLUNTEERS. Tennessee acquired its name, The Volunteer State, in the early days of the 19th century when General Andrew Jackson mustered large armies from his home state to fight the Indians and later the British at the Battle of New Orleans. The name became even more prominent in the Mexican War when Governor Aaron V. Brown issued a call for 2800 men to battle Santa Ana and some 30,000 volunteered. The dragoon uniform worn by Tennessee regulars during that conflict is still seen adorning the color guard at UT athletic events. The colors orange and white were selected by Charles Moore, a member of the first football team in 1891. They were the colors of the common American daisy which grew in profusion on The Hill. Tennessee players did not appear in the now-famous orange jerseys until the season opening game in 1922. Good choice? The VOLUNTEERS defeated the team from Emory and Henry by a score of 50-0.

Nickname: Vols

TEXAS A&M AGGIES

From its founding in 1876 until 1963, Texas Agricultural and Military was an all-male military school — a fact that has impacted many of their traditions. The Corps of Cadets is among the largest uniformed student groups outside the three U.S. service academies, and members are required to be in uniform at all official university functions, including athletic events. AGGIES was a common nickname for agricultural schools at the turn of the century, and Texas was no exception. Though many adopted new monikers as the century unfolded (for example, NC State became the WOLFPACK, and Colorado State became the RAMS), Texas did not. Reveille is the name of the AGGIES' mascot. Now an American Collie, the original Reveille was a stray brought to campus after being hit by a car filled with AGGIES returning from a football game. She earned her name the next morning when, apparently feeling better, she howled through the morning "Reveille."

TEXAS CHRISTIAN HORNED FROGS

A *New York Sun* article dated December 1, 1911, referred to the team from Texas Christian University as the PURPLE HORNED FROGS — followed by the comment "Gosh, what a name!" — and an upcoming confrontation against the Southern Methodist RED-AND-BLUE MUSTANGS. The HORNED FROG was adopted by the university in 1897 for the school annual. Gradually, the plural HORNED FROGS, now minus the PURPLE, also became the recognized nickname for TCU's varsity athletic teams. The final considerations were the CACTUS and the HORNED FROG, commonly known throughout the Southwest as the horned toad or horny toad. Both were the most typically Texas objects they could think of, but the name CACTUS had already been adopted by State University in Austin — now the University of Texas. For a while after TCU moved to Fort Worth when its main building burned down in Waco, the school was referred to as the CHRISTIANS. In 1980, the ESPN Sports Network selected the Texas Christian University's HORNED FROGS as the number 1 sport's nickname in the United States. The colors were selected in 1896. Purple to stand for royalty, and white for a clean game.

Nickname: The Frogs

TEXAS EL PASO MINERS

The University of Texas at El Paso was founded in 1914 as the School of Mines and Metallurgy. The first campus was destroyed by fire, and the school was moved just a stone's throw from the Rio Grande. In 1919 the institution became a branch of the University of Texas System, and in 1949 was renamed Texas Western College. When the school changed its name once again in 1967 to the University of Texas at El Paso, it looked back to its own history for a nickname — the MINERS. The UTEP LADY MINERS have competed in the WAC since 1990. School colors are white with blue-accent and the mascot's name is Paydirt Pete. Today, UTEP is the largest Hispanic-majority university in the continental United States.

TEXAS LONGHORNS

The first Longhorn cattle were brought to the New World by Christopher Columbus on his second voyage; Santa Domingo reportedly brought them to Texas which is where they are predominantly found. D.A. Frank wrote that in the fall of 1903, Alex Weisberg, who later became one of the more prominent lawyers in Dallas, was editor-in-chief of *The Texan* when D.A. was its sports reporter. One day Alex told him, "D.A., hereafter in every sports article, call the team the LONGHORNS and we'll so have it named." D.A. obeyed that instruction, and passed it on to his reporters after he became editor-in-chief. In 1907 the name became official, and the team has been called the LONGHORNS ever since. For over a hundred years of football, the school colors have been burnt orange and white. Today, the very impressive Longhorn steer named "Bevo" is the University of Texas mascot.

TEXAS TECH RED RAIDERS

Prior to 1930, the athletic teams from Texas Tech University were called the MATADORS, a cultural nod in the direction of the local Mexican influence — a matador being a bullfighter whose specialty is killing the bull with a sword thrust. It was the wife of then gridiron Head Coach Pete Cawthon who suggested a name change. Considering the red uniforms the football team wore, and the fact that the team was now travelling from coast to coast to challenge other university teams, she offered up the new moniker RED RAIDERS. School authorities went for it immediately, and the teams have been called the RED RAIDERS ever since.

Nickname: Raiders

TOLEDO ROCKETS

Referred to as the BLUE AND GOLD, MUNIES (for municipal university), and DWYER'S BOYS (after Coach James Dwyer), when the University of Toledo played then-powerful Carnegie Tech in football in 1923, Pittsburgh sports writers were surprised to learn that UT did not have an official nickname. As the game unfolded, writers pressed James Neal, a UT student working in the press box, to come up with something. The student labelled the team SKYROCKETS, obviously impressed by his alma mater's flashy performance against a superior team. The sportswriters shortened the name to ROCKETS, which has been used since. Many suggestions for UT's nickname have been considered through the years, including a Spanish theme of TOREADORS or BULLS, in honor of Toledo's namesake sister city in Spain. Others included COMMODORES, TURTLES, BANCROFT HIGHWAYMEN, and JEEPS. In 1961, UT procured a genuine rocket from the U.S. Army missile program. The one-ton rocket, which sits outside the Glass Bowl, carries two sets of fins and a propellant booster capable of guiding the missile to supersonic velocity. It was donated, in part, because of the University's affiliation with the Ordinance Corps of the U.S. Department of Army. Midnight blue and gold have been the school's colors since 1919.

TULANE GREEN WAVE

From 1893 to 1919, the athletic teams of Tulane were known as the OLIVE AND BLUE. In 1919, the *Tulane Weekly* began calling the football team the GREENBACKS. On October 20, 1920, Earl Sparling, editor of the *Tulane Hullabaloo*, wrote a football song which was printed in the newspaper. The song was titled "The Rolling Green Wave." Although the name wasn't immediately adopted, it began to receive acceptance. On November 19, 1920, a report of the Tulane — Mississippi A&M game in the *Hullabaloo* referred to the team as the GREEN WAVE. By the end of the season, the *Hullabaloo* was using the term GREEN WAVE to refer to all Tulane athletic teams, as were many daily newspapers, although as late as 1923, the name GREENBACKS was still in use. In its infancy, Tulane's mascot was a pelican riding a surf board, becoming an angry looking wave in 1964. The block "T" with waves arrived in 1986, and a mascot resembling the character "Gumby" is now the GREEN WAVE mascot.

TULSA GOLDEN HURRICANE

Did a HURRICANE really make it all the way to Tulsa? Sort of. Way back in 1922, a new football coach named Howard Archer came to Tulsa all the way from Pennsylvania. Before Archer's arrival local sportswriters referred to the school team as the KENDALLITES, the PRESBYTERIANS, TIGERS, the ORANGE AND BLACK, and the TULSANS. In the fall of 1922 they were being reigned as the YELLOW JACKETS, apparently due to the fact that they were wearing new yellow and black uniforms instead of the traditional orange and black. The coach was on the bandwagon immediately to give his team a more distinctive name. After hearing a remark in practice one day about how his team was "roaring through opponents," and because of their new jersey colors, he thought of the GOLDEN TORNADOES. He quickly found out however that the name had been taken by Georgia Tech in 1917. Archer quickly evolved the name from a tornado to a hurricane, and a team vote turned yellow into gold, and the team officially became the Tulsa GOLDEN HURRICANE.

UCLA BRUINS

Back in 1919 the University of California in Los Angeles was known as the "Southern Branch" of the University of California. The UCLA football team, then known as the CUBS because of their younger relationship to the California BEARS in Berkeley, was playing its first season against such powerhouses as the Occidental College freshmen and Manual Arts High School. Manual Arts defeated the CUBS 74-0! In 1922 the team won its first game, and celebrated by changing its name to the more aggressive GRIZZLIES. But in 1925, when the university joined the Pacific Coast Conference, a problem arose. The University of Montana, also in the PCC, had prior rights to the nickname GRIZZLIES. So UCLA, which had changed its name from the Southern Branch in 1927, became the BRUINS in 1928 and have been recognized as such with increasing importance and success over the years. The difficulty in obtaining and caring for live bears eventually led to the appearance of costumed student mascots. Joe and Josephine BRUIN make UCLA one of the few select universities that has both male and female mascots. While the nickname BRUINS seemed to be attached to the football team in the early years, the success of UCLA in as many as 18 different sports — most notably, basketball — has made BRUINS recognized the world over.

UTAH UTES

The state of Utah was named for the Ute Indians who lived in Utah prior to the arrival of white settlers. On April 9, 1865, tensions transformed into violence when a handful of Utes and Mormon frontiersmen met in Manti, Sanpete County, to settle a dispute over some killed cattle. The Indian delegation, which included a dynamic young Ute named Black Hawk, left, promising retaliation for a considered slight. The ensuing Black Hawk Indian War was the longest and most destructive conflict between pioneer immigrants and Native Americans in Utah history. The word "eutaw" means "dwellers in the tops of the mountains." The Beehive state has a beautiful state insect, the midnight butterfly. In deciding to pick a nickname with a nod to the state, however, the University of Utah selected UTES over all else. Playing in the Western Athletic Conference, the University of Utah campus is located in the capital city of Salt Lake City. School colors are crimson and white. With an enrolment of 27,100, Rice Stadium seats 32,500.

UTAH STATE AGGIES

Utah State University was originally founded March 8, 1888, as the Agricultural College of Utah. According to John Lewandowski of the Utah State Sports Department the nickname AGGIES is a natural extension of the school's founding as the state's land-grant institution. The Utah State Legislature changed the school's name to Utah State University on March 8, 1957. Athletic teams continued to be officially called the AGGIES, but fans and supporters of all types also refer fondly to their teams as BIG BLUE, a reference to the school colors of navy blue and white. Mr. Lewandowski says, "Our research does not indicate that any other nickname has ever been used, nor have we been able to find any history of the choosing of the nickname." Many agricultural schools have used the nickname AGGIES, and it seems it was simply a natural selection.

VANDERBILT COMMODORES

Beginning with the efforts of Cornelius Vanderbilt in the early 19th century, the Vanderbilt family amassed a fortune in the shipping and railroad industries. They became one of the wealthiest and most prominent families in the United States. Born in 1794, Cornelius Vanderbilt died in New York City on January 4, 1877, leaving behind a fortune of about 100 million dollars. He contributed a large sum of money to Central University, renamed Vanderbilt University, in Nashville, Tennessee. The school's athletic teams are also named in honor of Vanderbilt, who was a commodore — an officer ranking above a captain and below a rear admiral — in the U.S. Navy. The mascot, Mr. Commodore, wears white hair, a white beard, a coat with tails, and a big hat.

Nickname: Vandy

VIRGINIA CAVALIERS

Since being founded by Thomas Jefferson in 1819, the most prominent and widely accepted nicknames at the University of Virginia include CAVALIERS, WAHOOS, and HOOS, although V-MEN, VIRGINIANS, and OLD DOMINION have also been used. Although CAVALIERS, WAHOOS, and HOOS are used almost interchangeably to refer to teams and players, CAVALIERS is more often used by the media, while WAHOOS and HOOS are frequently used by Virginia students and fans. Legend has it that Washington & Lee baseball fans dubbed the Virginia players WAHOOS during the fiercely contested rivalry that existed between the two in-state schools in the 1890s. By 1940, WAHOOS was in general use around Grounds to denote University students or events relating to them. The abbreviated HOOS sprang up later in student papers and has gained popularity in recent years. In 1923, the college newspaper, College Topics, held a contest to choose an official alma mater fight song. "The Cavalier Song," written by Lawrence Haywood Lee Jr., Class of '24, with music by Fulton Lewis Jr., Class of '25, won. Although this song failed to become part of University tradition, "The Cavalier Song" inspired the nickname CAVALIERS.

Nickname: Cavs

VIRGINIA TECH HOKIES _____

The story leads back to 1896 when Virginia Agricultural and Mechanical College changed its name to Virginia Polytechnic Institute. With the name change came the necessity for a new cheer, and a contest was held by the student body. Senior O.M. Stull won first prize for his "Hokie!" yell, which was first used that fall and is still heard today. Later, when asked if "hokie" had any special meaning, Stull explained that the word was solely the product of his imagination! He put it in his cheer because he thought it sounded good. It soon became a nickname for all Tech students. Virginia Tech has the distinction of two nicknames, and they came to be known as the FIGHTING GOBBLERS thanks to the efforts of Floyd Meade. Meade appeared at Tech football games in the 1900s dressed as a clown for the entertainment of fans. The clown act grew tiring, and Meade began training a large turkey to pull him around in a small cart. Meade and his turkey first appeared on opening day

1912, and over the next few years made the Gobbler a part of Virginia Tech history. In 1962 the live turkey evolved into a costumed mascot, and the HOKIE BIRD'S antics at all Virginia Tech sporting events have long been loved by children and alumni alike. The official colors of Chicago maroon and burnt orange were selected in 1896 because they made a "unique combination" not worn elsewhere at the time.

WAKE FOREST DEMON DEACONS

Reports indicate that by the early 1920s, Wake Forest College nicknames were the BAPTISTS and THE OLD GOLD & BLACK. Most historians believe that the old gold and black color scheme of the athletic uniforms came from the connection with the tiger mascot, created by 19-year-old John Heck, and not, as some have proposed, from any association with the Bible. In 1923 Wake Forest had a major reversal of athletic fortunes, and it was felt that the nicknames of the time were not descriptive enough of the new-found spirit. After Wake Forest defeated rival Trinity (now Duke), school newspaper editor Mayon Parker first referred to his team as DEMON DEACONS, in recognition of what he termed their "devilish" play and fighting spirit. Wake Forest's news director Henry Belk liked the title and began using it extensively. In his deacon-top hat, tails, a black umbrella, the DEMON DEACON mascot has drawn praise from national media, such as NBC's Bob Costas, who said, "I love the Deacon. He's the mascot of protocol. I've never known him to be rude. He represents the gentility of the Old South, a very dapper guy. I think one day a year all Wake Forest men should dress as the Demon Deacon and walk — no, promenade — that way to class."

WASHINGTON HUSKIES

Washington's teams were called SUN DODGERS before the 1920s, originating when a college magazine of the same name was banned from campus and, in protest, students adopted the name for their teams. But the SUN DODGERS didn't do much for the Northwest's image, so a committee set out in 1921 to pick a new nickname. The decision came down to MALAMUTES and HUSKIES. The committee felt those were appropriate because of Seattle's nearness to the Alaskan frontier. The HUSKY was voted the most appropriate. Remnants of the SUN DODGER name remain, however. Before the 1920s, Washington's football mascot was a three-and-a-half-foot wooden statue named Sunny Boy, a sculptured replica of the happy-faced character, Sunny, who appeared in the University's humor magazine *Sun Dodger*. When Washington changed its mascot in 1923, Sunny Boy disappeared and was not discovered until 1948 in South Bend, Indiana! Twenty-three years later, Notre Dame promptly returned it. The HUSKIES have one football record that may never be beaten. From the last game of the 1907 season until the 1917 campaign, Washington did not lose one of its 63 games, winning 59 and tying 4. Another HUSKY first occurred on October 31, 1981, when cheerleader Rob Weller (yes, the same Rob Weller who hosted Entertainment Tonight) instructed the Washington crowd to start in one section and make a human wave. That's right, despite claims by others, the Wave can trace its origin to Husky Stadium.

WASHINGTON STATE COUGARS

Following the first football game between Washington State and California schools in 1919, an Oakland cartoonist portrayed the Washington State team as fierce Northwest COUGARS chasing the defeated GOLDEN BEARS. A few days later, on October 28, 1927, Washington students officially designated COUGARS as their nickname. During homecoming, Governor Roland Hartley presented Washington State students with a live cougar cub. The first cougar mascot was named Butch, to honor Herbert "Butch" Meeker of Spokane. He was Washington State University's gridiron star at the time, a diminutive halfback who played like a cougar. Governors have continued to present COUGARS to WSU over the years.

WESTERN MICHIGAN BRONCOS

In 1939, the Athletic Board of the then Western State Teachers College adopted the nickname of BRONCOS because the former name of HILLTOPPERS was often confused with similar monikers used by other colleges. Many suggested names were turned in for consideration at the time. The nickname BRONCO was submitted by John Gill, who was then the assistant football coach under M.J. "Mike" Gary. Gill later served as the BRONCO head grid coach and as Western Michigan University's associate athletic director until his retirement in 1969. The most popular BRONCO ever is Buster Bronco, the school's mascot, who works diligently to spread "Gold Pride" throughout the area.

Nickname: Broncs

WEST POINT BLACK KNIGHTS

Perhaps better known as the Army CADETS. With colors black, gold, and grey, and the motto Duty, Honor, Country, the United States Military Academy at West Point was founded in New York on March 16, 1802. Football had its birth in 1890, the result of a challenge from the U.S. Naval Academy. The Army CADETS lost that first game to the MIDSHIPMEN from Annapolis, but revenged that loss a year later. Since 1972 the Commander in Chief's Trophy has been awarded annually to the winner of the round-robin football competition among the Army CADETS, Navy MIDS, and the Air Force FALCONS. The CADETS nickname, a clear reference to military ranking, is not the only one Army has used. The first reference to the boys from the Point as the BLACK KNIGHTS was in a *New York Sun* article in December of 1944. It was in a poem written in support of the CADETS in their Army-Navy classic. "The Gold Crests gleam as the BLACK KNIGHTS ride, Out to uphold the Corps, and its pride." Four mules, heirs of a tradition that dates back to 1899, serve as the team mascots for the Corps of Cadets.

Nicknames: Army, Cadets, The Point, Dragoons, The Corps

WEST VIRGINIA MOUNTAINEERS

The origin of the state's name is from the English-named neighboring state of Virginia. Nicknamed the Mountain State, the motto is "Mountaineers are Always Free." West Virginia University was founded in 1867, and the game of basketball began intramural play one year later. The university adopted the MOUNTAINEERS moniker from the state, as the term had already been identified with the area for over a century. No other nickname was ever considered. Early WVU teams used the nickname SNAKES, although it is not now known why. The MOUNTAINEER mascot first roamed the sidelines in the late 1920s. Mascots wore the familiar coonskin cap and carried a rifle, but they dressed in coveralls and flannel shirts until the late 1940s. It was then that the genuine buckskin outfit made its debut. The rifle is a true flintlock that requires the user to become schooled in the amount of powder required to fire the charge.

WISCONSIN BADGERS

The University of Wisconsin in Madison nickname, BADGERS, was borrowed from the state. The territory was dubbed the "Badger State," not because of the animals in the region, but rather an association with lead miners in the 1820s. Prospectors came to the state looking for minerals. Without shelter in the winter, the miners had to "live like badgers" in tunnels burrowed into hillsides. The badger, a strong and belligerent animal, had been attending Wisconsin home games in a cage on the sidelines for a long time. On more than on occasion, the live badger stopped a football game for up to five min utes before a sideline hero recaptured the animal with a flying tackle. It was finally decided in the interest of fan safety that Wisconsin's beloved mascot be retired to the Madison Zoo. In 1946, William C. Shafer Jr. drew, on his feet, a badger wearing a sweater and carrying a football. This mascot was alternatively named Benny, Buddy, Bernie, Bobby, Bouncey, Regdab (BADGER backwards), and finally Bucky — short for Buckingham U. Badger.

Nickname: The Big Red

WYOMING COWBOYS

The nickname COWBOYS was applied to Wyoming athletic teams as early as 1891, two years before the first official football game. The story is that the Wyoming pick-up football team appealed to a 220-pound cowpuncher, Fred Bush, for help in a game against the Cheyenne SOLDIERS. Bush signed up for a course or two and came out for the team. When he trotted onto the field decked out in a checkered shirt and cowboy hat, someone yelled, "Hey, look at the cowboy!" Since many of the members of the team were also ex-cowboys, the name stuck. In the spring of 1895, the first ever University of Wyoming Alumni Banquet was held. Decorations for the event included brown-eyed Susans, a flower native to southeastern Wyoming. The Alumni was so impressed with the brown and yellow beauties that they decided to select them as the official school colors at UW And that familiar fight song sung by the fans after every Wyoming victory? Ragtime Cowboy Joe.

CANADIAN TEAMS

ACADIA AXEMEN

Acadia was the name of the French colony on the north-east coast of North America, from 1604 to 1713, and is the native name of Nova Scotia. Acadia University, founded in 1838 in Wolfville, Nova Scotia, was built initially by hand. The land was cleared and the trees felled by that pre-chainsaw tool — the ax. This action forms the heritage of the name of the university's men's athletic teams, the AXEMEN. The women's teams are know as the AXETTES, and they were national soccer champions in 1989. The AXEMEN of Acadia have won national athletic titles in swimming, basketball, hockey, and football.

ALBERTA GOLDEN BEARS

University of Alberta teams were called VARSITY from 1908 until 1929. Then male teams switched uniform colors from green with gold trim to gold with green trim, leaving intervarsity athlete's looking like "big gold people," which helped the development of the name GOLDEN BEARS. The mascot, GUBA, for Great University Bear of Alberta, debuted in the early 1970s. Meanwhile, the women's teams were called the HOOPSTERS, and other generic terms by the school paper *The Gateway*. The name PANDAS was suggested by Vera Pratt, a basketball player in 1943. She even outfitted a stuffed bear with school colors and called it "Pandy." In 1945, female students on campus held an election to name their teams, with four options: the GOLDEN PANDAS, TEDDY BEARS, the BRUINETTES, the PANDAS. The University of Alberta is currently one of three universities in Canada with distinct names for both its men's and women's athletic teams. The others are McGill, with its REDMEN and MARTLETS, and Waterloo with its WARRIORS and ATHENAS.

BISHOP GAITERS

No, it has nothing to do with the cousin of the crocodile. In fact, the Bishop's University GAITERS nickname does not refer to a beast of any description. Instead, in simplest form, a gaiter is a legging! To explain requires a brief examination of University history. Bishop's was founded by the Anglican Church — the Church of England. In earlier days, a School of Divinity prepared some graduates for holy orders and many faculty were referred to as CHURCHMEN. Part of the traditional garb worn by such individuals was the gaiter. According to Funk and Wagnalls, "gaiter" is defined as a "covering, as of leather or canvas, worn over the leg." As the first of Bishop's intercollegiate teams entered competition, one naturally looked to some unique attribute of the University as a nickname. By 1949, the use of GAITER became so prominent that the University officially changed its nickname from PURPLE AND WHITE, which was in reference to the school colors. The school mascot, not surprisingly, is an alligator.

BRANDON BOBCATS

Phys. Ed. Chair and former student Nancy Stanley tells us that early in the institution's history teams were referred to as the BLUE AND GOLD. After World War II, the school colors' moniker was replaced with the CAPS, and women's team CAPETTES. This may have been the initials for any of College Athletic Program Supporters to College Athletic Promotional Society to College Athletic Program. In 1967 Brandon College became Brandon University and went to the student body for a nickname change — reducing the many suggestions to two. The PLAINSMEN ended up the nickname of nearby Crocus Plains Secondary School, and the BOBCATS leapt into Brandon. The BU students union and athletic directorate liked the short, catchy, alliterative name, plus the fact the little cat is local. Originally, BOBCATS belonged only to the men's teams, and the women's were dubbed the BOBBIES. Since 1977, they have been referred to as the LADY BOBCATS. The BOBCATS basketball squad has been national champ four times, including the 1995-96 season.

BRITISH COLUMBIA THUNDERBIRDS

In November of 1933, the University of British Columbia *Ubyssey* newspaper sports department solicited from the student population suggestions for a "popular name or mascot" for the University teams. When the result of a vote produced SEAGULLS, disgruntled *Ubyssey* editors declared the contest invalid. A Pep meeting was called on January 31, 1934 to settle the name question once and for all. It was at this meeting that the nickname UBC THUNDERBIRDS was adopted. Almost 15 years later, a ceremony took place in the Old Varsity Stadium at half time of the 1948 Homecoming Football Game. The ceremony involved the presentation of a 16-foot high thunderbird totem to the University by Chief William Scow, who at that time was President of the Native Brotherhood of British Columbia and the hereditary chief of the Kwicksutaineuk Tribe. The presentation by Chief Scow represented something unique in sports today, official consent to use the THUNDERBIRD name and emblem. According to the old custom of his people, the THUNDERBIRD had, technically speaking, been illegitimately borrowed from his people and other west coast Indian tribes in 1934.

CALGARY DINOSAURS

Long before *Jurassic Park* made nicknames like RAPTORS contemporary, the University of Calgary teams were called DINOSAURS. Originally the University of Alberta at Calgary, the campus became autonomous in 1966. Students were looking for a name unique to the vicinity. Legend has it that while excavating the ground for the new campus in 1966 a huge skeleton was dug up. It belonged to a *Tyrannosaurus Rex*, the "terrible lizard" that ruled North America 65 milllion years ago. A nickname was born. Of course, the Calgary area is rich with dinosaur bones, and 90 miles from campus is the world famous Tyrell Museum and its impressive collection of prehistoric skeletons found in and around Alberta. Remembering that this was in the early 1980s, all before the dinosaur fad, there was a student uprising against the less than friendly moniker and T-Rex mascot, but that blew over — as did the female athletes referring to themselves as DINIES. In fact, Calgary DINOSAUR pins are more popular than ever at Canadian college athletic events.

Nickname: Dinos

CARLETON RAVENS

T. Scanlon wrote that without any explanation, the word RAVENS first appeared to describe Carleton University athletic teams on the front page of the student paper in 1948. It may be that the name was adopted simply because the Carleton players wore black uniforms, but whatever the reason, it was an appropriate choice. The raven often appears in mythology. It is a symbol to the Iroquois, to Arabs, to the English and to Indians. It is known as a wise all-knowing bird, a bird of death and destruction, a bird of battle. A raven sent by Noah discovered that the flood had not abated. The raven was the symbol of William the Conqueror and to the Norsemen who once ravaged England. It is believed by many that King Arthur still lives in raven form. It is the symbol of the English Crown: if the ravens leave the Tower of London, so legend says, the Crown will fall, and England, too. Once colored white, the raven was turned black by the god, Apollo, who was angered by bad news it carried. On the more pleasant side, it was a raven that fed Elijah the prophet, and Paul the hermit. Finally, the raven was made famous by Edgar Allan Poe in his poem about the bird which quoth, "Nevermore."

CONCORDIA STINGERS

The name STINGERS was chosen by the athletic director and assistant athletic directors in 1974. At that time Sir George Williams University, whose teams were known as the GEORGIANS, and Loyola College, with teams called the WARRIORS and TOMMIES, merged to become Concordia University. The people involved liked the sound and marketing of the World Hockey Association's Cincinnati STINGERS and patterned the Concordia squad along the same lines. The STINGERS even used a C-shaped logo a lot like that used by Cincinnati. In 1990 the STINGERS adopted a bee as their logo. Another consideration was the fact that STINGERS was easy to pronounce by both francophones and anglophones. Also, a STINGER may be a man or a woman, so there was no need for a female version of the nickname, like LADY STINGERS. With each and every team simply called the STINGERS, it would appear Concordia University was politically correct before it became the fashion.

Nickname: The Swarm

THE BLUE OF DAWSON

John Davidson of Athletics and Student Affairs tells us that in 1970, Dawson College players needed funding if they hoped to ice a hockey team, a must in wintry Montreal. The goalie at the time, Erwin "Irish" Brown, approached Eastern Airlines, then a major player itself at the Montreal International Airport. The airline agreed to help. At that time the Eastern Airline uniform was colored blue, and a unique deal was struck. Though no mention was ever made of the huge air carrier's gift to the College, all sports teams wore blue uniforms, and became known as THE BLUE.

Nickname: Blues

GRANT MacEWAN GRIFFINS

The name GRIFFINS was chosen by the students and staff of this Edmonton, Alberta institution in 1972, and it has been the one and only nickname ever used. Grant MacEwan Community College's athletic program had begun in 1971. The Griffin is a mythical creature with the body of a lion and the head of an eagle, and it is considered to bring good luck. In literature and legend, the creature has long stood for courage, swiftness, and excellence. Additionally, the Griffin is located in the MacEwan family coat of arms, and the college was named after J.W. Grant MacEwan, lieutenant governor of Alberta at the time the college was founded.

GUELPH GRYPHONS

The GRYPHON (or GRIFFIN) was a mythical creature known to the ancients as the guardian of treasures, particularly gold. It had the body of a lion, the head and wings of an eagle, and a tail often represented as a serpent. The GRYPHON was allied with the sun, which was drawn by GRYPHONS. They were said to inhabit the Asiatic Scythis, where gold and precious stones were abundant. Anyone intent on plundering these treasures would be torn apart by GRYPHONS, thus being chastised for his greed. The inspiration for the name of this frightful symbol is credited to Fred Gilbert, who, during the summer of 1966, suggested that a softball team playing under the university banner be called the GRYPHONS. Gilbert, who was then working on a master's degree in zoology, was a chairman of the Athletic Advisory Council for the campus and he suggested that the name be adopted by all of the University's teams. After a year's deliberation, the Council adopted the GRYPHON as Guelph's team symbol.

Nickname: Griffs

LAVAL ROUGE ET OR

Why RED AND GOLD? Because these colors were those of the coat of arms of the University of Laval. The name ROUGE ET OR has been associated with amateur sport in the Quebec region since 1947. It was then that Dr. Philibert L'Ecuyer and other elders of the University of Laval decided to form a hockey team that would evolve into the senior League of the city. It was hockey and the name ROUGE ET OR that put the University on the map. In the mid-50s a huge rivalry developed between the Laval team and those from neighboring Ontario. Still, in the 1980s, many Laval teams used different nicknames; L'ESSOR (volleyball), L'ESTRAN (handball), L'ESQUADRA (fencing), L'ALBATROS (diving), LE TRIASTE (athletics). In 1991, all teams came on board, and they now wear the ROUGE ET OR on their uniforms.

LETHBRIDGE COLLEGE KODIAKS

In 1958-59 the unnamed basketball team from Lethbridge Junior College found itself competing against other Alberta college and semi-pro clubs named Broder's PACKERS, Taber MARBEETS, Magrath ROCKETS, Hillspring ACES, and Carlton MAPLE LEAFS. It wasn't until 1962-63 that the blue and white KODIAKS men's basketball team took to the floor. The feeling on campus was that this extremely large Brown Bear — indigenous to the vicinity — epitomizes strength, courage, and stamina with an undying perseverance which ultimately ends in triumph and success. Team activities now include sports as diverse as equestrian events and snowmobiling!

LETHBRIDGE PRONGHORNS

The University of Lethbridge's original nickname was BOBCATS, for no particular reason. This was changed to CHINOOKS, to represent the chinook winds famous in Alberta — dry winds that blow down the eastern slopes of the Rocky Mountains. When the University developed their "Coat of Arms" there was a PRONGHORN in it, because this animal was unique to Southern Alberta. This antelope deer has curved horns, each with one prong. Then the Athletic Department decided to adopt the PRONGHORN for its teams, aligning itself with the school.

MANITOBA BISONS

The name Manitoba comes from the Cree words "manitou bou," meaning "the narrows of the Great Spirit," a reference to Lake Manitoba, which narrows at its center. The waves hitting the loose surface rocks of its north shore produce bell-like and wailing sounds, which the first aboriginal peoples believed came from a huge drum beaten by the spirit Manitou. The BISON nickname and symbol were adopted by the University of Manitoba in the 1940s, and the brown and gold uniforms have been appreciated by this campus of 24,000 ever since. The Bison is the Manitoban provincial symbol, which can also be seen on the flag. The Native Indian tribes that first settled Manitoba followed the herds of bison and caribou on their seasonal migrations. In the early 1600s they were joined by Europeans, who wanted to cash in on the fur trade that animals like bison provided, later settling in the province. It was in honor of this history that the bison was first recognized by the government on its flag, then the University with its nickname.

McGILL REDMEN

Montreal's McGill University, founded in 1827, played Harvard in the world's first international intercollegiate football game in May of 1874. And it was McGill's students that formed the world's first official hockey team on January 31, 1877. McGill even has a claim in basketball — it was McGill graduate James Naismith who founded the game while a teacher at Springfield College in Springfield, Massachusetts. Before 1930 the teams operated under a number of colorful monikers reported in the local sports papers. These included the RED-AND-WHITE, in reference to the school colors, the McGill HOCKEY CLUB, OLD McGILL, the MEN, the HOCKEYISTS, the RED SQUAD, the RED TEAM, and the BIG RED TEAM. But in the university's 1930 yearbook, and then again in a 1931 *Montreal Gazette* article, the sport's teams from McGill were being called the REDMEN. Again, the nickname was a reference to the school colors, worn proudly by all McGill students since the previous decade. Women's teams are referred to as the MARTLETS.

McMASTER MARAUDERS

The Department of Athletics and Recreation at McMaster University was surprised to discover there was no information readily available on the school history of their moniker, but were able to offer this. Up until 1948, the athletic teams at McMaster were called the RAMS, though no reason seems to have survived. The campus newspaper, called *The Silhouette*, began referring to the University sports teams as the MARAUDERS in their September, 1949 issue, and the nickname stuck. Besides the obvious alliteration, MARAUDERS has the historical definition which could be used to motivate any athletic team: to raid, plunder, and pillage!

MEDICINE HAT RATTLERS

Prior to 1984, the Medicine Hat College Athletics Teams went by the nicknames ANTELOPE for men, and KUDUS for the women. A Medicine Hat-based junior football team went by the name RAT-TLERS until that team was disbanded in 1979. After the collapse of that team, Medicine Hat College claimed the RATTLERS nickname for their own. Prior to that time a strong resemblance between the College's ANTELOPE/KUDUS logo and that of the nearby University of Lethbridge PRONGHORNS, another type of antelope, had left the Medicine Hat College without a unique identity for its athletic teams. The Prairie Rattlesnake (*Crotalus Viridus*) has a range which extends over much of southeast Alberta and southwest Saskatchewan. In many ways the name RATTLERS, and the symbols, signify attributes that are valuable in athletics. The rattlesnake is a creature of stealth and quickness. It is an efficient and merciless predator. While Medicine Hat College athletes and coaches do not regard themselves as coldblooded, they do hope to identify with the RATTLER'S "killer instinct" — dangerous creatures to be treated with respect.

MEMORIAL SEA-HAWKS

The Memorial University of Newfoundland SEA-HAWKS took flight in full uniform in 1990-91. The contest to suggest a logo and name was open to students, faculty, staff, and alumni. The total number of submissions was reduced to a final twenty, and from among them SEA-HAWKS was selected. "We were looking for a name and a logo which would symbolize our heritage, spirit, and future," said Keith Taylor, director of the physical education and athletics department. The Memorial SEA-HAWK is fashioned after the eagle, the osprey, and other birds of prey common around Newfoundland and Labrador. Similar to those majestic animals, this SEA-HAWK was designed to command respect and display athletic grace in flight and competition. The logo features a collegiate-style "M" with the SEA-HAWK superimposed facing west — the direction of its main source of competition. The symbol " - ", which separates the words "Sea" and "Hawks" represents the ocean and suggests the province's marine tradition and ocean heritage.

MOUNT ALLISON MOUNTIES

The Department of Physical Recreation and Athletics at Mount Allison University was good enough to research their nickname for us and came up with mixed answers. Some of the "local oldies" remember MOUNTIES coming from the school cheer. "Mount A" would be repeated out loud and in series at school athletic events, and eventually the yell went from "Mount A" to MOUNTIES. MOUNTIES stuck. Of course, the word is not without precedent in Canada where the Mounties provide the nickname for the Royal Canadian Mounted Police — the country's internationally known police force.

NEW BRUNSWICK VARSITY REDS

The athletics program within the Faculty of Physical Education and Recreation at the University of New Brunswick officially retired the nicknames for their twelve varsity teams on March 24, 1993. Until then, UNB had the distinction in modern college athletics of naming each sport team individually. At that time all teams became known as the UNB VARSITY REDS. The dictionary defines VARSITY as "the main team that represents a university," and REDS is a reference to the school colors. As a result of the name change, the Men's Cross Country Running team retired its HARRIERS nickname. Also, the Rugby Football Club, which was formed in the mid-60s but whose bloodlines could be traced to the turn of the century, released their beloved nickname. These IRONMEN had a rich tradition, complete with championship wins, tragic losses, and a fellowship that runs through its approximately 400+ players and alumni worldwide.

Nickname: Reds

NORTHERN ALBERTA OOKS

Opened in 1962, the Northern Alberta Institute of Technology had trouble settling on a nickname, so the Canadian Department of Indian Affairs and Northern Development decided to help out. NAIT was distinguishing itself by welcoming many northern Canadians as students, and it was at that time the most northerly institute of its kind, so the selection of a northern animal seemed appropriate. So it was that in the fall of 1964 that the Minister of Indian Affairs presented to the NAIT student body OOKPIK. Ookpik is Eskimo for Arctic Owl, and is the name given to the sealskin hand-crafted model of the Arctic Owl often used as a symbol of Canada at International Trade Fairs. Since its first arrival on campus the OOKPIK has had its name shortened to OOK, and the mascot has experienced a number of physical changes. OOK has been very popular with students from the rival Southern Alberta Institute of Technology, and was kidnapped on a regular basis until the early 1970s when the larger-than-life OOK-suit was finally put away for safekeeping.

OTTAWA GEE-GEES

According to Sports-Info at the University of Ottawa, the most often asked question on campus is "What the &$*#&@!'s a GEE-GEE?" The University's traditional colors have long been GARNET AND GREY in English, or GRENAT ET GRIS in French. Before the team had an official nickname, the sports teams were called by their colors. The Ottawa sports media, like all sports media looking for a shorter headline, began calling the team by the acronym for their colors, G.G.'s. Eventually, the official nickname became the GEE-GEES. A GEE-GEE has also been known to be a lead horse in a race, a breed of horse with a "formidable kick," but mostly as the lead horse in a team of horses. That is why a horse encompassing two letter "G"s was adopted as the official logo.

PRINCE EDWARD ISLAND
PANTHERS

Prince Edward Island is Canada's smallest province with a total area of only 2,184 square miles, and it was the home of Confederation in 1867. When the University of Prince Edward Island came into existence more than one hundred years later in 1969, the Athletic Department and the administration decided on the team name IS-LANDERS — a term long used to describe the citizens of the province. The school colors were red, white, and blue. But in the fall of 1970, the University of Prince Edward Island Student Union ran a referendum that would include the opinions of the entire campus. Other names were considered and most played with alliteration, but when the dust settled the students had voted on a team name of PANTHERS. The new colors are green, white, and rust.

QUEEN'S GOLDEN GAELS

Prior to the turn of the century, Queen's University athletic teams were called the TRICOLOUR, representing the three school colors of red, blue, and gold. These were chosen as they are contained in the official Queen's charter and flag. The nickname GOLDEN GAELS was allegedly coined in 1947 by a local *Whig-Standard* sports reporter, Cliff Bowering. It came at a time when the football team had made a change in their uniforms from the traditional sweater of tri-color bands of blue, red, and gold and off-white pants to a solid red pant with solid gold sweater and helmet. Bowering first used the term following a game between Queen's and the University of Western Ontario when he reported that "the GOLDEN GAELS of Queen's University" were thumped by Western 52-3 — a gael being a Celt of the Scottish Highlands. The phrase caught on and in the 1960s legendary Head Coach Frank Tindall changed the uniform to the solid gold pant, shirt, and helmet worn to this day by the football team. Initially only the gridiron squad was referred to as the GOLDEN GAELS, and all others were called TRICOLOUR.

REGINA COUGARS

The name COUGARS was first mentioned in the student newspaper in May of 1945. The men's basketball coach at that time, Dr. Sam Stewart, is credited with naming the then Regina College teams the COUGARS. There exists today no information as to why this moniker was selected, or if there were other considerations. Dr. Stewart, a Professor of Latin, is also credited with naming the junior/freshmen teams the CUBS. University records indicate basketball teams at Regina College as early as 1913-14, however, no nickname appears to have been associated with these athletes. Both men's and women's teams in all sports at the University of Regina use the nickname COUGARS.

Nickname: Cougs

RYERSON RAMS

The Ryerson Polytechnic teams were nameless as a group up until 1950-51. Prior to this time the football team was called the COMBINES, the basketball squad, the VAGABONDS, and the soccer team, because of their striped uniforms, the ZEBRAS. In 1950, the *Little Daily* began suggesting new nicknames to the student population, including ROCKETS, ROUGHRIDERS, RIDERS, and RUCKSTERS, with RANGERS the newspaper's favorite. In '51, in a similar spirit of alliteration, the men's football and hockey squads were calling themselves RAMS. It wasn't until 1961, when a ram was purchased for 25 dollars, that the school fully embraced the nickname. Renamed Ryerson Polytechnical Institute in 1963 (now called Ryerson Polytechnic University), the coat of arms was designed to show a ram on each side of the central shield. The live mascots, named "Eggy," are now up to number 11. Eggy III died heroically in 1981, killed by wolves at his farm, defending his flock of 40 ewes.

ST. FRANCIS XAVIER X-MEN

The captain of the 1901 rugby team, J.A. MacNeil from Sydney, Nova Scotia, was the first athlete to wear the "X" on his uniform. His mother sewed a large "X" on the front of his jersey, which was a big hit, and soon after the entire team then had an "X" put on their jerseys. Then, reporters announcing the scores at Saint Francis Xavier University hockey, rugby and football games began shortening the name to X-MEN. At that time, only men played team sports at SFX, and soon all of them were proudly wearing the "X." Then the "X" became the official symbol of the University at large, first appearing on a Degree ring in 1942. In 1996, 150 X-MEN and 75 X-WOMEN compete in everything from hockey to basketball to cross-country and boxing.

Nickname: St. F.X.

SAINT MARY'S HUSKIES

In 1960 the Siberian HUSKY became the official mascot for qualities which parallelled the team's motto, "In Pursuit of Excellence." Earlier, the teams were called the SAINTS, and the women's squads were nicknamed the BELLES until 1979. Originating in Northern Siberia, the breed has remained pure for over two thousand years. Huskies first appeared on the North American continent in 1909 for the "All Alaska Sweepstakes," a non-stop race from Nome to Candle and return (408 miles). Huskies are used as a form of transportation in northern areas, search and rescue dogs, seeing eye dogs, ski patrol dogs, and house pets; as well as racing dogs. Pound for pound, the Siberian Husky is said to be the strongest draft dog in existence. Like their namesake, the Saint Mary's University HUSKIES strive for gold, willing to work hard to get there, and always attempting to achieve their fullest potential.

SASKATCHEWAN HUSKIES

The University of Saskatchewan athletic program began play in the 1911-12 season. Legend has it that the program got its nickname from those fans that followed the football — actually, rugby — team. There was no real nickname in place, but it was noticed that players on the rugby team were typically larger and more muscular than the rest of the student body. Hence, they were referred to as husky. The nickname stuck — and certainly would've been unique in sports! But now, some 85 years later, the name HUSKIES refers to a dog. The University of Saskatchewan's athletic logo prominently features a Husky.

SIMON FRASER CLANSMEN

The university, which was to open on September 9, 1965 to 2,500 students, had been named after fur-trader and explorer Simon Fraser. In 1808, Fraser was the first European to travel to the mouth of the powerful British Columbia river that today bears his name. Fraser's ancestors were Scottish and the new university sought and was given permission by Lord Lovat, head of the Fraser Clan, to use modified versions of the Clan's motto "Je Suis Prets" (I Am Ready) and coat of arms. Seeing the Scottish heritage emerging strongly as the university went through its early planning stages, athletic director Lorne Davies chose CLANSMEN as the appropriate name for the football, basketball, and swimming teams which were to compete in the institution's very first semester. In the spring of 1966 a women's field hockey team was introduced as THE CLAN. SFU is the only Canadian university to be affiliated with an American athletic league — the National Association of Intercollegiate Athletics. The arrival of THE CLAN in some American cities — particularly in the South — has raised a few eyebrows, until the Scottish connection, as opposed to the racial one, is made clear.

TORONTO VARSITY BLUES

Sport historian Rick Kollins says that from its earliest days, University of Toronto had been known as VARSITY in recognition of its status as the first, and for many years only, accredited university in the province of Ontario. The nickname BLUES was not used until the 1930s. Previously, the BIG BLUE, the BLUE AND WHITE, and the VARSITY BLUE appeared interchangeably. The student newspaper attempted in 1936 to have the nickname BEAVERS adopted to counteract the popularity of Western Ontario's new entry in the intercollegiate league, the MUSTANGS, and throughout the 1936 season actually referred to the Varsity Seniors in print as the

BEAVERS. "Beavers Dam Good Against Upstart Mustangs!" was one headline. Toronto took its athletic traditions from the English tradition, chiefly Oxford and Cambridge, and thus for many years had no emphasis on developing a mascot. However, in the early 1980s, the athletics department introduced "True Blue," a beaver mascot. The beaver was chosen because there is a beaver on the University crest. Also, beavers had inhabited a stream, Taddle Creek, which flowed through the campus in the 19th century, near the present site of Varsity Stadium. The stream still runs underground. A former VARSITY football star and 1932 Olympian, Hud Stewart, developed a mythical history of "True Blue" from the turn of the century, and the mascot, although less than 20 years old in reality, has been accepted by Varsity fans as an integral part of the athletic tradition.

TRENT EXCALIBUR

The EXCALIBUR nickname has been used for Trent University of Peterborough, Ontario athletic teams since 1986. At this time a vote was taken on campus amongst a number of name suggestions, and this emerged the winner. EXCALIBUR is the name of the legendary sword of King Arthur. The Trent crest consists of the head of a sword surrounded by symbols that represent running water. This design comes from the fact that Trent is located on the banks of the Otonabee River and the sword is depicted in the City of Peterborough crest. Prior to 1986, Trent teams had been called the NATIONALS, but it was decided this moniker did not have the intrigue, interest, and symbolism required.

WATERLOO WARRIORS

"Why," you might ask, "would anyone name a university after a great battle?" Actually, the whole town in which the University of Waterloo is located is named after Napoleon's final defeat. In 1957 Waterloo College Associate Faculties was created to provide the technical university training that local business leaders thought Kitchener-Waterloo needed. It was a time of change for Ontario education, with universities moving from religious affiliation to government support, and in the spring of 1959 the province established the University of Waterloo. Though the present administration isn't sure who fashioned the actual names of WARRIORS and the female team's ATHENAS, they are certain the monikers were intended to represent the ideals of sportsmanship, athletic prowess, strength, and competitiveness. In 1975, students celebrated the first and so far only national championship when the WARRIORS won in Waterloo's chosen sport of basketball. WARRIORS and ATHENAS, along with the team colors of gold, black, and white, were the first selected by the University and have been around since the beginning.

WESTERN MUSTANGS

Quoting from a wonderful article by Bob Gage and Gary Kerhoulas, Canadian colleges were not so eager to adopt mascots and nicknames, but prefered to be identified by school colors. The University of Western Ontario in London, Ontario Arts and Med departments competed under the nickname PURPLE AND BLACK. The Divinity men however, wore purple, black, and white. A "colors" compromise eventually evolved, and PURPLE AND WHITE was born. In 1925 the *London Advertiser* made an editorial attempt at a new image, referring to the football team as the Western "U" BRONCOS — BRONCOS going nicely with Western. When the editorialists realized in 1926 their BRONCOS weren't going to catch on, they put forward a new symbol, the MUSTANGS. A newspaper competition ensued, with the *London Free Press* and *Western University Gazette* continuing to call the team from Western the PURPLE AND WHITE. The *Free Press* went even further, backing Coach Joe Breen's wish to call his team the PURPLE. The battle continued until 1930 when the *Gazette* wrote, "The Mustang is a descendent of the Arabian horses brought to America by the Spaniards. They strayed from their Spanish owners to run wild in the Western prairies. They have the best qualities of the Arabian steeds together with certain acquired characteristics when adapting themselves under new conditions. They are famous for their endurance. They are very difficult to tame but once broken are extremely intelligent." In 1930, Western students voted 20 to 1 in favor of the MUSTANG name.

WINNIPEG WESMEN

The University of Winnipeg WESMEN drew international attention in 1992-93 when the women's basketball team tied the North American record for consecutive wins at 88. While most other athletic teams bear names that are easily identifiable, animals and the such, many fans were wondering, "Why Wesmen?" Called United College prior to 1967, its link to the University of Manitoba meant the school teams were known as the JUNIOR BISONS. Intramural teams had a variety of names, such as the REDMEN and the COLLEGIANS. When the University of Winnipeg was established, it needed its own team name. The student council held a contest open to campus community, and it became a big event. The winning name was chosen by student Catherine Chase, "I entered the name WESMAN, made up from the Methodist Church's Wesley College and Manitoba College, the names of the two founding institutions. Oddly, it was decided to change the name slightly to WESMEN as a way of pluralizing it." This historical background explains why even the women's teams are proud to be called WESMEN.

YORK YEOMEN

The School of Physical Education decided that the York University sports teams should be named with a nod to history — British history, that is. The YEOMEN of the Guard were formed by King Henry VII. Fifty of the scarlet-uniformed men first made their official appeartance at his coronation in Westminster Abbey on October 30, 1485. An 18th century court historian, Samuel Pegge, wrote that King Henry recruited the YEOMEN on the "pretext of giving an uncommon eclat to that Ceremony," but actually the king was scared out of his wits by the "civil commotions" that had preceded his reign and he hired them as a bodyguard. They stayed with him 24 hours a day and even made his bed. These original YEOMEN no longer make the royal bed, but they still make a ceremonial appearance at state banquets. They also continue to search the vaults of the Houses of Parliament at the State Opening each November — a ritual that has become a tradition ever since an attempt on the King's life, the notorious Gunpowder Plot in 1605. In the city of Toronto the YEOMEN remain very active, however, defending the honor of York University.

BEST OF

SEAWOLF WHITE MULES BURN

HOYAS WIZ CLASH

TIDES KEYS

HATTERS SAGEHENS

THE REST

HOTSPURS

WAVES PAINTS

MUTINY

ARTICHOKES BANANA SLUGS HARDROCKERS

BEST OF THE REST

More interesting nicknames from the college and pro ranks, including minor league baseball, hockey, and British soccer.

Abilene Prairie Dogs
Alaska Anchorage Sea Wolf
Alaska Fairbanks Nanooks
Arkansas Tech Wonderboys
Asheville Tourists
Atlanta Knights
Baltimore Stallions
Bangor Blue Ox
Battle Creek Golden
   Kazoos
Bend Bandits
Boston Terriers
Bowdoin Polar Bears
California Maritime
   Keelhaulers
Chaminade Silverswords
Chattanooga Lookouts
Chicago Wolves
Chillicothe Paints
Cincinnati Cyclones
Cleveland Lumberjacks
Coastal Carolina
   Chanticleers
Colby White Mules

Connecticut Huskies
Dallas Burn
Delaware Fighting Blue
   Hens
Dickinson Red Devils
Durham Bulls
Endicott Power Gulls
Fort Wayne Komets
Fort Wayne Wizards
Frederick Keys
Georgetown Hoyas
Grand Rapids Mackers
Hardware City Rock Cats
Harvard Crimson
Hershey Bears
Houston Aeros
Illinois Blueboys
Indianapolis Ice
Irvine Anteaters
Johnstown Chiefs
Kalamazoo Kingdom
Kansas City Blades
Kansas City Wiz
Kissemmee Cobras

Las Vegas Thunder
Los Angeles Galaxy
Louisville Riverfrogs
Manitoba Moose
Metropolitan State College
   of Denver Roadrunners
Metro Stars
Michigan K-Wings
Milwaukee Admirals
Minnesota Arctic Blast
Missouri Kangaroos
Montreal Roadrunners
New Orleans Privateers
Norfolk Tides
Northern Kentucky Norse
North Florida Ospreys
Pacific Tigers
Peoria Rivermen
Pepperdine Waves
Pomona Sagehens
Quad City River Bandits
Rancho Cucamonga
   Quakes

Richmond Spiders
Roanoke Express
St. John's Red Storm
San Bernadino Stampede
San Jose Clash
Santa Barbara Gauchos
Santa Cruz Banana Slugs
Savannah Sand Gnats
Scottsdale Artichokes
South Dakota Tech
   Hardrockers
Southern Colorado
   Thunderwolves
Southern Illinois Salukis
Stetson Hatters
Tampa Bay Mutiny
Tarleton State Texans
Tehran Peruzee
Toledo Mud Hens
Trinity Christian Trolls
Washington Bears

BRITISH PREMIER LEAGUE

Arsenal Gunners

Aston Villa Villans

Blackburn Rovers

Bolton Wanderers

Chelsea Blues

Coventry City Sky Blues

Everton Toffeemen

Leeds United

Liverpool Reds

Manchester City Citizens

Manchester United Red
   Devils

Middlesbrough, The Boro

Newcastle United
   Magpies

Nottingham Forest

Queen's Park Rangers

Sheffield Wednesday

Southampton Saints

Tottenham Hotspurs

West Ham United
   Hammers

Wimbledon FC,
   The Dons

ABILENE PRAIRIE DOGS

In 1993, when Texas-Louisiana co-founders Byron Pierce and John Bryant were scouting the state for potential host cities for their fledgling league, Pierce came to Abilene. The Abilene BLUE SOX played their final game in the Big State League in 1957 before packing it in. The team had played 11 seasons in the Key City at the old Blue Sox Stadium, but America's fascination with air-conditioning and television put pro baseball on hold in Abilene for the next 38 years. When $850,000 in improvements were made to Abilene Christian University's Crutcher Scott Field, the PRAIRIE DOGS came to town. While PRAIRIE DOGS may not have been the first choice if a survey had been taken of the fans, Abilene businessman K.O. Long's suggestion in the name-the-team contest seemed to capture their imaginations (especially the young ones!). The quest for a friendly, approachable mascot ended when "Grounder" was introduced. Three local school children were winners in a name-the-mascot competition.

ALASKA ANCHORAGE SEAWOLF

Originally nicknamed the SOURDOUGHS, the University of Alaska Anchorage adopted the SEAWOLF moniker in 1977. The name SEAWOLF represents a mystical sea creature whose origin is linked with the Tlingit (pronounced Clink-it) Indians of southeastern Alaska. According to legend, anyone fortunate enough to view the SEAWOLF was subject to good luck. The exact nature or shape of the SEAWOLF, however, was left to the imagination and thus the creature has been depicted in many forms throughout the years. The SEAWOLF of today was introduced in 1985. Created by Clark Mishler & Associates Company of Anchorage in cooperation with a University committee, it represents an adaptation of a more traditional Alaskan totemic-like characterization of the mythical SEAWOLF. The most recent makeover of the SEAWOLF, a University-wide project, was taken on in order to update the look of the UAA mascot into a more recognizable and marketable image. The University has trademarked the logo.

ALASKA FAIRBANKS NANOOKS

The University of Alaska Fairbanks was founded in 1917. During the early years the athletic teams were called the POLAR BEARS, after the most dominant animal in the State of Alaska. When the basketball teams began traveling by air for their competitions (around 1970), the team's name was changed from POLAR BEARS to FLYING NANOOKS — which is the Athabascan Indian name for a Polar Bear. UAF believes that the "flying" part of the nickname was dropped within a couple of years as air travel became more prevalent. NANOOKS was chosen by a vote of the student body. Incredibly, each year the NANOOK athletic teams log more than 500,000 air miles traveling to competitions throughout the United States, paying off in 1994 with the NCAA Rifle Championship.

ARKANSAS TECH WONDERBOYS

Founded in 1909 as the Second District Agricultural School, the name was changed to Arkansas Polytechnic College in 1925, and then to Arkansas Tech University in 1976. It was in 1919 that Arkansas Tech upset the highly-favored Jonesboro AGGIES (now Arkansas State University) 14-0 behind a pair of 70-yard punt returns for touchdowns and two point-after kicks by 17-year-old quarterback John Tucker. The Jonesboro team had staked claim to the mystical state championship prior to the game. Henry Loesch, sports editor for the *Arkansas Gazette* in Little Rock, coined the name WONDERBOYS in complimenting the Tech team, then known as the AGGIES, in his post-game story. Tech's athletic teams have been known as the WONDERBOYS ever since.

ASHEVILLE TOURISTS

The Asheville Professional Baseball Club was first called the TOURISTS around 1924. Prior to that time, the team was known as the SKYLANDERS. The SKYLANDERS name was taken from the phrase "Land of the Sky," which is used to describe the western

North Carolina mountains where Asheville is situated. The name
TOURISTS developed because of Asheville's reputation as a tourists' mecca. The city is located at the conjunction of the Blue Ridge
and Great Smoky Mountains. Asheville is about 2,200 feet above sea
level and the home of the famed Biltmore Estate (George Vanderbilt's
250-room mansion) and the rustic Grove Park Inn. The region boasts
outstanding hunting, trout fishing, hiking, golf, and water sports.
Grandfather Mountain and Chimney Rock Park are other nearby
attractions. Downtown Asheville has many great examples of Art
Deco architecture of the early 20th century. In 1972 the TOURISTS
switched their affiliation to the Baltimore ORIOLES, who insisted
they change their name to the Asheville ORIOLES. This working
agreement lasted through the 1975 season when the renamed
TOURISTS became a part of the Texas RANGERS organization.
Asheville, playing in the South Atlantic League, has since seen its
parent club affiliation go from the ASTROS to the Colorado
ROCKIES, but the traditional TOURISTS name has endured!

ATLANTA KNIGHTS

For the International Hockey League, Atlanta franchise president
Richard Adler and wife Judi decided on KNIGHTS after looking
through the dictionary for names which appealed to them, and which
could be adapted appealingly to a logo. Remaining a family affair,
Judi's father designed the team logo featuring the skating suit of ar-
mour. Established in 1992-93, the KNIGHTS made IHL history
when they became the first pro team to employ a female goaltender
in a regular season game when Manon Rheaume of Quebec played
against Salt Lake on December 13, 1993. In 1996 the franchise was
moved north to Quebec City, replacing the National Hockey
League's NORDIQUES, who had become the Colorado ROCKIES.

BALTIMORE STALLIONS

The Baltimore NO NAMES? For a brief period, that's right! Baltimore's expansion Canadian Football League team lost its first choice

for a nickname in court before its first game! Even though the NFL
COLTS had left town for Indianapolis, the newest franchise in the
one-hundred-year-old Canadian league was told it could not lay
claim to the storied Baltimore moniker. It also lost merchandise that
could not be sold because it bore the banned COLTS name. But
thanks to the stylized horse head with a flowing main — the CFL's
most popular logo — being nickname-less didn't hurt merchandise
sales. And to no one's surprise, the CFL's shortlived Baltimore COLT
franchise merchandise has become quite a collector's item. The history went like this: on March 1, 1994, owner Jim Spiros named his
Canadian Football League the Baltimore COLTS. By the end of
April the National Football League sued for the use of the name —
after all, Indianapolis was still using it. In June an injunction was put
on Baltimore, and they called their team the Baltimore CFL CLUB
to ride it out. Fans began calling their home team the CFLs and the
CFLers. Then the *Baltimore Sun* held a name-the-team contest, and
40 percent of respondents wanted to keep the simple CFL name.
Meanwhile, the National Football League was looking at expansion
in five cities: Baltimore BOMBERS, Memphis HOUND DOGS,
Jacksonville JAGUARS, Carolina PANTHERS, and the St. Louis
STALLIONS. But when the National Football League St. Louis ap-
plication panned out, it had the RAMS moved to Missouri. This
freed up the St. Louis patent on the nickname STALLIONS, because the franchise would be inheriting its Los Angeles moniker. As
it turned out in Baltimore, STALLIONS had been the fan's second
choice, and MUSTANGS was third. On July 7, the Baltimore STAL-
LIONS were born. And on November 19, 1995, the STALLIONS
from Baltimore became the first American team to win the Grey Cup
in 83 years. This team became the Montreal ALOUETTES in 1996.

BANGOR BLUE OX

The Greater Bangor Baseball Inc. offices were flooded with suggestions to name the new Eastern Maine minor league team. In a week-
long contest over 1,200 entries made their way to Bangor Baseball
headquarters. The most popular nominations included nicknames
involving life in Maine, including BUNYANS, BLACK FLIES,

TIMBER KINGS, TIMBER BARONS, and LUMBERJACKS. On February 27, 1996, it was announced that the club would be known as the Bangor BLUE OX, its logo characterized by Babe, Paul Bunyan's legendary companion. General Manager Dean Gyorgy said the team wanted a look that was both strong and fun, and something that reflected the flavor and history of the Greater Bangor region. The BLUE OX was submitted by 16 fans ranging in age from 8 to 61.

BATTLE CREEK GOLDEN KAZOOS

Originally the MAD HATTERS, a Class "A" affiliate of the St. Louis CARDINALS in 1994, was one of the more cleverly named sports franchises in minor league sports. No city-wide name-the-team contest here, just a bolt of fanciful inspiration on the part of the ball club's owners. The moniker was a whimsical nod in the direction of one of author Lewis Carroll's most endearing characters, the Mad Hatter of *Alice in Wonderland* fame. But the club moved to Battle Creek, and re-christened themselves the GOLDEN KAZOOS. Battle Creek shares its fan base with Kalamazoo, 18 miles away, and the club felt it important that both sites be referred to in the new nickname — Kalamazoo's nickname is KAZOO. As for GOLDEN, GM Tim Cullen said, "We want to emphasize the golden era of the sport." The KAZOOS play in the Midwest League.

BEND BANDITS

Playing in the Independent Western Baseball League since 1994, the town of Bend, Oregon BANDITS and their mascot "Rowdy" the Rebel Raccoon had their names selected from over 1,000 entries. BANDITS was the most popular by a 2-1 margin over several other names, including the CASCADERS, the LAVA BANDITS, the MOUNTAINEERS, and the TIMBERJACKS. Originally, there were over 75 names from which to choose. BANDITS was selected for three reasons: it was genuinely the most popular choice; it was alliterative with "Bend"; it was easier to create a logo from the shorter nickname.

BOSTON TERRIERS

Not to be outdone by the Yale BULLDOG and the Princeton TI-
GER, Boston University students selected the Boston TERRIER as
their football nickname and mascot shortly after the sport received
official University recognition in 1917. The terrier is one of the few
dogs actually bred in the United States. Interestingly enough, it was
in 1869, the year the University was incorporated, that a Boston
dog-breeder crossed the English Terrier with a bulldog and came up
with this American favorite.

BOWDOIN POLAR BEARS

The POLAR BEAR symbolizes the spirit of exploration, and refers
specifically to the active role Bowdoin College played for well over
100 years in exploring the Arctic. Scores of Bowdoin faculty members, students, and alumni made trips to the Arctic on missions of
exploration and of scientific research. The most famous of these explorers were Rear Admiral Robert E. Peary and Rear Admiral
Donald B. MacMillan. Peary, Class of 1877, became the first man
to reach the North Pole on April 6, 1909. MacMillan, Class of 1898,
was Peary's chief assistant on that historic expedition, and he later
made 26 voyages of his own to the Arctic. The move toward making the POLAR BEAR the mascot of Bowdoin was made by
MacMillan, who in 1915 presented a mounted polar bear to the
college as a mascot. That polar bear is preserved in a large glass case
in the lobby of Bowdoin's Morrell Gymnasium. A life-size statue
of a polar bear stands in the Hyde Plaza on the Bowdoin campus.
The statue, erected in 1937, was a gift of the Class of 1912 as a
memorial to its deceased members on the occasion of their 25th
reunion. The base and statue were carved by sculptor Frederick
George Richard Roth, and the nose of the polar bear on the statue
points to the north.

CALIFORNIA MARITIME KEELHAULERS

Playing in the California Coastal, the California State University Maritime Academy sport's teams are proud to be the only athletic team in the world named after a form of punishment. In many European navies, keelhauling was considered second only to hanging in terms of severity. Hands were tied to one end of a spar (the mast, yard, boom, or gaff), while feet were tied to the other end. The unfortunate captive was then dragged under the keel of the ship, and if he didn't drown, he was usually cut so badly by the barnacles he bled to death, or died from infection. Founded by a special act of legislation in 1929, the California Nautical School was known informally as the SEA HORSES, and MARINERS. In 1973-74, the student council held a name-the-team contest, and considered names such as SEA HAWKS and SEA SNAKES. Then known as the California Maritime Academy, nicknamed "Keema" by students, they also considered CRABS for the alliteration. But KEELHAULERS and all the notoriety that came with it was the winning entry. The mascot is a pirate.

CHAMINADE SILVERSWORDS

Chaminade University of Honolulu athletic teams are called the SILVERSWORDS. This is the name of a rare plant found on Haleakala, a dormant volcano on the neighboring island of Maui. The flowers of this exotic plant are said to resemble the Cross, the symbol of the Christian faith. The SILVERSWORD grows from four to 20 years before it produces one single flower, from one to nine feet! The basketball team is also synonymous with the nickname the GIANTKILLERS. The name comes from Chaminade's series of great basketball upsets, including what is possibly the greatest college hoops upset in history, the 1982 defeat of Ralph Sampson and the #1 nationally ranked University of Virginia CAVALIERS.

CHATTANOOGA LOOKOUTS

In 1888, and still with amateur status, the Chattanooga club was called the SULLIVANS. Then in 1909, O.B. Andrews obtained a South Atlantic professional franchise for Chattanooga, and the games were played at Chamberlain Field. Johnny Dobbs was Manager and the team was given its new nickname, the LOOKOUTS, at this time. It was as a result of a fan contest, won by W.O. Powell. It was named at that time after Lookout Mountain right there in Chattanooga. The LOOKOUTS went on to win the South Atlantic (Sally) League pennant, walking off with the first half. The team from Augusta won the second half. In the playoff, the story goes that when the LOOKOUTS went to Augusta, their pitcher was kidnapped! Now more than a hundred years old, the Chattanooga LOOKOUTS are a Double "A" affiliate of the Cincinnati REDS, and play in the Southern League.

CHICAGO WOLVES

Established in 1994-95, the International Hockey League WOLVES moniker was the choice of team President and General Manager Grant Mulvey, who "wanted to make sure that this team had a name that would last forever, a name that would weather all trends and obstacles...we went through lists and lists of possible names and then one day the name WOLVES came up, and it stuck for good." The Chicago WOLVES sold out their first-ever home game on October 14, 1994, which at the time was the 10th-largest crowd in league history.

CHILLICOTHE PAINTS

The PAINTS nickname and team logo were chosen to stay within the theme set by the Frontier Professional Baseball league. The moniker originated as the result of a name-the-team contest, along with help from the owner and friends. The Paint Horse is documented as being the preferred horse by the American Indians, considered by many authorities to be the greatest horsemen who ever lived. The

Paint Horse and Chillicothe are part of the tradition of the Old Frontier. The Paint Horse is known to be a combination of versatility, strength, and aggressiveness with an extra dash of color and individuality which is displayed in the logo: a horse with "painted" markings and colorful war feathers flowing from the horse's mane. The feathers have accents of red and gold tones. The Paint Horse is to symbolize the team spirit and is known as the "Sport Model of the Horse World."

CINCINNATI CYCLONES

The dictionary definition of the word CYCLONES loosely suggests a windstorm with a violent, whirling movement; tornado or hurricane; a storm with strong winds rotating clockwise in the Southern Hemisphere, counterclockwise in the Northern Hemisphere, about a moving center. CYCLONES was actually carried over from the team's days in the East Coast Hockey League. Moving to the International Hockey League, owner Doug Kirchoffer recognized that the name would sound good alongside Cincinnati, and was one that would certainly lend itself to an active logo. Established in 1992-93, Cincinnati had already been home to the MOHAWKS from 1952-58.

CLEVELAND LUMBERJACKS

Lumberjacking might not be the first thing a fan would think of when Cleveland is mentioned, but this 35-year-old franchise actually started in Muskegon, Michigan. The lumberjacking industry was prevalent when the city of Muskegon was formed, so it was no surprise that more than 600 people submitted it as their entry in a name-the-team contest, conducted in 1984 when current owner Larry Gordon bought the franchise. LUMBERJACKS remained in place when the franchise moved to Cleveland in 1992. It played under the name ZEPHYRS from 1960-65, the MOHAWKS from 1965-84, and finally the LUMBERJACKS from 1985.

COASTAL CAROLINA
CHANTICLEERS

In Chaucer's *Canterbury Tales*, more specifically, the "Nun's Priest Tale," we become acquainted with the Chanticleer. It was a proud and fierce rooster who dominated the barnyard. "For crowing there was not his equal in all the land. His voice was merrier than the merry organ that plays in church, and his crowing from his resting place was more trustworthy than a clock. His comb was redder than fine coral and turreted like a castle wall, his bill was black and shone like a jet, and his legs and toes were like azure. His nails were whiter than the lily and his feathers were like burnished gold." Additionally, he was greatly feared and mightily respected by all. CHANTICLEER was chosen to be Coastal Carolina's mascot after a group of Coastal students and their English professor brought up the idea of a new mascot in the late 1960s. At the time, Coastal athletic teams were known as the TROJANS. CHANTICLEER gave Coastal a mascot which resembled big brother's Southern Carolina GAMECOCK, but still gave the College its own identity.

COLBY WHITE MULES

Colby College historian Ernest Cummings Marriner wrote: "The POLAR BEAR of Bowdoin and the BLACK BEAR of the University of Maine antedated the Colby WHITE MULE by several years. In his senior year, Joseph Coburn Smith was editor of the *Colby Echo*, just as Frank Johnson had been 33 years earlier. Like Johnson, Joe was interested in the honest promotion of athletics. On November 7, 1923, Joe published an editorial suggesting that, because Colby football teams so often upset predictions of the newspaper dopesters, Colby no longer appeared as a 'dark horse' but ought to be symbolized by a WHITE MULE! A group of students got busy, located a white mule on a Kennebec farm, borrowed the animal for the Bates game on Armistice Day in 1923, and placed the animal, properly caparisoned in blue and gray, at the head of the band and student body as they marched onto the field." From dark horse to WHITE MULES — Colby won.

CONNECTICUT HUSKIES

The HUSKIES nickname was chosen in 1934 after the editor of the student newspaper questioned why the University of Rhode Island had a mascot (a ram) and UConn did not. Soon it was suggested that the HUSKY would be the perfect mascot because of the "frigid hills" of the Storrs campus. The actual dog which symbolizes the mascot is named Jonathan after Connecticut's Revolutionary War-era governor, Jonathan Trumbull. The first dog, which was brown and white, boasted a great-grandfather who journeyed to the North Pole with Admiral Robert E. Peary in 1909. He is buried on the campus next to the step of old Whitney Hall across from the Storrs Congregational Church.

DALLAS BURN

Most of the franchises in the new Major Soccer League are being sponsored by large running shoe companies, and the BURN franchise is no exception, supported by Nike. They sent us this: The Dallas BURN logo system starts with the cowboy of the asphalt West; the loners, outsiders, and rebels found on cycle jackets and gas tanks. With a street-inspired, aggressive typeface and a fire-breathing mustang, the BURN logos reflect the raw horsepower of the team and the speed of the game — all mixed together in the combustion chamber of a hot Texas field. Brings new meaning to the phrase "getting burned on the pitch."

DELAWARE FIGHTING BLUE HENS

The University of Delaware's FIGHTING BLUE HENS is a name that stretches back over 200 years of Delaware history. On December 9, 1775, the Continental Congress resolved that a military battalion was to be raised from the lower three counties along the Delaware River. The second company of the Delaware Regiment was composed of men from Kent County and was under the command of Captain John Caldwell, who was an avid fan and owner of gamecocks. The militia often amused themselves by staging cockfights with these birds, which were of a breed known as the Kent County Blue Hen, having some blue plumage. These Blue Hens' chickens quickly developed a reputation for ferocity and fighting success, as did Captain Caldwell's men, nicknamed the BLUE HEN CHICKEN company. In 1939 the Blue Hen Chicken was named Delaware's official state bird. The University of Delaware's College of Agriculture maintains a breeding group of the Blue Hen Chicken on its campus farm. The mascot's name is YoUDee.

Nickname: Hens

DICKINSON RED DEVILS

The nickname RED DEVILS was first applied to a Dickinson College football team, playing in the Eastern College Athletic Conference, in the 1930 season. Despite losing by a 27-6 score to a heavily favored George Washington University squad, Dickinson impressed a sportswriter from the Washington, D.C. area with its fighting spirit and he gave it the name it still bears today. In 1936, the Dickinson Board of Athletic Control changed the name to COLONIALS, but a student petition sent to college president Fred Corson convinced him to sanction the name RED DEVILS as the official college moniker. The colors red and white were Dickinson's colors from the beginning. The colors had been adopted soon after the Revolutionary War. In 1903, Dickinson switched from red and white uniforms to black uniforms with white and red stripes because the color on the red uniforms would run when wet! They switched back 25 years later.

DURHAM BULLS

Not just a great movie! Unlike so many "Johnny-come-lately" minor league teams who have chosen unique names, the name Durham BULLS dates back to the 19th century! The first use of the word BULL in conjunction with Durham came as the name for a brand of locally-produced tobacco. It was called "Bull Durham" tobacco, and our research indicates that as the Duke family searched for a

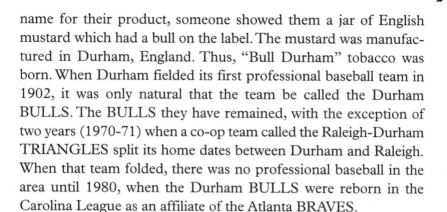

name for their product, someone showed them a jar of English mustard which had a bull on the label. The mustard was manufactured in Durham, England. Thus, "Bull Durham" tobacco was born. When Durham fielded its first professional baseball team in 1902, it was only natural that the team be called the Durham BULLS. The BULLS they have remained, with the exception of two years (1970-71) when a co-op team called the Raleigh-Durham TRIANGLES split its home dates between Durham and Raleigh. When that team folded, there was no professional baseball in the area until 1980, when the Durham BULLS were reborn in the Carolina League as an affiliate of the Atlanta BRAVES.

ENDICOTT POWER GULLS

Endicott College, a senior college in Beverly, Massachusetts, with its enrolment of 800 students, has its campus located right on the Atlantic Ocean. This geographical reality was the primary reason a student vote in the early 1980s turned to the sea for the school's first official nickname, and the unique POWER GULLS was the end result. Other considered and rejected names included RIP TIDE and the CLIPPERS. School colors are also water-related: royal blue, kelly green, and white.

Nickname: Gulls

FORT WAYNE KOMETS

The dictionary definition of the word "comet" suggests a heavenly body in the solar system, having a starlike nucleus with a luminous mass around it, and, usually, a long, luminous tail that points away from the sun. One of the original owners of the Fort Wayne International Hockey League franchise, Ernie Berg, had a wife named Katherine. When the results of a local contest produced the name COMETS, Berg, in keeping with his wife's name, converted the team nickname to be spelled with a "K." The KOMETS are the IHL's most-established franchise, joining in 1952-53, the league's eighth year of operation.

FORT WAYNE WIZARDS

After almost two months without a name, the Fort Wayne professional baseball affiliate of the Minnesota TWINS playing in the Midwest League found its identity on October 22, 1992. In early
September, the name-the-team contest was announced to have fans
of Fort Wayne submit suggestions for the nickname of a baseball
team. With the promotional help of a local restaurant, radio station,
television station, and Delta Airlines, more than 20,000 entries were
reviewed during the five-week promotion. With more than 1,500 different names entered, the screening committee had a difficult time
making a short list of finalists: CAVALRY, KEKIONGAS, SAND-
BAGGERS, and SUMMIT CITY PIONEERS. Paula King's submission of WIZARDS was randomly drawn from all of the other
contestants who entered WIZARDS. She received two WIZARDS
season tickets and two round-trip airline tickets to any Delta Airlines
destination in the United States. "Amazing Baseball" was the theme of
the inaugural season for this northeast Indiana Midwest League entry.

FREDERICK KEYS

Prior to the 1989 season, the Maryland Baseball Limited Partner-
ship ran a name-the-team contest in the local paper. Some of the
entries included the Frederick FLINTSTONES, FALCONS, FLY-
ERS, and FLAMES. The organization picked the Frederick KEYS
from an entry by Bob Reed. The name is in honor of Francis Scott
Key, the author of the National Anthem who is from the area and is
buried across from the team's current stadium. For having the winning entry, the Frederick KEYS, a Class "A" affiliate of the Baltimore ORIOLES, gave Bob two season box seats for life. The
Frederick KEYS play in the Carolina Baseball League.

GEORGETOWN HOYAS

Georgetown was founded in 1789, the same year George Washington took office. Its colors are blue and grey, adopted at the end of

the Civil War to signify the union of the North and South. In the days when all Georgetown students were required to study Greek and Latin, the University's teams were nicknamed the STONE-WALLS. A student, using Greek and Latin terms started the cheer "HOYA Saxa." HOYA is from the Greek word "hoios," meaning "such a" or "what a." The neuter plural of this word is "hoia," which agrees with the neuter plural of the Latin word "saxa," meaning rocks; thus we have "hoya," substituting the "y" for an "i," which translates into "What Rocks"! The name proved popular and the term HOYAS was eventually adopted for all Georgetown teams. Among many famous Georgetown alumni are President Bill Clinton and John J. Sirica, the judge who presided over the Watergate trials.

Nickname: G'Town

GRAND RAPIDS MACKERS

Minor league basketball came to west Michigan when Grand Rapids was awarded an expansion franchise in the Continental Basketball Association for the 1989-90 season, and the team was nicknamed the HOOPS. After the 1993-94 season, the HOOPS were sold to the inventors of the nationally known Gus Macker 3-on-3 outdoor street basketball tournaments. Accordingly, the team's nickname and colors were changed to reflect the owner's business ...hence the name MACKERS. Team colors for the HOOPS were purple, green, and orange. The MACKERS adopted Macker Maroon and Gus Gold with a Navy accent. The National Basketball Association parent clubs were the Detroit PISTONS and Phoenix SUNS in 1990-91, but are now the PISTONS and Washington BULLETS.

HARDWARE CITY ROCK CATS

Hardware City is the nickname for New Britain, Connecticut! The reason is that Stanley Tools makes its home there. When the city ended its 12-year affiliation with Boston and welcomed the TWINS, a new name was needed. The Double-A club hired Guy Gilchrist, the ultra-hot graphic designer of the Portland SEA DOGS, to come up with a new logo and the Hardware City ROCK CAT was born. He was a cat with sunglasses, an electric guitar, ponytail, and an ear-ring. Team owner Joe Buzas became concerned that fans wouldn't know where "Hardware City" was. He decided the name would re-main Hardware City, but New Britain would appear on the road uniforms. Even the original logo was toned down. "We took out the earring," said director of media relations Chris Whalen. "But the first shipment of T-shirts still had the old logo." Might turn out to be a collector's item someday.

HARVARD CRIMSON

Founded in 1636, Harvard University is the oldest institution of higher learning in the United States. This storied house of academia is a member of the Ivy League, along with Brown, Cornell, Colum-bia, Dartmouth, Princeton, Yale, and the University of Pennsylva-nia — a clique of northeastern universities identified with academic achievement and social prestige. Their only official association is on the football field, where they have played mostly each other since 1900. The Ivy League once implied gridiron valor as well as the right academic stuff; now their teams are relatively weak, though in some cases ardently supported. Perhaps the most important date in Harvard football history occurred on May 6, 1875. That was the day Harvard undergraduates held a plebiscite on the University's color and chose crimson. As was often the case in the last century, the team color became also the team name. Had the vote gone the other way, Harvard athletic teams would be known as the MA-GENTA, the student newspaper still would be named — as it was then — the *MAGENTA*, and the fight song might be "The MA-GENTA in triumph flashing." Instead, CRIMSON was supported by a large majority and also became the name not only of the news-paper but of Harvard's representatives on the athletic field.

HERSHEY BEARS

The sport of ice hockey came to Hershey, Pennsylvania during the depths of the Depression in 1931. The first game was played on

February 18, 1931, when Penn A.C. faced off against Villanova in the Convention Hall/Ice Palace. The first team officially to call Hershey its home was the Swathmore A.C., playing in the 1931-32 season. They continually played before sellout crowds. It was then determined by Milton S. Hershey and John B. Sollenberger that hockey was here to stay. The following season, the Hershey B'ARS joined the Amateur Hockey League and played regularly scheduled games against teams from Baltimore, Atlantic City, and Philadelphia. At the start of the 1936 season, the club was officially renamed because the Hershey B'ARS was considered too commercial. The name BEARS originated from being referred to as "the BEARS from Penn Woods" when the team played at Madison Square Garden. The BEARS were also the first, on December 19, 1936, to skate onto the ice of newly built Hershey Sports Arena, now referred to as the Hershey Park Arena. Since that time, over six hundred men have proudly worn the Hershey BEARS sweater.

Nickname: Chocolate and White

HOUSTON AEROS

Playing in the International Hockey League, this Houston franchise was established in 1994-95. The nickname AEROS was not new, as it was also used by Houston's entry in the World Hockey Association, which won league championships in 1974 and 1975. The moniker originally represented the Texas city's connection to the aerospace industry, with Houston being the site of the Johnson Space Center. Today's AEROS incorporate a World War Two theme as the logo includes a star found on the wings of WWII bombers. The Houston AEROS are the southern-most team in IHL history.

ILLINOIS BLUEBOYS

Tom Rowland, former football star for the Illinois College BLUEBOYS, was drafted by the Green Bay PACKERS in 1968. There's a story that when he stood on his chair in the training room one night and prepared to make the traditional rookie speech, he panicked. "I stood up and shouted 'I am Tom Rowland of the Illinois College TIGERS,'" Rowland recalled. "Hall of Fame player Ray Nitschke was sitting there looking at me with no teeth. There was no way I was saying BLUEBOYS." Reflecting on the incident in 1993, Rowland was the track and wrestling coach back at the college and was trying to change the nickname to the FIGHTING BLUE. But since the moniker comes from the days when Illinois students fought in the Civil War and were known as Blue Boys, the traditionalists at this oldest school in the state, established in 1829, would not bend.

INDIANAPOLIS ICE

Established in 1988-89, the International Hockey League franchise in Indianapolis chose the name ICE after a name-the-team contest. "We were happy to see the ICE on top," said team President Ray Compton. Other choices in the final fan balloting included the CAPITOLS, WARRIORS, SILVER STREAKS, TORNADOES, and the PURPLE HAZE. Indianapolis was a hockey town long before the arrival of the ICE, including IHL franchises the CHIEFS from 1955 to 1962, and the cleverly nicknamed CHECKERS, who took over in 1984 until 1987.

IRVINE ANTEATERS

Playing in the Big West, the advent of the ANTEATER at the University of California at Irvine was in 1965, the year that the University opened. As a fledgling intercollegiate athletics program was initiated, the search for an official nickname began. Pat Glasgow and Bob Ernst, two water polo players, are regarded as the main instigators for the campaign to select the ANTEATER as mascot, with some inspiration from the Johnny Hart comic strip "B.C." The two student-athletes, along with the marketing creativity of fellow student Schuyler Hadley Bassett III, organized an intense promotional effort and by student election time only the ANTEATERS, EAGLES, UNICORNS, GOLDEN BEARS, and SEAHAWKS had obtained the required 100 signatures to be included on the ballot. The ANTEATERS emerged victorious in the final tally with 55.9 percent of the vote. Bassett borrowed the war cry "Zot!" from the Anteater in the "B.C." comic strip and established his own fraternity, Zeta Omega Tau. The successful campaign led to a piece on the nickname in an issue of *Sports Illustrated* and into the news-commentary segment of the well-known Huntley-Brinkley newscast. To this day, the ANTEATERS remain popular, being listed as one of the top five nicknames in national polls conducted by ESPN and Collegiate Directories, Inc.

JOHNSTOWN CHIEFS

Another Hollywood-inspired nickname. The first name to be considered was JETS, after the former Johnston JETS who spent more than 30 years of pro hockey playing in the former Eastern Hockey League and North American Hockey League. After club officials failed to secure the name JETS from the franchise's former owners, they decided on CHIEFS. This name came from the most famous hockey movie of all time, *Slapshot,* starring Paul Newman, which was filmed in Johnstown in 1977-78. While the club was known as the Charlestown CHIEFS in the movie, it was the Johnstown CHIEFS that took to the ice in what is now the East Coast Hockey League. In their ninth season in 1996, the CHIEFS are carrying on a tradition of over 55 years of pro hockey in the city of Johnstown.

KALAMAZOO KINGDOM

The city of Kalamazoo waited a couple of years to receive its first outdoor pro soccer franchise. In 1994, the Kalamazoo PRIDE were supposed to play in the USISL, but never materialized. In 1995 an ownership group formed the Detroit WHEELS and the Grand Rapids EXPLOSION in the USISL. This group also owned the rights to field the Kalamazoo KOSMOS in 1996, but sold those rights. This newest ownership group announced that its team would be called the SPEEDSTERS, but due to negative reactions, hired a marketing firm that produced the Kalamazoo KINGDOM nickname. Other teams playing in the Central Premier Division are: Ann Arbor ELITES,

Austin LONE STARS, Colorado Springs STAMPEDE, Detroit DYNAMITE, Des Moines MENACE, Lexington BANDITS, Mid-Michigan BUCKS, Oklahoma City SLICKERS, Omaha FLAMES, Sioux City BREEZE, and Wichita BLUES.

KANSAS CITY BLADES

The moniker BLADES came out of a name-the-team contest, but wasn't the number one choice of Kansas City fans. Their choice was JAZZ, but was rejected in part because the name was already used by the Utah franchise in the National Basketball Association. Ironically, the National Hockey League San Jose SHARKS rejected their fan favourite, the BLADES, because of its "insinuation" of violence. "First of all, we wanted a name with strong hockey connotations. This clearly identifies us as a hockey club," said BLADES owner Russel A. Parker. Established in 1990-91, the BLADES posted the largest single-season turnaround in IHL history in 1991-92, posting 116 regular season points, a 62-point improvement over the previous season.

KANSAS CITY WIZ

Kansas City, an Adidas-supported franchise in Major League Soccer, had been reduced to five nicknames; the RIVERCATS, ROUGHRIDERS, WIZ, TWISTERS, and QUEST after a month-long campaign in the *Kansas City Star* asking fans for their ideas. 3,200 responded, six suggested WIZARDS, which became a variation of the eventual winner. Nine-year-old Sarah Starr of Lee's Summit was chosen the Grand Prize winner of the promotion and received two season tickets to the WIZ's premier season at Arrowhead Stadium. General Manager Tim Latta said he liked WIZ for four reasons: flexibility, creative license, visual appeal, and marketability to young audiences. "It was also very important for us to choose a name that was unique," Latta said, "Its biggest strength, aside from its visual appeal, is that it offers us a great creative springboard. Our youth program will be known as the "WizKids," our mascot will be some form of Merlin the Magician, and one of our premier giveaway nights may be WIZbees (Frisbees with the WIZ logo). And we have the flexibility of using WIZards when we want to."

KISSIMMEE COBRAS

Kissimmee ASTROS? Can you imagine the locker room jokes! Houston brought its minor club to Kissimmee in the Florida State League in 1988, but decided to use the county name — Osceola — rather than the city name. In 1995 the team decided to switch back to the city's name, and dropped its parent club ASTROS nickname. The Kissimmee COBRAS was chosen for the alliteration and marketing possibilities. In fact, 16 of 21 minor league teams with new nicknames for 1995 opted for flash and fun over traditional organization monikers such as the YANKEES or PIRATES. Reason? Big merchandising dollars. "I think traditional baseball marketing ideas get thrown out the window in Florida, and especially here in the world of Mickey Mouse and Shamu the Killer Whale," COBRAS General Manager Tim Bawmann said. "This seemed an opportunity to make ends meet and it's been great so far — we've had to re-order hats and T-shirts."

LAS VEGAS THUNDER

The dictionary defines thunder as "the sound that follows a flash of lightning, threatening, menacing, to make, or move with, a sound like thunder." Owner Hank Stickney chose THUNDER from among 500 ideas submitted by fans in a name-the-team contest. "Anyone who has seen a hockey game knows how you 'feel the thunder.' It's an exciting, aggressive name, and it has some flash and dash," Stickney said when he established the franchise in 1993-94. The THUNDER then went on to post the best record for a first-year International Hockey League team with 115 points (52-18-11) en route to the Huber Trophy as regular season champions.

LOS ANGELES GALAXY

Playing in the World Soccer League, this Nike-supported franchise sent us this information: The logo system for the Los Angeles GALAXY revolves around the one part of the cosmos that LA can rightfully claim — the sun. Spinning and energetic, the logo not only conveys the warmth and action of the city, but the intensity and movement of the game. The team's colors of orange, yellow, blue, and black underscore the theme, while the retro-typeface echoes Art Deco LA. As for the mascot/character — well, its creators dubbed it "Twizzle." It's some kind of astral-whirly, and it means business.

LOUISVILLE RIVERFROGS

This nickname was generated from inner-office conversations which spanned some five months. The name FROGS was originally suggested by Asst.GM Greg Galiette. The name was refined to RIVERFROGS through office brainstorming. Then the nickname was given to Creative Alliance, a local advertising agency, to be included with any other names the agency wanted to suggest. The final three names brought back to the board of directors were RIVERFROGS, VULTURES, and PIRANHAS. RIVERFROGS won out because it was considered "kid friendly" and would have tremendous across-the-board marketing implications. The name is different, yet not intimidating to kids or adults. Louisville's previous East Coast Hockey League team, the ICEHAWKS, had become the Jacksonville LIZARD KINGS in 1994, opening the door for the RIVERFROGS.

MANITOBA MOOSE

MOOSE season expanded to the city of St. Paul in the fall of 1994. But, unlike the hunting seasons held in northern Minnesota, this Minnesota MOOSE season is played on ice, and they are targets only for other International Hockey League teams. The MOOSE was the favorite nickname of the fans in the name-the-team contest conducted by the *Pioneer Press* and the favorite of majority owner Kevin MacLean. The MOOSE received 1,031 votes, 57 more than the runner-up, MUSTANGS. Other suggestions included the MAL-LARDS, WIZARDS, BOBCATS, and TOMCATS. "The people have spoken," MacLean said, happy the fans preferred the same nick-name that he did. "This is a name we can have fun with and fun is a big part of the IHL's approach to hockey." In fact, a team executive was heard to say at the time, "We don't know if Bullwinkle will be available for the opener, but we've got a call in for Rocky." The Twin Cities has hosted two previous IHL franchises — the Minneapolis MILLERS and the Saint Paul SAINTS, both from 1959-63. In 1996, the National Hockey League Winnipeg JETS left town to become the Phoenix COYOTES, and the IHL's MOOSE was moved north to fill the void.

METROPOLITAN STATE COLLEGE OF DENVER ROADRUNNERS

These ROADRUNNERS were students, named for the necessity of dodging the traffic as they made their way between campus build-ings! Playing in the Colorado Athletic Conference, the Metropolitan State College of Denver nickname of ROADRUNNERS did not originate with this desert bird, and was not chosen to refer to the ath-letic prowess of any of the school's sports teams. In the old "rent-a-campus" days, Denver residents watched students dodge traffic to get to and from classes, and "roadrunning" became the term used to describe the process. Horror stories still abound of close calls with traffic, and it was a rare day that students did not hear horns blaring at people dodging cars. While the first mascot was actually a Mus-tang, the swift Roadrunner was soon adopted as a more fitting mas-cot. With the building of North Classroom to replace the East Bank facilities, and the closure of Lawrence and Larimer streets, "roadrunning" is no longer an integral part of life here. Students will have to think up a different excuse for being late to class.

Nickname: Metro

METRO STARS

This Nike-supported franchise in the new World Soccer League sent us this: The logo system of the New York/New Jersey Metro STARS taps into the electric energy of the city. The non-stop action of a town without a closing time. And, of course, the ever-present taxi — the fastest way to get from point A to point B, but not necessarily the safest or the sanest. Painted the same colors as those Gotham go-carts, the STARS' logos carry a hood ornament icon, a gas-guzzler-era typeface and the sheer guts of your average kamikaze cabbie.

MICHIGAN K-WINGS

When Kalamazoo joined the International Hockey League in 1974-75, the team was 40 percent owned by the National Hockey League Detroit RED WINGS — a senior club named in memory of the WINGED WHEELERS, an amateur Montreal Athletic Association team that the Detroit Red Wings first team president, James Norris, played on in the 1890s. Local fans became so familiar with the nickname, which is also used in the arena name, that it has remained intact, even though the team has been affiliated with the Dallas STARS (formerly the Minnesota NORTH STARS) franchise for several years. The K-WINGS, short for Kalamazoo-WINGS, have the league's most senior owners in Martha and Ted Parfet.

Nickname: Wings

MILWAUKEE ADMIRALS

Named after a fridge? That's right, and why not for a hockey franchise? Established in 1977-78, the Milwaukee ADMIRALS were actually formed in 1970, playing as an independent amateur team. One of the owners at the time, Erwin Merar, owned an appliance dealership and decided to name the hockey team after his top-selling line, which happened to carry the brand name ADMIRAL. Current owners Lloyd and Jane Pettit bought the team in 1976, kept the name, and a year later entered the International Hockey League. Prior to the 1994-95 season, the ADMIRALS had hosted 11 of the 12 largest crowds in league history, the largest being a turnout of 17,875 on February 4, 1994 versus Peoria.

MINNESOTA ARCTIC BLAST

The Minnesota MOSQUITOS, no. How about the ICE, LOONS, or POLARS? Those were some of the concepts that design and marketing partners Michael Vacanti and Richard Valentine had to work with for Minnesota's new Roller Hockey International franchise before the team management decided on the ARCTIC BLAST. "They really liked the idea of the polar bear so we went with that concept," said Valentine. "Plus it also helps to have an animated character as a mascot." Vacanti added, "We wanted them to have an NHL-NBA level logo that had durability, and was rather irreverent." After creating the pencils of the grinning polar bear and blasting puck he put it on the computer, developed the background and came up with the colors silver, black, and blast blue. The black and silver combination has been a popular one for both the Chicago White Sox and Los Angeles Kings when they opted for uniform and design changes. "Colors play a big part in merchandising and marketing of a team. Teal has been over-done lately so we wanted to do something different," said Vacanti. Different and fresh is what they came up with as the ARCTIC BLAST is being perceived as a fresh and unique approach to sports franchise identity. The team is presently on sabbatical from the Roller Hockey International League.

Nickname: The Blast

MISSOURI KANGAROOS

The KANGAROO issue was first brought up in 1936 when the editors of the University (then named Kansas City University) newspaper decided it was time for a mascot for, of all things, the debate team. There were no organized athletic teams at the time, and the fire was lit later that year when an article appeared in the *Kansas City Star* titled "Kangaroo May Go to KCU...Student Editors Believe University Should Have a Symbol." Even the Kansas City Zoo contributed to the ground swell when they purchased two baby kangaroos. In 1937, the University yearbook, *The Crataegus* decided the kangaroo was not an appropriate school symbol. Just as the criticism began to mount and support for the kangaroo was beginning to wane, a famed cartoonist came to the rescue. A University humor magazine had been established, and on its second cover was a cartoon of one Kasey (K.C.) the Kangaroo alongside none other than Mickey Mouse! Only one other college in the nation uses KANGAROOS as its nickname, Austin College in Sherman, Texas, and one other uses the creature as its mascot — the Akron ZIPS. The University of Missouri, Kansas City is annually listed among the top ten most unusual mascot names in Division One across the country.

Nickname: The Roo

MONTREAL ROADRUNNERS

This Montreal entry into the Roller Hockey International League was managed and co-owned by Yvan Cournoyer, a former hockey star with the Montreal Canadiens of the National Hockey League. The speedy right winger earned a reputation as one of ice hockey's fastest skaters. He also earned a nickname, the roadrunner. The roller blading franchise was named after him. A newspaper contest was held by the *Montreal Gazette* and the *Journal de Montreal,* and the nickname ROADRUNNER actually finished in second place behind the Canadiens' most famous son Maurice Richard and his nickname, the ROCKET. But Cournoyer was going to be behind the bench, making the ROADRUNNER selection most appropriate. Cournoyer has since moved on, but his namesake franchise lives on.

NEW ORLEANS PRIVATEERS

Cruising over the blue waters of Lake Pontchartrain, a silver and blue privateer patrols its boundaries from the old barracks of Camp Leroy Johnson on the East Campus to Hangman's Tree, not far from Bienville Hall on the Main Campus. The "armed" vessel, originally created to attack and capture enemy ships, was the Louisiana State University in New Orleans's way of drifting apart from the mother institution, Louisiana State University in Baton Rouge — and their TIGERS. One student complained, "We not only did not have an identity that was distinct from Baton Rouge, we really had no identity at all." In the fall of 1964, students' entries in the mascot suggestions varied from spiky reptiles to hairy mammals. The final vote reduced all entries to these finalists: PANTHERS, DOLPHINS, PRIVA-TEERS, MARLINS, and MARINERS. But there was a lot of thought about the PANTHER and the Black Panther movement of that time in the U.S., and the student body changed its mind, wanting something that was new and really didn't have anything conjured up. In a final runoff election, the PRIVATEER emerged victorious, receiving 583 votes to 423 for the DOLPHINS. Freshmen nicknames were changed from BABY BENGALS, the final reference to the Baton Rouge TIGERS, to PRIVATEER PLEBES.

Nickname: Bucs

NORFOLK TIDES

Now playing in the International League, Norfolk had been without professional baseball since the TARS of the Piedmont League folded on July 13, 1955. The Portsmouth MERRIMACS finished that season, but then the league went out of existence. A South Atlantic League exhibition game was held in Portsmouth at Lawrence Stadium and was followed by a study to bring baseball back to the area. A Tidewater franchise in the South Atlantic League was granted in 1961 to William McDonald of Miami. The name TIDES was selected in a contest conducted by *The Virginian-Pilot*. MARINERS was the name of choice, but editor Robert Mason liked the sound and alliteration of Tidewater TIDES. The team operated in the South Atlantic League for two years, then in the Carolina League for another six. In 1969, the METS moved their Triple "A" interests to Tidewater, and the TIDES have been a New York affiliate ever since. When the METS sold the franchise in 1992, the new group dropped the Tidewater name in favor of Norfolk, giving the Norfolk TIDES a national geographic presence.

NORTHERN KENTUCKY NORSE

Norse warriors took their shields and swords into battle on large warships with dragon figureheads, used to intimidate their opposition.

The name Norse is given to the men and women of the Scandinavian countries of Norway, Sweden, and Denmark situated in the northern-most region of Europe. NORSE has been the nickname of Northern Kentucky University student-athletes and athletic teams since the NKU intercollegiate athletics program was started in 1971. The name NORSE, selected in a campus-wide contest that year, is a fitting nickname for NKU's students and athletic teams since the University is the northern-most university in Kentucky and is located at the highest spot in northern Kentucky. "Heyu" is the school's mascot, unveiled in 1992.

NORTH FLORIDA OSPREYS

The osprey was adopted officially as the University of North Florida nickname and mascot in November 1979 by an election conducted by the Student Government Association. The osprey received 47 percent of the votes, winning over other suggestions ARMADILLO, SEA GULL, MANATEE, and SHARK. It's not unusual to see an osprey gliding majestically over the campus. Described as "trendy birds" in National Geographic magazine for their success in adapting to suburban neighborhoods, osprey are also into recycling. Children's toys, styrofoam containers, cork buoys, and doormats are many of the items they use to construct their gigantic nests. Ospreys, like UNF alumni, reside on all the world's continents — except Antarctica.

PACIFIC TIGERS

Nicknames for American college athletic teams began as early as the 1860s. When University of Pacific played Santa Clara College in baseball in 1866, the *San Jose Mercury* called the team the UNIVERSITIES, since UOP was California's first chartered university (1851) among several state colleges. Occasionally another name would surface, such as DIRIGO (?) in 1885, but they were short-lived. TIGER was first used in the fall of 1908, when football replaced rugby at Pacific. The nickname evolved because the uniform jerseys and socks were black with orange stripes, making the team look like tigers. The *Pacific Pharos* reported: "New suits have been ordered and when the team appears in action they will wear the TIGER stripes, which will be of great assistance to the players because they can locate their own men without any difficulty." The students expressed hope that the TIGER moniker would inspire the team to play with the same intensity and fierceness as the jungle cat. Not only was TIGER used to describe the team, but the student body embraced this animal persona as its own identity. The main campus location spreads over 170 acres along the Calaveras River in a peaceful setting in a residential area of Stockton, approximately 80 miles east of San Francisco in the San Joaquin Valley.

PEORIA RIVERMEN

Established in 1982-83, it wasn't until 1984 that the Peoria Civic Center Authority selected RIVERMEN from several entries suggested by citizens through a phone poll conducted by the *Peoria Journal-Star*. It was considered an appropriate moniker by the International Hockey League franchise given that the Illinois River runs next to Peoria's downtown district. The RIVERMEN set a still-standing pro hockey record by putting together an 18-game winning streak early in the 1990-91 season, which culminated in a Turner Cup championship.

PEPPERDINE WAVES

Playing in the West Coast Conference, Pepperdine University was founded in 1937. Now at its present address on the Pacific Coast Highway in Malibu, California, the school adopted WAVES as the nickname for its athletic teams even though it was located at that time in South Los Angeles at Vermont Avenue and 79th Street. A school history says the moniker was proposed by a group of students who were from Tennessee and became captivated by the beach, which was eight miles away. The WAVES compete in team colors of blue and orange.

POMONA SAGEHENS

The tradition of athletics at Pomona is nearly as old as the College itself. Pomona was one of the founders of intercollegiate competition in Southern California, and the first issue of the student newspaper, printed in 1889, refers to the College's tennis team and courts as the BASEBALL NINE. The sagehen, a bird native to desert regions of the Southwest, was selected as the College nickname and mascot in 1917. In 1923 Pomona played against the University of Southern California in the first football game held at the Los Angeles Memorial Coliseum, which Pomona lost 23-7. Today, the Pomona College SAGEHENS remain true to one of the original assumptions of intercollegiate athletics: that college athletes must be students first. Interestingly, Pomona combines its forces with Pitzer College to field varsity athletic teams in 19 NCAA Division III sports, including men's football and women's basketball.

QUAD CITY RIVER BANDITS

Back in July of 1991, when word got out of a contest to rename the Quad City ANGELS, suggestions came in from places as far away as Guam and as unusual as the Iowa State Penitentiary. "When people think about the ANGELS," Quad City owner Rick Holtzman said, "they think about the California ANGELS. We wanted to give the franchise more of a Quad City identity." Everyone was thrilled with RIVER BANDITS. RIVER because the one significant aspect of the Quad Cities is the Mississippi, and BANDITS because it has a certain amount of mystery and flair. "The key was to develop a name that is marketable both internally and nationally, and I think we've found that." RIVER BANDITS, a Class "A" affiliate of the Houston ASTROS playing in the Midwest League, was selected by the Quad City staff from the more than 1,000 entries and 800 different names suggested by the Quad City fans. Bob Heimer of Davenport was the only one to suggest the precise name, "I actually submitted about ten different names. With RIVER BANDITS I was looking to combine the Mississippi River with the one-armed BANDITS of riverboat gambling." Team colors are red and black.

RANCHO CUCAMONGA QUAKES

The Ventura COUNTY GULLS were sold to a group of investors that moved the team to San Bernardino in 1987. The San Bernardino SPIRIT entertained fans at Fiscalini Field until the 1992 season when the city of Rancho Cucamonga told majority owner Hank Stickney of its intention to build a brand new, state-of-the-art ballpark. The rights to the name San Bernardino SPIRIT were sold, and Stickney moved the franchise into temporary trailers just outside the construction area of the new ballpark. Fans were asked to select a name for the new team and on September 30, 1992, it was announced that six people had suggested the nickname QUAKES. Team management chose the very Californian moniker as the winner from over 200 different names. The QUAKES nickname in turn lent some of its theme to the naming of the new stadium. And so the Rancho Cucamonga QUAKES won its first game on April Fool's Day, 1993, at the Epicenter! On July 15, 1993, the QUAKES, a Double "A" affiliate of the San Diego PADRES, broke the year-old California League attendance record of 218,444 previously held by the High Desert MAVERICKS. Other nicknames the QUAKES enjoyed over the years include the CRUSHERS, PADRES, ORIONS, LIONS, ORIOLES, and DODGERS.

RICHMOND SPIDERS

From 1876 until 1893, the University of Richmond carried the nickname COLTS into its athletic contests, so dubbed for their play as an "energetic group of young colts." In the summer of 1894, a new nickname was born. A baseball team comprised of UR athletes and city residents adopted the name SPIDERS. Star pitcher Puss Ellyson's lanky arms and stretching kick confused batters to such an extent that *Richmond Times-Dispatch* writer Ragland Chesterman used the name of that clever creeping insect, the spider, to fittingly describe the erudite members of the team. So was created one of the nation's unique nicknames. To this day, the University of Richmond is the only school in the country which sports the SPIDERS nickname.

ROANOKE EXPRESS

The Western Virginia town of Roanoke is proud of its old railway ties, and wanted a nickname that celebrated this fact. Playing in the East Coast Hockey League, it was Jack Bogaczyk of Hockey Roanoke Inc. that instigated a name-the-team contest through the local newspaper. Finalists included the LOCOMOTIVES and the SHOOTING STARS. At one of the initial EXPRESS organizational meetings, Owner Joe Steffen brought along a Barcelona DRAGONS football jersey. The DRAGONS, a member of the once defunct (but now re-born) World League of American Football, presented a dark, forest-green base team color that was immediately accepted. The idea of a train coming out of a star was also uniquely tied in with the history of Roanoke. Considerations of the type of train to be used included going with the history and power of an old steam locomotive, or to take a futuristic approach with a more streamlined, high speed train. The EXPRESS were the first team in the ECHL to utilize a puck in their logo. It's carried in the train's "mouth."

ST. JOHN'S RED STORM

In June of 1994 St.John's University joined the movement away from nicknames found potentially offensive to Native Americans — they'd been called the REDMEN from the time the school was located in Brooklyn, New York. Polled by a committee composed of students, alumni, and administrators, RED STORM was selected because it was very original, and no other school in the country had a name close to it. Another reason the name was selected was that the name lent itself to a very sharp and marketable logo. Other considered names included RED RAIDERS, rejected because Colgate University and Texas Tech were already using it, and RED DRAGONS, rejected because the school was not very receptive to it.

Nickname: Johnnies

SAN BERNARDINO STAMPEDE

The San Bernardino SPIRIT didn't just want a new name and logo, it wanted an entire theme to market itself around. So the SPIRIT changed its name to the San Bernardino STAMPEDE. The move continues the recent trend of singular sports nicknames. It gives the club a more marketable logo — a stampeding horse — and the chance to create a Western theme at its new ballpark. Many fans preferred the nickname SPIRIT, which had represented the team since it joined the California League in 1987. STAMPEDE General Manager Jim Wehmeier said the club wanted to make a clean break, "The SPIRIT went out as 1995 league champions, so we're retiring the name on a winning note. We're also moving to a new stadium, so it's a logical time for the transition to a new name." The city is building a 5,000-seat stadium which has been dubbed "The Ranch." "We were looking for something very wholesome and family-oriented," said co-owner Donna Tuttle. "There is strength to a stampede, mass and energy...And instead of picking an animal, we wanted a whole Western theme."

SAN JOSE CLASH

A Nike-supported franchise in the new World Soccer League, the CLASH media department sent us this reason for its name selection: The driving spirit of the San Jose CLASH is the scorpion — quick, lethal, and mean. A striker that hits without warning. An attacker whose defense is just more attack. With shapes and colors that reflect the diverse ethnic make-up and heritage of the Bay Area, the logo system is derived from the soil it represents. And together with the team's name, it promises strong and decisive action in every San Jose match.

SANTA BARBARA GAUCHOS

It was in 1921 that the then-called Santa Barbara State introduced its first football team. Called the ROADRUNNERS in honor of the bird that frequented the Riviera campus, the team was forced to play its home games on the all-dirt field of the original, clapboard Pershing Park — a facility normally used for horse shows. Coach Spud Harder complained at the time, "We'd have to play with horse dung all over the place. I wouldn't let my players on the field without having inoculations for tetanus." Since the growing roadrunner population was also defecating all over the school's campus, it wasn't too surprising that the university changed its nickname. A student election was held to pick the new moniker, and the campus coeds — enamored with Douglas Fairbanks Sr. in the movie "El Gaucho" — stuffed the ballot box in his honor. Beginning with the 1934-35 school year, Santa Barbara State's sport's teams were known as LOS GAUCHOS. GAUCHO describes a cowboy of mixed Indian and Spanish ancestry.

SANTA CRUZ BANANA SLUGS

Perhaps you noticed? In the award-winning film "Pulp Fiction," 1970s demigod John Travolta immortalized the SLUG T-shirt by wearing it throughout the last few scenes of the film. For many years, the BANANA SLUG served as the unofficial mascot and nickname for the University of California at Santa Cruz. The students felt the SLUG mollusk (once under consideration as the official state mollusk of California) represented many of the strongest elements of the campus: contemplation, flexibility, non-aggressiveness, and an iconoclastistic challenge toward the status quo. The SLUG is also indigenous to the region and shares a symbiotic relationship with the California Redwood that populates the campus. In 1981 the school Chancellor made SEA LION the official nickname in order to make the campus more mainstream, sparking a student revolt five years later. When reinstating the BANANA SLUGS moniker, it bested the SEA LIONS at a 12-1 ratio in a student referendum. Leaders of the pro-SLUG movement even appealed to late night czar David Letterman in their case (SLUGS being nocturnal creatures, of course). In 1992, *Sports Illustrated* magazine named the BANANA SLUGS the nation's best college nickname. The students of Santa Cruz are proud to tell you that BANANA SLUGS are hermaphroditic, and can actually mate with themselves if necessary.

Nickname: Slugs

SAVANNAH SAND GNATS

Affiliated with the LA DODGERS, Savannah's minor-league baseball team has settled on a new nickname, the SAND GNATS. "It's pretty good for us down here," said director of marketing Nick Brown, "With all the humid weather, we've got those gnats. Either us or Charleston almost had to grab the nickname." Brown said the name was picked in voting by the public through the news media. Seventy percent of those voting chose SAND GNATS over four other prospective names — HAMMERHEADS, THRASHERS, SHADOW, and SEA TURTLES. SHADOW was a distant second in the results, announced February 13, 1996. The Class A team, formerly affiliated with the St. Louis CARDINALS, switched to the DODGERS in December of 1995.

SCOTTSDALE ARTICHOKES

What was intended as a protest has become a college sports legend. Students and the government elected to represent them felt athletics should be low on the Scottsdale Community College budget list, putting them in conflict with the administration who saw the future written on the white chalked grid of a football field. The year was 1970, a new decade born of the protests and campus turmoil of the 1960s, and the SCC students felt they were being sold out by yet another establishment false promise. The administration, while hearing the vague footsteps of dissension, went ahead with plans for making SCC a national junior college athletic power. It asked an infuriated student government to run an election to find a nickname, so they reacted by giving the students three self-parodying choices: the ARTICHOKE, the RUTABAGA, or the SCOUNDRELS. The shocked administration tried to declare the election null and void when ARTICHOKE won. They held another election, pitting DROVERS against the vegetable. ARTICHOKE won big. For the majority of students entering SCC today, the nickname is no more than a quirky reminder of a time when students chose academic reputation over athletics.

SOUTH DAKOTA TECH
HARDROCKERS

South Dakota is a name from the Sioux Indians. Lakota or Dakota is a word meaning "friends" or "allies." The HARDROCKER nickname was derived from the Gold Miners who came to the area in the mid-1870s. The Black Hills is the home of the largest gold mine in North America operated by Homestake Mining. The miners mined hard rock in attempting to find gold, thus the name HARDROCKERS was adopted by the school in the early 1920s to recognize them. "Grubby" is the official mascot of the South Dakota School of Mines and Technology HARDROCKERS. He is a miner and symbolizes those mining engineers that were the first graduates of South Dakota Tech.

Nicknames: Rockers, Miners

SOUTHERN COLORADO
THUNDERWOLVES

The previous nickname, INDIANS, was selected by the student population in 1933 at the old Pueblo Junior College, which became the University of Southern Colorado. When a change was sought, a campus-wide committee received recommendations from the community and student population. The USC New Look Committee forwarded three finalists — THUNDER, THUNDERWOLVES, TRAILBLAZERS — to the university president who selected THUNDERWOLVES because "the name reflected the university as a modern, forward-looking institution which strives to be an excellent regional university; the name sent a message out of state that the university is located in the beautiful state of Colorado; the name served as an effective image for publications, stationery and banners, as well as for tee shirts, jackets, mugs, bookstore supplies, and other marketable items." The university moved to its new location in 1964, adopted its new nickname in 1995, and adopted its motto at the same time, "shake, rattle, and howl!"

Nicknames: The Pack, T-Wolves

SOUTHERN ILLINOIS SALUKIS

In 1967, the Southern Illinois University at Carbondale basketball coach Jack Hartman wrote, "Old Duke has its DEVILS, St.Louis plays its BILLS, Texas Western digs the MINERS like there's gold in them thar hills. But from Loo'ville on the bluegrass to St. Peter's on the bogs, the scene was bad last winter, they all went to the DOGS." The SALUKI is an ancient breed of Arabian dog, a choice consistent with a bit of local lore — the southern one-third of Illinois is often referred to as Egypt! This was the result of a drought that dried streams and fields of wheat in the early 1800s all over Illinois — but not the South! A similar "miracle" had once occurred in Egypt, and appears in the Bible. In Egypt at that time, Salukis were the finest animals a family could own. Known for their speed and hunting skills, Salukis are the oldest pure-bred dogs, dating back to 3600 B.C. Other nicknames considered in 1951 were REBELS, KNIGHTS, FLYERS, MARAUDERS, and MAROONS.

Nickname: Dogs

STETSON HATTERS

Originally named DeLand Academy, Stetson University was re-named after the famous Philadelphia hatmaker John B. Stetson in 1889. The nickname HATTERS, stemming from Mr. Stetson's business, started at the turn of the century. Other schools in the Trans America Athletic Conference include, among others, the Campbell University FIGHTING CAMELS. Formerly the HOR-NETS, the new name was derived from a mis-heard comment which included school founder Dr. James Archibald Campbell's surname. A student poll in the early 1960s resulted in Georgia State PANTHERS being selected, replacing the old OWLS nickname — a reference to the Night Owl image of the former Georgia Tech Night School. The PANTHER choice made good local sense as the teams already played many of their contests in the area still known as Panthersville. The Florida Atlantic University campus was des-ignated a Burrowing OWL sanctuary in 1971 by the Audubon So-ciety because of the birds of prey that live there. The feisty bird, traditionally associated with wisdom and determination, serves as the University's mascot and nickname. Centenary College was formerly nicknamed the IRONSIDES, but was re-christened the GENTLEMEN in 1921 by then-College President George Sexton; and the Samford University BULLDOG, a name newswriters earliest recollections place somewhere around 1930.

TAMPA BAY MUTINY

Another shoe manufacturer, this one Nike, is supporting this Major Soccer League franchise, and sent us this: The Tampa Bay MUTINY logo system doesn't have any rebellious sailors. No three-masted galleons. No rolling oceans. Just little green winged cyber-mutants from the dark blue depths of space. Inspired by the futuristic visions of video games, the logos and type suggest a mega-high-tech, ominous force on the field. The logos' designer will even point out that the character isn't controlling the ball with its feet, but with its mind — soccer reaches the fourth dimension! Not your typical pirate story.

TARLETON STATE TEXANS

Back in 1925 when the college was known as John Tarleton Agricultural College, the athletic teams were called the PLOWBOYS, a name selected by then athletics director W.J. Wisdom. Now playing in the Lone Star Conference, in 1961 college officials decided to have a contest to come up with a new athletic nickname to reflect Tarleton's new status as a four-year college. The top three vote-getters were TEXANS, ROCKETS, and PACKRATS. Although cognizant of current events — in 1961 the space race was about to take full bloom in Texas — ROCKETS finished second! The Tarleton TEXANS women's athletic teams have traditionally been known as the TEXANNS. This nickname was adopted in the late sixties and borrowed, actually, from Ranger Junior College, which had taken to calling its female athletic teams the RANGE-ANNS.

TEHRAN PERUZEE

Iran's most popular soccer club is based in the capital city of Tehran, playing in the Iranian National Football League. When the team was formed it was named in honor of an ancient king named Korosh, or Cyrus, who ruled Iran some 2500 years ago from the capital of his kingdom, the city of Shiraz. The family name Haghamaneshian was the most powerful for many years. They built a magnificent palace which they called PERSEPOLIS. So, more than two thousand years later, when it came time to name the local soccer franchise, they chose to honor this ancient king by naming their new heroes the PERSPOLICE, after his place of residence. The club's name stayed the PERSPOLICE until the mid-1980s, when non-religious names honoring Iranian royalty became unpopular. The name was then changed to PERUZEE, which means "winner" in the Persian language.

TOLEDO MUD HENS

Playing in the International League, the Toledo MUD HENS are probably the most famous team in all of minor league baseball, but there's a persistent dilemma with the team's fame — nobody seems to know what a MUD HEN is. This Detroit TIGER triple "A" affiliate told us that a MUD HEN is a marsh bird with short wings and long legs that inhabits swamps or marshes. Such birds have been known as marsh hens, rails, or MUD HENS. Teams from Toledo have also been known as the WHITE STOCKINGS, SWAMP ANGELS, BLACK PIRATES, and GLASS SOX. The Toledo baseball club earned its present nickname in 1896, and it has kept it — with those few minor exceptions — ever since. In that year the team played at Bay View Park, and the marshland outside the field was frequented by these strange birds. The abundance of MUD HENS near the park brought about the nickname and the rest, as they say, is history. Alumni of this Triple "A" Detroit TIGER affiliate include Jim Thorpe, Frank Viola, and Kirby Puckett, but the MUD HENS persona is so strong that even famous non-players have been seen in a Toledo uniform. Actor Jamie Farr brought the uniform and the MUD HENS nickname nation-wide fame in his role as Toledo-born Max Klinger of M★A★S★H.

Nickname: Hens

TRINITY CHRISTIAN TROLLS

Trinity Christian College is the only college or university from among 3,200 in the U.S. to have the TROLLS nickname. In 1966, Dr. Peter Steen, Trinity's professor of theology and basketball coach, made a request of the college's first president, "We're starting a basketball team, and we need a name!" President De Jong's family, which included three sons and wife Joanne, began to ponder the problem. Joanne suggested using the dictionary, "We'll work for a name with alliteration, using the TR in 'Trinity' and find some noun from the tr's to use with it." Soon they came upon TROLL: in Scandinavian folklore, any of a race of supernatural beings, variously conceived of as giants or dwarfs, living underground or in caves. They loved it! The Trinity TROLLS would need supernatural powers to develop into a viable team, and there was hope that they would soon emerge from their cave of anonymity to become a team which would cheer and enliven student life at this fledgling college.

WASHINGTON BEARS

There are 31 four-year colleges and universities using the BEAR nickname, ranking it in the top ten for most common names, with EAGLES topping the collegiate list. The earliest nickname for the University's athletic teams was PIKERS, a name whose roots lie in the 1904 World's Fair! The Pike, which ran along Lindell Boulevard. between DeBaliviere and Skinker, was the World's Fair's amusement section. After the Fair, when the University moved to the Hilltop campus, the new campus' proximity to the Pike led to the tradition of using the nickname PIKERS to refer to both athletic teams and Washington University students in general. The teams were known as the PIKERS until 1926, when Chancellor Herbert S. Hadley called a meeting of the students, suggesting the name be changed to the BEARS, and the name has been used ever since. While no longer used in connection with sports, the name PIKERS lives on as the name of the male a cappella ensemble.

BRITISH PREMIER LEAGUE

ARSENAL GUNNERS

Initially known as DIAL SQUARE after a workshop at the Royal Arsenal — where most of the original team worked — the club began life in 1886 under founder Daniel Danskin, a Scotsman from Kirkcaldy. From the earliest days until 1891 it played under the name Royal ARSENAL, an obvious nod in the direction of the gunnery. The leading light at the time was former Nottingham Forest player Fred Beardsley, who got his old club to help out by giving him some spare red shirts and a football. Apart from a brief trial with red and light-blue stripes in 1895, the team played in an all-red strip until 1933. A pig farm was among the local venues used until the club moved to the Invicta Ground at Plumstead in 1890. Becoming professional as Woolwich ARSENAL in 1891, the club was elected to the Football League's Second Division two years later. Not long afterwards, it bought a ground at Manor Field. Promoted to the First Division in 1904, increasing debts forced the club into liquidation in 1910 — only to be rescued by property developer Henry Norris, who initially suggested a merger with Fulham. Relegated in 1913 after winning only one home game, a new start was made, despite vociferous local opposition, at Highbury in North London. From 1914, the club was re-christened "THE" ARSENAL until, in 1927, it adopted the simple ARSENAL name which has become famous throughout the world. A favorite nickname, again in reference to the club's origins in a gunnery, is THE GUNNERS. The club holds the record for an unbroken run in the top-flight of English football.

ASTON VILLA VILLANS

Legend has it that Aston Villa began life on a foggy winter night with a meeting of cricket fans under a gaslight on an anonymous street corner in Birmingham in 1874. Members of Villa Cross Wesleyan Chapel, they were keen to find a way of keeping fit during the close season. The club's first proper ground was reportedly at Aston Lower Grounds amusement park, where rival attractions included a variety of performers such as trick-cyclists. Moving to a field in Perry Barr in 1876, the team rapidly captured the local imagination and decided to build Villa Park as its permanent home. In 1888, Villa joined the newly-formed Football League instigated by Villa committee member Scotsman William McGregor, a wealthy draper who had moved to Birmingham in 1870. The VILLANS — the nickname a wordplay on their location — soon made their mark with four First Division championships in less than a decade: 1894, 1896, 1897, and 1899. Another followed in 1910. The VILLANS were proud of their collection of star names, including the unforgettable Charlie Athersmith — who, so the story goes, played one rain-hit game carrying an umbrella.

BLACKBURN ROVERS

It was the creation of two former grammar school pupils Arthur Constantine and John Lewis, and its first pitch was a field with a pond or cow pit in the middle — which had to be covered with planks before kick-off! Narrowly beaten FA Cup finalists within two years, they won the trophy for the first time in 1884 at the Oval. The Pall Mall Gazette described the fans flooding down to London for the final as "a northern horde of uncouth garb and strange oaths." ROVER refers to a person who roves, or wanders. Only the second Northerners to win the cup — Blackburn OLYMPIC had been victorious the previous year — ROVERS supporters released the carrier pigeons they had brought specially with them to welcome the team onto the pitch! Victory celebrations included a reception by Blackburn Brass Band, with the team being pulled through the streets in a carriage drawn by six superb grey horses.

BOLTON WANDERERS

Under schoolmaster and captain Thomas Ogden, the club dates from 1874 — when its president was local vicar Rev J.F. Wright. To become a member you had to pay two-and-a-half pence. When the Vicar of Christ Church attempted to put too many restrictions on how church premises could be used, the club broke away and, in 1877, formed Bolton WANDERERS. For the next 18 years they had no permanent home — consistent with their nickname. Initially called the REDS, because of their original red-and-white quartered shirts, they experimented with several strips. For a time in the early 1880s, they even played in white shirts with red spots because they thought it made players look larger and more intimidating. One of the original 12 members of the Football League in 1888, they remained in one of the top two Divisions until the Seventies. After a period of decline, accompanied by the 1946 Burnden Park disaster in which 33 fans died, success returned in the Fifties. Promotion to the Premier League marks the return to former glory days after a 30-year downward drift, culminating in 1987 when — for the first time — the TROTTERS descended to the lowest division in the League.

Nickname: Trotters

CHELSEA BLUES

The club was formed in 1905 after Fulham rejected an offer from H.A. Mears, the owner of Stamford Bridge, to use the athletics stadium there. From the early days, Chelsea enjoyed a glamorous image — helped by the ground's closeness to London's West End and the use of celebrity players. Even so, they found it difficult to shed a reputation for unpredictability. Losing to Sheffield UNITED in the 1915 FA Cup final, Lord Derby presented the medals to both sides as the First World War raged on. He told the players, "You have played with one another and against one another for the Cup. Play with one another for England now." In 1937, despite a disappointing season at home, Chelsea was the first English club to play in a European tournament, losing the final to Italian side Bologna. After the Second

World War, the Fifties marked the start of a new era. Manager Ted Drake added vigor to the side with the introduction of notable young players who inevitably became known as DRAKE'S DUCKLINGS. In 1955, the BLUES, a reference to the team's colors, won their First Division championship. But soon they found themselves relegated and charismatic Scotsman Tommy Docherty was brought in to revive the club's fortunes. Under him, in 1965, Chelsea became the first London club to win the League Cup.

Nickname: Drake's Ducklings

COVENTRY CITY SKY BLUES

Formed in 1883 by workers at the Singer's bicycle factory, the club was first known simply as Singer's FC. It changed to its current name in 1898, the year before Highfield Road became its permanent home — and seven years after its first trophy win: the Birmingham Junior Cup. It was not until 1919 — by way of the Birmingham and District League and then the Southern League — that the club joined the Football League's Second Division. In those days, they played in blue-and-white quartered shirts. The Sixties remain the club's most memorable heyday, under Manager Jimmy Hill and chairman Derrick Robbins. With a reputation for its modern outlook and unafraid of innovation, the club successfully pioneered a more fan-friendly and commercial approach. Inspired by an impressive new kit for players, Coventry City developed the SKY BLUE theme and nickname with special trains for travelling fans and SKY BLUE radio to provide pre-match entertainment.

EVERTON TOFFEEMEN

Nicknamed after the city of Everton's world famous toffee, the origins of Everton FC (Football Club) go back to an English Methodist congregation called New Connexion, founded in 1797! They decided in a meeting in 1868 to renew their social activities in the Liverpool area by building a new chapel there. The following year, they bought some land on Breckfield Road North, between St.

Domingo Vale and St. Domingo Grove. This was located near the district of Everton (originally Ofer Tun), which had become part of the City of Liverpool in 1835. So, like many other Premier League teams, Everton began life as a church team. They were called St. Domingo's and were founded in 1878. The team first played using homemade goalposts in Stanley Park. Expanding and changing to their current name a year later, the team earned an early nickname as the BLACK WATCH because of their black shirts with white sash. The world-famous royal-blue strip was adopted, after several experiments, from 1901. Quick to take advantage of employing professional players, the TOFFEEMEN were among the twelve clubs which were original members of the newly formed Football League in 1888. Since then, the club has been in the top flight for all but four seasons. In 1892, the TOFFEEMEN moved from Anfield to its permanent Goodison Park home. In August of 1936, the British Broadcasting Company chose Everton's away game against Arsenal to be the first football match to be broadcast in Britain.

LEEDS UNITED

The club began in October 1919 as a result of the disbanding of Leeds City, which refused to allow the Football League to inspect its accounts during an investigation into illegal payments to players. After Leeds City, founded in 1904, was expelled from the League, the plan had been to join with Huddersfield Town, which was suffering a financial crisis. But in the end, solicitor Alf Masser decided Leeds should continue to have its own club, "uniting" the area. Returning to the First Division in 1964, Leeds wore an all-white strip made famous by Real Madrid.

LIVERPOOL REDS

Liverpool can thank arch rivals the TOFFEEMEN from Everton for their creation. In 1892, Everton failed to strike a deal with John Houlding, the owner of Anfield, and left for Goodison Park instead. Playing its first Football League game in 1893, the team was dominated by 10 Scotsmen. Only goalkeeper Bill McOwen was born in England. REDS is a reference to jersey colors. Never having been lower than the Second Division, Liverpool's record is unparalleled. Throughout its distinguished history, fans have been able to watch an array of talented players, whose earliest stars were goalkeepers Sam Hardy and Elisha Scott as well as Billy Liddell. Even heavyweight boxer Joe Louis signed with the REDS in 1944, although he never played a match.

MANCHESTER CITY CITIZENS

Founded as Ardwick FC in 1887, the modern club dates from 1894 when its predecessors were forced into bankruptcy. Even earlier roots can be traced back to 1880 when St. Mark's Church in West Gorton supplemented its cricket section with a footballing counterpart. Having amalgamated with Gorton ATHLETIC in 1884 as Gorton FC, the club changed its name when it moved grounds to Ardwick three years later. Whatever its antecedents, the new Manchester City — otherwise known simply as the CITIZENS — were soon, thanks to such players as Billy Meredith, the premier club in the city.

Nicknames: Blues, Man City, Citizens, City

MANCHESTER UNITED
RED DEVILS

The seeds for Manchester United's future success were sown when workers with the Lancashire and Yorkshire Railway decided to form a team of their own in 1878. It was run by the Dining Room Committee of the Carriage and Wagon Works, and was known as the Newton Heath Lancashire and Yorkshire Cricket and Football Club. At this time the club was nicknamed the HEATHENS, a play on Heath. Only after Newton Heath went bankrupt did Manchester United emerge from the ashes in 1902. Having joined the Football League in 1892, the club has played in one or other of the top two divisions ever since. Just before the Second World War Manchester stole the nickname RED DEVILS from the neighboring Salford

Rugby League, a rugby team. Salford had visited France where the locals were taken with their vigorous approach to the game, and nicknamed them the ROUGE DIABLE. The moniker stuck, and because both teams played in red and shared a signifigant fan base, Manchester United lifted the nickname. During the war, heavy bomb damage meant Manchester United had to temporarily abandon its Old Trafford ground and play matches at their Manchester rivals' Maine Road stadium. Quickly dominating English football after the war, the new team won the First Division in successive seasons before the 1958 Munich air crash claimed the lives of eight players.

MIDDLESBROUGH, THE BORO

A tripe supper at the Corporation Hotel marked the beginnings of Middlesbrough FC, which was actually founded a year after the idea was supposedly mooted at the tripe table. Formerly established in 1876 at a meeting in the Talbot Hotel, it is one of the North-East's oldest clubs. The BORO nickname is a good-natured mispronunciation of the last half of Middlesbrough. After spells as a professional and then an amateur team, the BORO — by then twice winners of the Amateur Cup — fixed permanently on professionalism in 1899. Three times winners of the old Second Division, BORO — also known as the IRONSIDES because of the area's industrial base — earned a place in the Premier League when it was established.

Nickname: Ironsides

NEWCASTLE UNITED MAGPIES

Founded in 1881, the club — originally known simply as STANLEY — changed its name to Newcastle EAST END before becoming known as Newcastle UNITED in 1892 — after a meeting in Bath Lane Hall. By then, rivals Newcastle WEST END had disbanded and the club took over St. James' Park as its home. Elected to the Second Division in 1893, the MAGPIES, which is a diminutive of Margaret, and the name for a genus of chattering birds, was heavily dependent on Scottish players. The club soon won promotion for what turned out to be a 36-year stay in the First Division, ending in relegation in 1934. After a 14-year absence, they returned to the top flight only to be demoted again in 1961. The pattern continued to repeat itself; up in 1965, down in 1978, up in 1984, down in 1989. One hundred years after being elected to the Second Division, the MAGPIES won promotion to the First Division of the premier league. With the return of former club star Kevin Keegan as Manager, TYNESIDERS hope 1995 will be the year their club adds new gleam to the collection of trophies bequeathed by the stars of the past.

Nickname: Tynesiders

NOTTINGHAM FOREST

One of the oldest football clubs in the world, Nottingham FOREST has its origins in a meeting at the Clinton Arms in Nottingham in 1865. Founded simply as FOREST Football Club, members had previously met there to play "shinny," an early form of hockey. The FOREST referred to in the club name was FOREST Racecourse or Recreation Ground, where it was originally based. Shortly after its foundation as a football club, players bought themselves RED caps to wear on the field. Hence the team's colors. The Trent Bridge cricket ground was one of a number of temporary homes before FOREST moved into the City Ground in 1898. The club badge has a history all of its own. There is no record of an official badge or crest being in existence before the Second World War, but shortly after that the club adopted and then adapted the City of Nottingham Coat of Arms, the only difference being the letters NFFC replacing the castle on the original design. The badge first appeared on the club shirts in 1957. By the early 1970s the commercial aspects of the game were beginning to surface, and the need for a new badge became apparent. This is because the club couldn't obtain a copyright for an existing coat of arms, so FOREST decided to change the badge to enable them to copyright it. A competition was organised by the local paper, the *Nottingham Evening Post*, in the summer of 1973. The winning entry was chosen from over 800 entries and was submitted by David Lewis who was a lecturer in graphic art at Nottingham Trent University. Firsts for FOREST? A referee's whistle was first used in a FOREST game for signalling stoppage, replacing the previous method of waving a white flag. Shin pads were first worn by FOREST player Sam Widdowson in 1874 on the outside of his socks. Goal posts and crossbar were first used officially at a FOREST ground in 1891.

Nickname: The Reds

QUEEN'S PARK RANGERS

Starting out as St. Jude's Institute, the club was formed in either 1885 or 1886 when St. Jude joined forces with Christchurch RANGERS. The Rev. Gordon Young, of the Church of St. Jude, is credited with playing an important role — along with Scotsman Jack McDonald who, from his home in west London, recruited boys from the local Droop Street Board School. The club adopted the existing name in 1887, because most players came from the district known as Queen's Park. In England, RANGER refers to the chief official of a royal park or forest. An early wanderlust meant the club had several homes before settling at Loftus Road in 1917. With two temporary moves to White City, the club has had 18 different grounds in its century-old history. One of the founding members of the Third Division in 1920, the RANGERS, or QPR, or simply the R's, only made it to the top flight in 1968. Since then, always playing in one of the two top divisions, the RANGERS have been widely regarded as one of London's top sides.

Nicknames: QPR, R's

SHEFFIELD WEDNESDAY

Few clubs can claim origins as distant as Sheffield WEDNESDAY. The club was formed in the early 19th century by cricketers who wanted to play during the winter. Their jobs required work on Saturdays and their days off came on WEDNESDAY. In 1867 the Sheffield WEDNESDAY Cricket Club was then transformed into the WEDNESDAY Football Club, joining other local football clubs like the Sheffield FC and Hallam FC, though it rarely played on a WEDNESDAY. The term OWLS comes from the original home ground at Owlerton — which the OWLS renamed Hillsborough at the start of the First World War. In the Seventies, WEDNESDAY dropped to the Third Division, their reputation damaged by a headline-grabbing bribe scandal. They only managed to avoid the ignominy of descending to the Fourth Division by a single point. So bad was their performance, one fan tried to sue them under the Trades Descriptions Act! In more recent times, the OWLS have restored their pride and built on the success that began with their League Cup victory in 1991. Two years later, only the Arsenal GUNNERS — twice — prevented them achieving a remarkable League Cup and FA Cup double.

Nickname: Owls

SOUTHAMPTON SAINTS

With links to the Young Men's Association connected with Southampton St. Mary's Parish Church, a curate was elected the club's first president in 1885. It was this early relationship with the parish that gave the SAINTS their nickname. The team was formed largely of players from Deanery FC, which had been established by schoolteachers five years earlier. Although the Dell was already its home ground by 1898, the SAINTS did not join the Football League — as founder members of the Third Division — until 1920. Southampton are Southern England's only representative in the Premier League.

TOTTENHAM HOTSPURS

According to the various publications on the history of SPURS, the club was started by schoolboys — mainly former pupils of Tottenham Grammar School and St. John's Presbyterian School — who were reading Shakespeare and were particularly interested in Henry Percy, who lived at the time of the Wars of the Roses. The exact date of the first match played is not known but research has established the first recorded match played was on August 30, 1882, when a team called RADICALS beat them 2-0. Unlike many clubs over these last hundred and some years, the SPURS have never moved far from their roots and have always played within one mile of where they first began. Why HOTSPUR? That was the name of the cricket team, taken from Harry HOTSPUR, the nickname of Henry Percy (1364-1403), eldest son of the Earl of Northumberland (his name was derived from the riding spurs he wore). In 1898 SPURS had moved to their present world-famous park at White Hart Lane. In 1901 SPURS won the FA Cup. Even though Wembley Stadium had not been built as yet, the first game of the final match against Sheffield UNITED at Crystal Palace drew 110,000 fans! The club's world famous ball-and-cockerel emblem is believed to have its origins in cock-fighting, because combative cocks were fitted with tiny spurs.

Nickname: Spurs

WEST HAM UNITED HAMMERS

The HAMMERS, wordplay on Ham — also known as the IRONS — began life as the Thames IRONworks team formed in 1895 by employees of a shipyard whose managing director Arnold Hills came up with the idea of setting up an amateur club. They entered the FA Cup in their inaugural season at Chatham, and the London League in their second. Although the impoverished club was eventually wound up in June of 1900, it was relaunched a month later as West Ham UNITED. The new club maintained the shipyard connection until 1904, when it moved to Upton Park. Although they never won the First Division, they have had more success in the FA Cup, winning it three times in 1964, 1975, and 1980. In 1965 they added the European Cup-Winner's Cup to their trophy cupboard. Traditionally respected for their stylish play, the best-known of West Ham UNITED's stars of recent times were the 1966 World Cup trio of Bobby Moore, Geoff Hurst, and Martin Peters.

Nickname: Irons

WIMBLEDON FC, THE DONS

Founded in 1889 by old boys of the Central School, and known originally as Wimbledon OLD CENTRALS, few had paid much attention to the DONS — an abbreviation of the club's location — progress before they entered the Fourth Division in 1978. Replacing Workington Town in the Football League, their rise through the divisions continued to astonish onlookers and culminated in their arrival in the top flight in 1986. Notable for their strong team spirit and the tenacious no-nonsense style epitomised by Vinnie Jones and John Fashanu, the club was among the founders of the Premier League in 1992. Having abandoned their Plough Lane ground, the DONS — the nickname is clipped off of the end of Wimbledon, through the players still use the moniker of THE CRAZY GANG — now share Selhurst Park with Crystal Palace.

Nickname: *The Crazy Gang*

SPORT SURFER'S INTERNET GUIDE

GENERAL

Sports Schedules
Access to professional football, hockey, basketball, and baseball schedules from this single menu.
Gopher:
    Name: Ball State University
    Address: gopher.bsu.edu
    Choose: Professional Sports Schedules

Sports Statistics
Statistics for NFL, MLB, NHL, and NBA.
Anonymous FTP:
    Address: ftp.wustl.edu
    Path: /doc/misc/sports/*

Sports Web Page
World Wide Web:
    URL: http://www.sfgate.com/sports/
    URL: www.awa.com/arena

World Wide Web of Sports
Sports information, results, and schedules, including NFL, MLB, NHL, NBA, and more. Updated regularly to cover major sporting events around the world.
World Wide Web:
    URL: http://tns-www.lcs.mit.edu/cgi-bin/sports

BASEBALL

Baseball Archives
Anonymous FTP:
    Address: etext.archive.umich.edu
    Path: /pub/Sports/Baseball
World Wide Web:
    URL: http://wuarchive.wustl.edu/pub/baseball/

Baseball Information Center
For baseball fans worldwide — discussion groups, baseball collectible info, stats, rosters, and team reports.
World Wide Web:
    URL: http://www.gems.com/ibic/

Baseball Schedule
Get the day's game schedule for your favorite MLB teams.
Gopher:
    Name: University of Colorado Boulder
    Address: gopher.colorado.edu
    Choose: Professional Sports Schedules
     | Major League Baseball Schedule
Telnet:
    Address: culine.colorado.edu
    Port: 862

Baseball Server
Coverage from the American and National Leagues, major league standings, season-to-date transactions, statistics, and facts. Updated daily.
World Wide Web:
    URL: http://www.atm.ch.cam.ac.uk/sports/baseball.html
    URL: http://www2.nando.net/SportServer/baseball

Baseball Teams
Stats, standings, and other team information.
Usenet:
    Newsgroup: alt.sports.baseball.*
    Newsgroup: rec.sport.baseball.*
World Wide Web:
    URL: http://www.yahoo.com/Entertainment/Sports/Baseball/Teams/

Major League Baseball Schedules
Get the day's baseball schedule.
World Wide Web:
    URL: http://tns-www.lcs.mit.edu/cgi-bin/sports/mlb/schedule

BASKETBALL

Basketball Server
Read the *NBA Daily Report,* see scores, news statistics, archives, and scheduling.
World Wide Web:
    URL: http://www.netgen.com/sis/NBA/NBA.html

Basketball Statistics

Draft information, playoff schedules and rankings, team records, results, scores, and statistics.
Anonymous FTP:
    Address: ftp.wustl.edu
    Path: /doc/misc/nbastats/facts
Usenet:
    Newsgroup: alt.sports.basketball.nba.*
    Newsgroup: alt.sports.basketball.pro.*
    Newsgroup: rec.sports.basketball.pro

NBA Schedule

Get the day's game schedule for your favorite NBA teams.
Gopher:
    Name: University of Colorado Boulder
    Address: gopher.colorado.edu
    Choose: Professional Sports Schedules
    | National Basketball Association Schedule
Telnet:
    Address: culine.colorado.edu
    Port: 859

FOOTBALL

American Football

Scores, history, and news on both college and professional football.
World Wide Web:
    URL: http://www.ch.cam.ac.uk/sports/gridiron.html

Football Resources

Details of college and professional football, updated daily with news, notes, and complete game coverage. Includes a section on the National Football League.
Anonymous FTP:
    Address: ftp.vnet.net
    Path: /pub/football
Usenet:
    Newsgroup: alt.sports.football.arena
    Newsgroup: alt.sports.football.pro.*
World Wide Web:
    URL: http://www.cs.cmu.edu/afs/cs/user/vernon/www/nfl.html
    URL: http:www.netgen.com/sis/NFL/NFL.html

Football Stadiums
A list of the U.S. football stadiums and the teams that play there.
Anonymous FTP:
Address: ftp.spies.com
Path: /Library/Article/Sports/stadium.lis
Gopher:
Name: Internet Wiretap
Address: wiretap.spies.com
Choose: Wiretap Online Library
| Articles
| Sports
| Stadium Listing

NFL Draft Information
Complete listings of all the draftees and the teams that picked them.
World Wide Web
URL: http://www.netgen.com/sis/NFL/draft

NFL Schedules and Scores
Get the day's game schedule for your favorite NFL teams.
Gopher:
Name: University of Colorado Boulder
Address: gopher.colorado.edu
Choose: Professional Sports Schedules
| National Football League Schedules
Telnet:
Address: culine.colorado.edu
Port: 863

NFL Server
Information and schedules for each of the NFL teams.
World Wide Web:
URL: http://www.ink.org:8087/nflstat.html

NFL Talk
A meeting place for football fans.
Internet Relay Chat:
Channel: #nfl

Canadian Football League
Rules, referee signals, history, schedules, and a glossary.
World Wide Web:
URL: http://www.engr.wisc.edu/-dwilson/rsfc

Football Resources
Details of college and professional football, updated daily. Includes a
section on the Canadian Football League.

Anonymous FTP:
  Address: ftp.vnet.net
  Path: /pub/football
Usenet:
  Newsgroup: alt.sports.football.arena
  Newsgroup: alt.sports.football.pro.*
World Wide Web:
  URL: http://www.cs.cmu.edu/afs/cs/user/vernon/www/nfl.html
  URL: http:www.netgen.com/sis/NFL/NFL.html

HOCKEY

Hockey
Schedules for the NHL, links to the web pages of various hockey teams and team statistics.
Usenet:
  Newsgroup: alt.sports.hockey.echl
  Newsgroup: alt.sports.hockey.fantasy
  Newsgroup: alt.sports.hockey.ihl
  Newsgroup: alt.sports.hockey.nhl.*
World Wide Web
  URL: ftp://ftp.u.washington.edu/public/hockey/homepage.html
  URL: hhtp://www.netgen.com/sis/NHL/NHL./html

Hockey Discussion
A meeting place for hockey players and fans.
Internet Relay Chat:
  Channel: #hockey

NHL Schedule
Get the day's game schedule for your favorite NHL teams.
Gopher:
  Name: University of Colorado Boulder
  Address: gopher.colorado.edu
  Choose: Professional Sports Schedules
    | National Hockey League Schedule
Telnet:
  Address: culine.colorado.edu
  Port: 860
World Wide Web:
  URL: http://www.cs.ubc.ca/nhl

COLLEGE

Big Eight College Football
Read statistics and information on the Big Eight college teams.
World Wide Web:
  URL: http://www.ink.org.8087/bigeight

College Football
Read polls from CNN and *USA Today*. Links to other football sites
are available.
World Wide Web:
  URL: http://www.math.ufl.edu/-mitgardt/rsfc.html

Football Resources
Details of college and professional football, updated daily with news,
notes, and complete game coverage. Includes a complete roundup of
NCAA Division 1 football.
Anonymous FTP:
  Address: ftp.vnet.net
  Path: /pub/football
Usenet:
  Newsgroup: alt.sports.football.arena
  Newsgroup: alt.sports.football.pro.*
World Wide Web:
  URL: http://www.cs.cmu.edu/afs/cs/user/vernon/www/nfl.html
  URL: http:www.netgen.com/sis/NFL/NFL.html

College hockey
Scores, team information, and schedules for your favorite college
teams.
Listserv Mailing List:
  List Name: hockey-l
  Subscription Address: listserv@maine.maine.edu

  List Name: hockey-d
  Subscription Address: listserv@maine.maine.edu

  List Name: info-hockey-1
  Subscription Address: listserv@maine.maine.edu

  List Name: hockey-3
  Subscription Address: listserv@maine.maine.edu